U.S. Immigration and Citizenship Q&A

Debbie M. Schell
Richard E. Schell
Kurt A. Wagner
Attorneys at Law

SPHINX® PUBLISHING
AN IMPRINT OF SOURCEBOOKS, INC.®
NAPERVILLE, ILLINOIS
www.SphinxLegal.com

Copyright © 2003 by Debbie M. Schell, Richard E. Schell, and Kurt A. Wagner
Cover and internal design © 2003 by Sourcebooks, Inc.®

All rights reserved. No part of this book may be reproduced in any form or by any electronic or mechanical means including information storage and retrieval systems—except in the case of brief quotations embodied in critical articles or reviews, or in the case of the exercises in this book solely for the personal use of the purchaser—without permission in writing from its publisher, Sourcebooks, Inc.

First Edition, 2003

Published by: **Sphinx® Publishing, An Imprint of Sourcebooks, Inc.®**

<u>Naperville Office</u>
P.O. Box 4410
Naperville, Illinois 60567-4410
630-961-3900
Fax: 630-961-2168
www.sourcebooks.com
www.SphinxLegal.com

This publication is designed to provide accurate and authoritative information in regard to the subject matter covered. It is sold with the understanding that the publisher is not engaged in rendering legal, accounting, or other professional service. If legal advice or other expert assistance is required, the services of a competent professional person should be sought.

From a Declaration of Principles Jointly Adopted by a Committee of the American Bar Association and a Committee of Publishers and Associations

This product is not a substitute for legal advice.

Disclaimer required by Texas statutes

Library of Congress Cataloging-in-Publication Data

Schell, Debbie M.
  U.S. immigration and citizenship : Q&A / by Debbie M. Schell, Richard E. Schell, and Kurt A. Wagner.-- 1st ed.
    p. cm.
  Includes index.
  ISBN 1-57248-362-8 (alk. paper)
  1. Emigration and immigration law--United States--Miscellanea. I. Title: US immigratgion and citizenship. II. Title: United States immigratgion and citizenship. III. Schell, Richard E. IV. Wagner, Kurt A. V. Title.

KF4819.6 .S335 2003
342.7308'2--dc22
                                        2003019864

Printed and bound in the United States of America.

VP Paperback — 10 9 8 7 6 5 4 3 2 1

ACKNOWLEDGEMENT

We would like to thank the many individuals whose contributions and support have made the writing of this book possible. We wish to give great thanks to Andrea, Anna Lena, and Nathan for their love and support. We also wish to thank Bruni and Doreen for their devotion and substantial contributions.

Further, we acknowledge the encouragement and moral support of numerous family members, friends and colleagues from Austria, Alabama, Des Plaines, Evanston, Lombard and Polo. Finally, we wish to give a special thanks to Dianne and Mike at Sphinx for their faith in us and support for the project.

Contents

Introduction ix

Chapter 1: Defining Family 1
   Marriage
   Children
   Extended Family

Chapter 2: Visiting the United States 25
   Entering the United States
   As a Tourist
   On Business
   Permissible Activities
   Staying in the United States
   For Medical Treatment

Chapter 3: Working in the United States 81
   Getting Started
   Foreign Companies
   Managing Your Own Business
   Teaching, Research, School, and Training Programs
   Domestic and Agricultural Workers

Chapter 4: Immigrating Based on Employment 137
    Working Permanently in the United States
    As a Teacher, Researcher, Artist, or Other Creative Occupation
    Due to Investments or Family Business

Chapter 5: Immigrating Based on Family 157
    Lawful Permanent Residents
    Family-Based Preferences
    Engagements to be Married
    Green Card Lottery

Chapter 6: United States Citizenship 203
    Qualifying
    Applying
    Determining Factors
    Gaining and Losing Naturalization

Chapter 7: Bureau of Citizenship and
              Immigration Services 237
    Changes in Immigration Laws and Procedures
    Being Excluded from Entering the United States
    Being Removed from the United States
    Special Registration

Chapter 8: Benefits Available to Immigrants and
              Nonimmigrants 271
    Rights and Benefits of Visiting Foreigners
    Rights and Benefits of Permanent Residents
    Rights and Benefits of Asylees and Refugees

Chapter 9: Consular Processing 289
  Visa Processing
  Dealing with the U.S. Consulate

Appendix A: Visas 313

Appendix B: Finding Forms. 337

Appendix C: Official Government Websites 339

**Appendix D: Associations and Non-Profit
              Immigration Organizations.** 343

Appendix E: BCIS Offices 345

Appendix F: Abbreviations 349

Index 351

About the Authors. 365

Introduction

Why is it sometimes better to be a spouse?

How can I stay 20 years old forever?

What happens to my visa if I lose my job?

I met my wife on the Internet, can she come to the United States?

What's the new V Visa and how do I get one?

If I go home to take care of my Mother, will I lose my Green Card?

Can I get U.S. citizenship through my dead grandfather?

This book answers these questions and many others in a way that we hope will take some of the mystery out of the complexity of U.S. immigration and citizenship law and is in a format designed to make it easier to access the information.

Most immigration books require readers to categorize themselves in order to find the information he or she wants. "Let's see...am I a nonimmigrant business visitor or a temporary intracompany transferee..." Our approach, is to let the reader find the information based on what he or she wants to do or is doing in the United States. Do you want to visit the U.S.? Work in the U.S.? Study in the U.S.? Then just ask the question and find what you need.

Under each main activity question (How do I live…work…play…), you will find a short review of the immigration law and procedure applicable to that activity followed by questions and answers. The questions range from general questions about the activity to specific questions about particular aspects and problem areas. Because the questions are based on real-life cases and the most common issues, you should be able to find information directly applicable to your situation.

We have tried to avoid abbreviations and acronyms wherever possible so that you don't have to continually look up the names of organizations or agencies we write about. The only exception to this is the Bureau of Citizenship and Immigrations Services, an agency of the Department of Homeland Security, which is the primary immigration authority in the United States. We use the abbreviation BCIS for this agency throughout the book. The BCIS is the successor of the famous Immigration and Naturalization Service or INS.

This is a Q&A book, so let's start right off with a Q&A—

Q How do I use this book?

A There are four ways to use this book depending on your needs:

1. If you know what you want to do in the United States, or have a specific question you want answered, just go directly to the chapter that most closely matches your activity.
2. If you want a complete overview of the types of visas available, who qualifies for them, and what forms you need to fill out to get them, go to Appendix A.
3. If you want to find out where to get forms, see Appendix B. Offical government websites and associations and nonprofit immigration organizations can be found in Appendices C and D, respectively. BCIS offices are located in Appendix E. Finally, helpful abbreviations and acronyms are located in Appendix F.
4. If you want to see how U.S. immigration affects the daily lives and futures of people all over the world, read the book like a novel from start to finish. Many of the questions read like mini-dramas where the answer can determine someone's future.

We sincerely hope that this approach will make U.S. immigration law accessible to you and help you achieve your goals in the United States.

This book also contain various appendices that may, in fact, be the most important part of the book for you. You can use them long after the information in the chapters has been outdated by new laws. You can get up-to-the-minute information and help.

However, one word of caution, and, also, a request for help—Internet links are sometimes very short lived. They may change without notice or simply disappear altogether. New links and new websites are being added every day. If you find a link that no longer exists or you find other sites that might be of interest and help to future readers of this book, please share them with us. We would appreciate hearing from you. Send your updates or suggestions to:

Law Offices of Kurt A. Wagner
Post Office Box 3
Des Plaines, Illinois 60016

www.WagnerUSLaw.com
wagner@wagneruslaw.com
schell@wagneruslaw.com

THANK YOU

Debbie M. Schell
Richard E. Schell
Kurt A. Wagner

WARNING AND DISCLAIMER

Every effort has been made to make this book as accurate and up-to-date as possible, but the accuracy of the information contained herein cannot be guaranteed by the authors or the publisher. Immigration laws and regulations change frequently, sometimes daily, and typographical errors may occur. This book is sold for informational purposes only, it does not create an attorney client relationship and is no substitute for legal advice. Any reliance on the information in this book is taken at your own risk. You should consult a competent immigration attorney before making any decisions or taking any action on an immigration matter.

1.

Defining Family

In this chapter, we answer questions about how U.S. immigration law defines family relationships. This is the first chapter of the book for a reason. Your eligibility for a visa may depend on your family relationship. Your eligibility to sponsor a family member may depend on your family relationship. Your eligibility to come with or join a family member who has a visa certainly depends upon your family relationship.

How do you know if you have the proper family relationship? Most of the time, you can rely on your common sense. You know who your husband is, who your wife is, who your children are, who your parents are, and who your brothers and sisters are. You know this because you got married, grew up together, and live together. Everyone knows their family.

Most of the time, when you look at an immigration form and are asked to fill in your spouse's or your brother's name, you won't have any problem with the answer. But, like with almost everything about immigration law, there are subtleties and complexities that make it worthwhile to know ahead of time if you will have a problem.

This chapter is important for everyone because proving the family relationship is the first hurdle to overcome in any family-based visa application and in keeping your family together if you want to work, live, study, or teach in the United States. This chapter is especially important for families with adopted children, stepchildren, half broth-

ers or sisters, or any family relationship that is somewhat less than what the BCIS might consider traditional.

This chapter is also important because of changes in the law after September 11, 2001. For example, the Child Status Protection Act helps families that have been waiting a long-time for immigrant visa applications keep their children in child status. The U.S.A. Patriot Act makes the spouse and children of anyone inadmissible on terrorist-related grounds also inadmissible to the United States.

MARRIAGE

Q I am getting married next week to my fiancée in Mexico. We are both Mexican. I have been offered a job in the United States, and, of course, we want to go together. Can we?

A Yes, of course. Once you are legally married in Mexico, your husband or wife becomes your *spouse* for U.S. immigration purposes on any visa application you make after the marriage takes place. The work visa that you want to use to come to the United States, specifically allows for your spouse to accompany you.

Defining Family

Q I am a U.S. citizen and plan to marry a non U.S. citizen in the U.S. For purposes of immigration, when does my future husband become my husband?

A Your future husband becomes your *spouse* on the date of your marriage. On this same date your new spouse becomes your *immediate relative* for purposes of immigration preferences. Also, if your future husband is not currently in the United States, you should check the regulations governing a fiancée visa (K Visa). The K Visa is for fiancées of U.S. citizens who are coming to the United States to get married within ninety days of arrival.

Q What is a valid marriage?

A A valid marriage, for purposes of U.S. immigration laws, is one that is properly conducted and legally enforceable under the laws of the country where it is entered into and where both parties to the marriage were physically present at the ceremony. You should know that if the marriage was performed outside the United States and you plan to use your marriage as the basis for your spouse's immigration to the United States, you may have to start your processing at the U.S. consulate in the country where you got married.

Q What kind of documents can I use to prove that my husband and I are legally married?

A The most important document is the original or certified copy of the marriage certificate issued by city hall or the appropriate authority in the country where you got married. If you are applying at the U.S. consulate for a visa on the basis of your marriage, the consular officer will tell you what documents you need and if a translation into English is required. If there is any question as to whether your marriage is in fact a real marriage (a *bona fide marriage*), you may be asked to produce other documents. Some of these documents might be copies of joint tax returns, photographs of your children, photographs of you and your spouse at social events, driver's licenses for both spouses, real property deeds showing both names, life insurance policies showing your spouse as beneficiary, religious marriage certificate if you were also married in a church, evidence of trips taken together as husband and wife showing, for example, hotel registrations.

Q I was surfing on the Internet and found a website where I can find a bride. I have corresponded with one of the candidates for about six months. We both feel that we are ready to get married, even though we have never met. I would like to marry her and bring her to the United States. The website offers a service where we can get married over the web and get a marriage certificate in her home country. Once we are married, can I then bring her to the United States as my wife?

A No, she is not yet your wife in the eyes of the immigration service. This type of situation is becoming more and more popular in these days of the World Wide Web, but so-called *mail-order* brides have been around for a long time. However, U.S. immigration law is not ready to accept long-distance marriages, virtual or otherwise. The law says that to be classified as a *spouse*, both the husband and the wife have to be *physically present* at the wedding ceremony and have to be in the presence of each other at the ceremony. The law will recognize a long-distance wedding ceremony like yours if you *consummate* the marriage.

Q I met my wife over the Internet and we got married in her country, even though I could not travel to be there. This was all arranged for us and we are legally married. I checked with the BCIS and they told me that I could not bring my wife to the United States as my spouse, but had to bring her as my fiancée. Is my wife now my fiancée and not my spouse? Do we have to get married again in the United States in order for my wife to become my spouse?

A No. You and your wife were married by *proxy* because you were not present. For immigration purposes the marriage will not be recognized until it is *consummated*. Once you bring your new wife to the United States on a fiancée visa and start to live together, your wife will automatically become your spouse for immigration purposes. That is because the law now recognizes the marriage as valid. You do not have to get married again in the United States.

Q In my country it is quite common for cousins to marry. If I marry my first cousin can we get an immigrant visa to the United States as husband and wife?

A This will depend on two things. First, the law of your country must recognize and not prohibit marriages between first cousins. Second, the law of the U.S. states where you intend to live must not prohibit marriages between first cousins.

Q My wife and I have been separated for about four years. She lives in our home country. I have a Green Card. We do not want to get back together, but she would like to come to the United States. Can I bring her to the States as my spouse?

A Yes. As long your marriage is still valid and you did not get married just to qualify for U.S. immigration benefits, your wife is still your spouse for immigration purposes. You can file an immigration petition on her behalf. It does not matter that you no longer live together. It also does not matter if you do not live together when she gets to the United States.

Defining Family

Q My husband and I broke up two years ago. We signed a legally binding separation agreement according to the rules of the courts in our country, but we haven't yet gotten a divorce. I am working as a nurse in the U.S. and my husband wants me to sponsor him for a visa so that he can come to the United States before we get our divorce. Can I do this?

A No. Because you signed a separation agreement that is recognized by the courts of your country, you are *legally separated* and your husband is no longer your spouse for immigration purposes, even though you have not obtained a final divorce.

Q I am a U.S. citizen. My future husband was married before, but has separated. He and his ex-wife have a legal separation agreement. If we get married, can I bring my husband with me to the United States as my spouse?

A No, not unless the separation agreement signed by your future husband and his ex-wife is recognized in the state where you live as the same as a divorce. Normally, your future husband will have to obtain a divorce from his ex-wife in order to be considered your spouse for immigration purposes.

Q My boyfriend and I certainly feel that we are just as married as any couple. Can my boyfriend qualify as my husband for the visa?

A Yes, but it will depend upon the law of your home country. U.S. immigration law recognizes living together or *cohabitation* (sometimes referred to in the U.S. as a *common law marriage*) as being a valid marriage if certain requirements are met. You must show that your living arrangement gives you the same legal rights and duties as those in a lawfully contracted marriage, and that your cohabitation is recognized by local laws as being the same in every respect as a traditional legal marriage. Generally, this requires that the relationship can only be terminated by divorce; there would be a right to alimony; you would have the right to inherit from your boyfriend unless he has made a will stating otherwise; and, you would have right of custody if you have children.

Q I have a Green Card on the basis of my employment. When I got my immigration visa I was told that I could bring my wife. But at that time I was not married. Now, I have just gotten married to someone I knew before I left my country. Is she automatically my wife?

A Yes and no. She is your wife and spouse by virtue of a legal marriage conducted with both of you present, but she does not automatically derive the status of *spouse* on your immigration visa. A spouse or child acquired through a marriage that occurs after the admission of the principal visa applicant is

Defining Family

not entitled to *derivative status* provided by the original visa application. You will have to file a new petition to bring your spouse to the United States.

CHILDREN

Q I have been looking at a lot of immigration forms lately trying to see where my family fits in. Sometimes I see things that apply to my child and sometimes to my son or daughter. What's the difference? Aren't my son and daughter my children?

A No. For purposes of U.S. immigration, your son and daughter are only *children* if they are unmarried and under twenty-one years of age. The law provides more protection and more immigration options to children than it does to older sons and daughters.

Q My husband has a son by his first marriage. His son was 13 when we got married. Can I put his son down as our child on my application for a temporary work visa to the United States?

A Yes. A stepchild who is under the age of 18 at the time of the marriage that created the relationship is a *child* under U.S. immigration law.

Q I am a U.S. citizen living in Jamaica. I was married for ten years to a Jamaican, but we are now divorced. He had a son by a previous marriage who he brought into our marriage and who lived with us. His son was only 2 at the time. I have always considered my stepson to be my son and that is the way we lived. Now that I am divorced, I would like to move with my son back to the United States. Can I do this?

A Yes. Because your son was under 18 when you married your ex-husband and established the relationship with your stepson, your stepson is considered your child for immigration purposes. Your divorce will not change this as long as your marriage was valid when it took place and a family relationship continues between your stepson and yourself. Your stepson will continue to be your child for immigration purposes until he turns 21.

Q I have a child, but I am not married. I have the chance to study in the United States, and, of course, I need to take my son with me. He's only 5. Can I do this?

A Yes. A child born out-of-wedlock is considered the child of its *natural mother*. Your name on the birth certificate is enough to prove the relationship. Once you qualify for your student visa, your son can get a visa to accompany you.

Q I was working in Germany and lived together for a short time with a German man. The relationship didn't work out, but we had a child together. We never got married. My daughter has German citizenship at birth because of my boyfriend. I'm concerned now that maybe it will be difficult for me to get a visa or even U.S. citizenship for my daughter because she was born out-of-wedlock. Will this be a problem?

A No. For immigration purposes your daughter is your child. You should make certain, however, that you have the birth records to prove you are the mother. Your marital status will not make a difference.

Q I was in the military in Germany. I had a brief relationship with a German woman and found out later that she got pregnant and had a baby. I'm now back in the United States and would like to try to get my child U.S. citizenship. Is this possible?

A Yes, but it may be quite difficult. The child your girlfriend had in Germany is considered *illegitimate* under U.S. immigration law. As the *natural father* of an illegitimate child you have the possibility of applying for an immigration benefit for the child only if you had a *bona fide father-child relationship* with the child. This would require, for example, having lived in the same household for a considerable portion of the child's life or taking care of the child's needs. However, if you can get your former girlfriend to work with you to *legitimate* the child under German law, your child could get *child* status under U.S. immigration law.

Q: My girlfriend and I have a child together, but we are not married. I have the chance to do a three-month training course in the United States and thought it would be a great experience for our daughter (who is 15) to come with me. Can I put her down as my child on the visa form?

A: Only if she is considered your *legitimate* child under the law of your home country or if you can prove that you have a bona fide father-child relationship with her. Many countries recognize a child as the legitimate child of its father and mother even if the parents are not married as long as the parents are registered as the parents on the birth certificate and the relationship enjoys the same legal protections as a marriage. You should check to see if this is the case for you. You should also check with the U.S. consulate in your home country to see what documents you should have available to prove the relationship.

Q: I am a U.S. citizen. I have applied for an immigration visa for my son. I filed the *Petition for Alien Relative* (Form I-130) about four months ago, but haven't heard anything. I noticed on the form that my son is only a child until he is 21. He is now 20. What happens if I don't get an answer from the BCIS before he turns 21?

A Your son will still be considered your child even after he turns 21. In 2002, the *Child Status Protection Act* was made law. The Act was specifically designed to prevent a child from *aging out* due to BCIS processing delays. It does this by using the date of filing of the I-130 petition to determine the age of the child. You filed your petition when your son was 20 years old. So now your son will stay 20 *forever*, at least as far as the BCIS is concerned for purposes of the immigration petition, and his status as an *immediate relative* of yours.

Q I have had a Green Card for over six years. I filed a petition to bring my daughter to the United States. We are still waiting for approval. I know this takes a long time. She is now 19 and I am worried that we might not get the visa until after she is 21 and that then she would not get it. Is there anything I can do?

A Yes. You should consider becoming a *naturalized* U.S. citizen. You have been a Green Card holder for more than five years, so you can apply for naturalization. The advantage is that the new *Child Status Protection Act* allows your daughter to remain classified as a child if you naturalize while she is under 21.

U.S. Immigration and Citizenship Q&A

Q Our son is 19, and is now getting divorced. We, as U.S. citizen parents, would like to get him an immigrant visa for the United States. I was told that there is a long wait if your children are married. Does his divorce make any difference?

A Yes. The divorce makes a big difference. Under the new *Child Status Protection Act,* married children of U.S. citizens can use the date of divorce to determine which category they can immigrate under. In other words, on the date of his divorce, your son was no longer the *married son or daughter of a U.S. citizen,* but became a *child* again. This will be to his advantage, because as a married son of a U.S. citizen he could have a fairly long wait for a visa, but as a child, he is an immediate relative and there will be no wait.

Q In the year 2000, I filed a petition to bring my daughter to the United States. I have a Green Card. My daughter was 19 when I filed. She is now over 21. Will this be a problem?

A No. The new *Child Status Protection Act* may be able to help you out. The law allows your daughter to calculate her age based on the date when the priority date of the petition (Form I-130) becomes current MINUS the number of days the petition is pending. This sounds somewhat complicated, but, basically, means you can deduct the number of days your petition has been pending from your daughter's age when the petition finally becomes current and a decision is made.

Defining Family

For example, in your case, it could be that petitions with your priority date in 2000 will become current in 2004. Your daughter would then be 23. But the petition was pending for four years, so for immigration purposes, your daughter is still 19 (23 year old – four years of waiting). The only catch is that your daughter must immigrate and acquire legal permanent residence status in the United States within one year of the petition being approved.

Q When I was a Green Card holder, I applied for my son who is 26 to immigrate to the United States. I just finished naturalizing as a U.S. citizen. Does this make any difference to my son?

A Yes. Your son still is classified as an *unmarried* son because he is over 21 and therefore cannot be a child. But, he is now an unmarried son of a U.S. citizen. This will put him in a different *immigration preference category* with a much shorter waiting time. In fact, based on visa availability in June 2003, your son's waiting time could be reduced by five years. Plus, you do not have to do anything to get this benefit, the conversion is automatic under the law unless your son requests that the transfer not take place.

U.S. Immigration and Citizenship Q&A

Q Why would my son not want to be converted to a better preference category?

A There are no good or bad categories of immigration preferences, just differences in the time it takes for a petition to become current so that a decision is made on it. Petitions for unmarried sons and daughters of Green Card holders from some countries are getting current faster than petitions from U.S. citizens for unmarried sons and daughters in those countries. For example, in June, 2003, the priority date being processed for petitions for unmarried sons and daughters of Green Card holders was 1994, but for U.S. citizen parents of unmarried sons and daughters the date was 1990–a wait four years longer. Thus, for most people, the *better* preference category is the one with the shortest waiting line.

Q My husband has received a job offer in the United States and, of course, we want to take our daughter with us. We adopted her when she was only 1. Is there any problem getting a visa for her?

A No. U.S. immigration law recognizes legally adopted children as children as long the child was adopted under the age of 16 and has been in the legal custody and resided with the adopting parents for at least two years.

Defining Family

Q Can my husband and I adopt a child abroad and bring him or her back to the United States?

A Yes. U.S. immigration law allows you to either: adopt a child abroad and bring him or her back to the United States as your child or to bring an orphan to the United States to be adopted here. But, either you or your husband must be a U.S. citizen to file the petition for this visa.

Q My husband and I are U.S. citizens and want to adopt a Romanian child. We have already arranged with an orphanage in Romania for the adoption. When does our new baby become our child for immigration purposes?

A As soon as the adoption in Romania is complete you can apply for an immigration visa and list your new baby as your child.

Q My husband and I are adopting a baby from another country. An agency has made all the arrangements for us. It is difficult for my husband to get away from his job, so I would like to travel to the other country to pick up our new child. Can I do this?

A Yes, but you will have to make arrangements ahead of time in your *state* to adopt the child in the United States. These pre-adoption requirements will be necessary in order to get a visa for your child. This is because your husband is not going to *physically* see the child until you come back. In order for a child to be adopted abroad for U.S. immigration purposes, both parents must see the child before the visa can be issued.

If both parents do not see the child before adoption, this is a *proxy adoption abroad* and requires the child to be re-adopted in the United States under the law of the U.S. state where the child will live.

Q **I am not married, but I would like to have a child. I am thinking of adopting a baby overseas. How do I do this?**

A U.S. immigration law requires that you must be at least 25 years old in order to file a petition to bring an adopted child to the United States if you are unmarried. You must also be a U.S. citizen. You then have two choices on how to go about adopting your baby: you can either adopt the baby overseas or bring the baby back to the United States for adoption here. Either way, you will have to make sure that you have complied with all local laws regarding the adoption and/or taking legal custody of your baby. The international adoption process itself can be quite complicated depending on the country where you adopt your baby.

To start the visa process, you will need to file Form I-600 *Petition to Classify Orphan as an Immediate Relative* with the BCIS. Once this is approved, you will need to file a visa application at the U.S. consulate in the country where your baby lives. In order to issue the visa the U.S. consulate will require:

➢ notification of approval by the BCIS of your petition (Form I-600);

- a visa application completed by you;
- an interview with you and the child;
- proof of adoption or legal custody;
- a medical examination of the child and a signed medical examination report;
- the child's birth certificate and passport (from the country of the child's nationality); and,
- photographs of the child.

The process requires good planning and attention to detail. Contact the U.S. consulate as soon as possible and schedule a meeting with the consular officer before the required interview. This will give you a chance to get a list of the visa requirements and necessary forms for the specific U.S. consulate that will process your child's visa and help you avoid any surprises at the end of the process.

Q: What kind of documents can I use to prove that my husband and I are legally married?

A: The most important document is the original or certified copy of the marriage certificate issued by city hall or the appropriate authority in the country where you got married. If you are applying at the U.S. consulate for a visa on the basis of your marriage, the consular officer will tell you what documents you need and if a translation into English is required. If there is any question as to whether your marriage is in fact a real marriage (a *bona fide marriage*), you may be asked to produce other documents. Some of these documents might be copies of joint tax returns, photographs of your children, photographs of you and your spouse at social events, driver's licenses for both spouses, real property deeds showing both names, life insurance policies showing your spouse as beneficiary, religious marriage certificate if you were also married in a church, evidence of trips taken together as husband and wife showing, for example, hotel registrations.

EXTENDED FAMILY

Q I am now a naturalized U.S. citizen. I would like to bring my parents to the United States to live with me. We are a normal family in the sense that my mother and father got married and then I was born. I assume that they are my parents for immigration purposes, but I just want to make sure there is not something tricky here. Am I right?

A Yes, don't worry, both of your parents are indeed your parents. But, you are right to check, because these things are not always obvious in U.S. immigration law. In the case of who can be recognized as a *parent* under U.S. immigration law, a parent, father or mother, is a parent based on the existence of any one of the following relationships:
- a legitimate child;
- a stepchild;
- a child legitimated under the laws of the father's place of residence;
- an illegitimate child if the relationship is with the natural mother;

Defining Family

- an illegitimate child if the relationship is with the natural father and the natural father had a bona fide father-child relationship with the child; and,
- an adopted child if adopted before age 16.

Q Over twenty years ago, I had to give up my baby for adoption. She was adopted by Americans. She has now gotten touch with me and we are both happy to finally know each other. She would like me to come to America. She said that she could apply for a visa for me as her mother. Can she do this?

A No. U.S. immigration does not allow the natural parent of an *adopted* child to get any immigration benefit or status from the adopted child. In effect, once you gave up your baby for adoption, she was no longer your child, and your were no longer her mother for purposes of U.S. immigration.

Q My parents never got married. My natural father left my mother when I was about 5 and never had any contact with us. I have since become a U.S. citizen. Now my natural father wants me to sponsor him to the United States as my parent. Can I do this?

A No. A natural father who has abandoned, deserted, or irrevocably released his child is not considered a *parent* under the immigration laws.

Q My natural mother was a U.S. citizen, but my natural father was not. Due to family problems, I was put up for adoption when I was 5. I was adopted by a nice American couple. However, by the time I reached 18, I did not want to live with my adoptive parents. I left and they disowned me. After a while I got back in touch with my natural father and am thinking of bringing him to the United States. Would this even be possible?

A It is entirely possible that your natural father could be considered your *parent* for U.S. immigration purposes. In order for this to happen, you will have to show:
- that you received no U.S. immigration benefit from your adoptive parents;
- that you had at one time a bona fide father-child relationship with your natural father;
- that your adoption was terminated; and,
- that your natural father is once again recognized by law as your father.

You obtained your U.S. citizen through your natural mother, so you received no immigration benefit from your adoptive parents. You had a family relationship with your father. Your adoption has been terminated. So, if your father is now legally recognized in your home country as such, he is once again your father for purposes of U.S. immigration law.

Q I am now a naturalized U.S. citizen. I understand I could petition to bring my brother to the United States. The problem is that our parents never got married. Can I still do it?

A Yes. Because you and your brother have the same mother and same father, U.S. immigration law recognizes that he is your brother even though you were born out-of-wedlock.

Q I have become a U.S. citizen. I have a half sister. Is she my sister for immigration purposes?

A Yes. if you and your half sister have the same mother. Brothers and sisters who have the same mother, but different fathers, are *brothers* and *sisters* for U.S. immigration purposes. If you had the same father, both you and your half sister would have to show that you had a qualifying *child* relationship with your common father.

U.S. Immigration and Citizenship Q&A

Q My parents adopted a child when I was growing up. I am now a naturalized U.S. citizen and have been living in the United States for about fifteen years. Is my adoptive brother really my brother?

A Yes. An adoptive brother or sister of a U.S. citizen who is at least 21 years of age is considered a brother or sister for purposes of U.S. immigration law. This is true as long as the adoptive sibling was adopted into your family before he or she reached the age of 16.

2.

Visiting the United States

Millions of people from around the world visit the United States each year. They come as tourists, to visit friends and relatives, to attend sporting events, to attend conferences, to have business meetings, and to receive medical treatment.

In this chapter, we look at nonimmigrant visas that allow you to visit the United States temporarily for a wide range of reasons, but not to work in the United States. These visas include visas for visitors on business (B-1 Visas) and tourists (B-2 Visas). These are the most widely used visas. The B-1 business visitor visa is also one of the most misunderstood visas. We also discuss the Visa Waiver Program that allows citizens of certain countries to enter the United States temporarily for business or pleasure without the need to get a visa at the U.S. consulate beforehand.

This chapter is also one of the most important chapters in the book, because it discusses two concepts of utmost importance to visitors to the United States: (1) the need to overcome the assumption of immigrant intent and (2) the act of entering the United States.

The concept of "immigrant intent" is important because you, as an applicant for a U.S. visa, are presumed to have the intent to stay and live permanently in the United States, unless you can convince the consular officer or the immigration officer at the border otherwise. Business visitors and tourists generally do this by having a round-trip *airline ticket and close connections to their home country. The Q&As that follow will help you understand how this works in practice.*

Entering the United States is important, because it is a separate process from getting a visa. A visa may be seen as the right to travel to the United Sates and present yourself at the border to be inspected and admitted to enter the country. The visa is evidence that you qualify to enter the country, but the inspector at the border can decide otherwise. That moment at the border, when the inspector from the Bureau of Customs and Border Protection makes the decision to let you enter the United States is the most crucial point in allowing you to do what you want in the United States.

Years of planning and waiting have sometimes been wasted because of misstatements made at the border. This chapter will show you what kind of things can make you ineligible for admission to the United States.

Finally, in this chapter, we discuss all the new (and not so new) security measures that are swirling around you as a visitor to the United States as you move through the visa application and issuance process and enter the country. Programs like the "National Security Entry-Exit System" and the post-9/11 "Visitor and Immigration Status Indication Technology System" have made visitor visa processing and entry longer and more complicated.

ENTERING THE UNITED STATES

Q I want to visit the United States. I have heard that if I visit the United States immigration service will assume I want to live in the United States is that true?

A Yes. United States immigration law makes the very broad assumption that an alien coming to the United States is an immigrant unless he or she can show that he or she fits into one of several nonimmigrant categories. In other words, you are assumed to have *immigrant intent* unless you prove otherwise.

Q I want to visit my sister in America. My sister says that if the inspectors ask me if I intend to stay in the United States, I must say no. If I tell them I don't want to live in the U.S., will that matter if someday I want to get my Green Card?

A No. The fact that you tell the immigration inspector on this visit that you do not intend to stay in the United States has no effect on a later application for a Green Card if your intentions change.

U.S. Immigration and Citizenship Q&A

Q What is a nonimmigrant visitor visa?

A A *nonimmigrant visitor* to the United States is a person who wants to enter the United States for a specific business purpose, tourism, or personal reasons, and when that purpose is done he or she will return home. The visas that allow such visits are called B-1 Visas for business visitors and B-2 for tourists.

Q I am coming to the United States on business to meet our U.S. clients. If one of them offers me a job in the United States, I would take it. Should I tell the border inspector this?

A No. You can enter the country as a nonimmigrant visitor and later decide to *adjust your status* so that you can work or live permanently in the United States. If you tell the immigration inspector at the border that this is something you would like to do, he or she may decide you have *immigrant intent* and not allow you to enter the country on a visitor's visa.

Q What is the very first thing I must know about coming to the United States?

Visiting the United States

A First and foremost, you should be aware that while citizens have a clear and recognized right to enter and exit their own country, visitors do not. So, as a visitor to the United States, you need permission from the U.S. government to enter the United States. A visa is the permission of the government of the United States for you to travel to the United States and present yourself at the border for inspection and admission to the United States.

Q **Does a visa mean I will get into the United States?**

A No. Admission to the United States is a *two-step process*. The U.S. State Department issues visas; the BCIS decides at the border whether you can enter the United States. The visa is evidence that you meet the requirements for entry, but the BCIS can keep you out if they believe you do not really meet the requirements for entry.

Q **I have heard that after 9/11 there will be background checks on me before I can enter the U.S., is that true?**

A Yes. There have always been some background checks on aliens who want to come to the U.S., but, it has definitely gotten more rigorous.

Q Can you tell me why there are so many delays in processing visitor visas?

A In general, the length of time it takes to process your visitor visa will depend upon your nationality, background, personal circumstances, the U.S. consulate you apply at, and the stated purpose of your trip.

Q What is a background check and how does it work?

A For most visitors to the United States, a *background check* is nothing more than a search of U.S. government databases. This is to determine if the U.S. government has any information about you that would force the BCIS to keep you out of the United States. These databases include the State Department system known as CLASS (Consular Lookout and Support System) and another U.S. government list known as TIPOFF.

The BCIS also has a system known as the IBIS (Interagency Border Inspection Service). Currently, if you come into the U.S. by air or sea, the BCIS must check your name against a list of terrorists. If you come by land, they may not do this unless you are male, over 16, and from a list of countries that the U.S. screens more carefully.

Q What happens if my name matches any of the U.S. consulate or BCIS lists?

A If this happens at a U.S. consulate, the background check on you will be expanded beyond the database check. You will probably be asked to supply additional information that the consular officer will verify. If this happens at a U.S. border, you will be asked to produce documents or evidence that you are not the same person as the person on the list. You may be asked to go to a separate room where you will be interviewed in order to determine if you are the person on the list.

Q What does being *admitted* into the United States mean for me?

A It means that you were inspected and then authorized to come into the U.S. by an immigration officer. If you are not legally admitted into the United States, you have not officially entered the country. This dramatically effects the possible rights you may have for a review of certain immigration-related decisions. It also makes you inadmissible for future entry into the United States.

Q What is the difference between a single entry and multiple entry visitor visa?

A A *single entry visa* enables you to visit the United States for business or pleasure—one time. As soon as you arrive in the United States, the visa has been used. You no longer have permission to come back into the United States. Of course, you have permission to stay here until the date stamped in your passport. A *multiple entry visa* is one that can be used for more than one entry into the United States. It may be issued indefinitely or for some specific number of years. It enables you to visit the United States as often as you want while the visa is valid, but the length of each stay in the United States is limited to the term appropriate for the visa—usually six months.

Q What exactly do I have to do to enter the U.S.?

A To do it legally, you must arrive at a designated point, a *port-of-entry*, and be inspected by a BCIS officer.

Q I visit the United States regularly. I'm worried because my job requires me to travel in the U.S., but whenever I do now, I get hassled by airport security. What should I do?

Visiting the United States

A You are not alone, the U.S. has started using lists to screen people for engaging in certain activities like driving trucks to simply riding as a passenger on a plane. Sometimes presumably this works and prevents terrorists from getting on planes. Other times it seems to just cause problems for ordinary people like you who are just going about their business. Our advice is to try to stay calm, keep your documentation ready, and cooperate fully with the security people. This will usually keep delays as short as possible.

Q My family and I are flying to Disney World in the summer. Do the airlines screen my name or is it just the BCIS?

A Currently, the airlines use their computers to crosscheck passengers' names with computerized lists of suspected terrorists that are on the Transportation Security Administration's (TSA) *no-fly list*.

Q What should I do if I suspect that I am entered by mistake on a *no-fly list*?

A The Transportation Security Administration (TSA) has an *ombudsman* that can be reached at 571-227-2283. You can work with them to fill out a *passenger identification verification form*. This form contains biographical information such as your social security number, address, and date of birth.

U.S. Immigration and Citizenship Q&A

Q What is Viper?

A After the first bombing of the World Trade Center in the early 1990s the State Department responded by setting up a program known as *Visa Viper*. The U.S. government was responding to the fact that some people who had helped attempt to blow up the World Trade Center were in the U.S. lawfully. So far, they've run tens of thousands of names of suspected persons through this database. Then the names get entered into the CLASS system and the TIPOFF database. The CLASS system is a database the U.S. uses to find people who might pose a threat to the United States or have misused their visas. It stands for the Consular Lookout and Support System.

Q It seems like all of the security stuff is really getting the go ahead right now. Did the government handle foreign visitors differently before?

A Yes, it sure did. Once 9/11 proved the U.S. was a terrorist target, the government started spending huge amounts of energy and money and also passed many new laws relating to entry into the United States. The *Enhanced Border Security and Visa Entry Reform Act of 2002* was passed. The Act mandated many changes. In addition, after 9/11, the U.S. enacted the *U.S.A. Patriot Act* which contained huge amounts of money and programs for increasing U.S. security. This has resulted in more data being gathered on visitors, more background checks, and more airport and border security.

Visiting the United States

Q I have heard the U.S. is going to initiate new screening procedures at the border is this true?

A Yes, it is. The U.S. is currently considering many different screening devices including several which use biometrics.

Q What is a biometric device?

A A *biometric* device uses some unchangeable, physical characteristic of a person to attach the person to their identity firmly. You may change your name, but it's unlikely you'll be able to change your retinal pattern or ear lobe or fingerprint.

Q Why is the BCIS so interested in biometrics?

A There are two factors driving *biometrics*. First the BCIS hopes it will finally allow them to cut down on document fraud. Second, any way of increasing border security has to be fast. BCIS and its previous incarnations have always had a dual mission: keep illegals out, but let legitimate business travelers in. Any system which adds more than a second or two to processing times at the border, particularly the land border entry points, could bring U.S. trade, particularly under the free trade provisions of the *North American Free Trade Agreement (NAFTA)* to a standstill.

Q Where would the biometric data come into play for visitors like me?

A Visa processing, in its simplest form, amounts to the foreign national going to a U.S. embassy or consulate and applying for a visa. Second, the consular official reviews the application. This used to not require an appointment, but now appointments will be required. Third, the consular official will put the applicant's name through a database which lists the names, ages, and *biometric* information on people who would be denied entry. Then, if it passes, the person gets a visa. Finally, the State Department sends the applicant's name on to BCIS as approved. It is in the application stage, that aliens can be expected to supply biometric information such as a fingerprint or retinal scan or hand print among others. Upon arrival, the alien fills out an I-94 and the alien gets the departure part of the form. Upon departure, the alien's biometrics can be compared to what is on file in order to firmly identify the departing alien.

Q What is the VISIT system?

A VISIT stands for *Visitor and Immigration Status Indication Technology System*. The system is designed to track and record people entering and exiting the U.S. It is also supposed to be able to monitor an individual's visa status while they are in the U.S. as well.

Q When will the VISIT system be in place?

A VISIT is supposed to be in place by January 1, 2004. At the end of the process, all the U.S. agencies are supposed to have *biometric* applications in place and all of them are supposed to be able to share data with each other.

Q Will VISIT be able to alert BCIS if I overstay?

A Not yet and not by itself. One of the goals is to have VISIT merge with the other programs so the BCIS will know right away if people overstay their visas. Of course, the programs may not know if it was a legitimate renewal or it was truly an *overstay*, so always keep proof of your status on hand.

Q I visit the United States at least three times each year. What will it be like for me when VISIT is up and running?

A The effect you feel will depend on your nationality and the purpose of your visits. For example, one piece of good news is that VISIT will replace *Special Registration* for nationals of certain countries. (See pages 264–269 for additional information on Special Registration.) In the start up phase, the government will rely on what procedures are in place now. The government will begin collecting two fingerprints and a photograph from visitors. The government is supposed to be experimenting with earlobe recognition software, so that's one of the reasons why they need the photo. Also, the photos are digitalized for computer storage. Then they'll place this information into what used to be the INS computers so it can finally wind up in IBIS, which is the *Interagency Border Inspection System*. Theoretically, the FBI uses this to access most wanted information. Then this information goes to the Department of Homeland Security so it knows what visitors and students are doing during their stay in the U.S.

Q **What is the National Security Entry-Exit Registration System?**

A In the early 1990s, in response to growing terrorist threats, the U.S. Congress mandated that the then INS (now BCIS) should create a means of tracking alien entry and exit into the U.S. After 9/11, the government ramped up its efforts and produced NSEERS (National Security Entry-Exit Registration System) in response.

Q **What do all these new security measures and checking systems mean for me as a visitor to the United States?**

A The U.S. used to be one of the most easy-going countries around in terms of alien visitors. Many European countries routinely require foreigners to register with the local police stations. The U.S. does not. Even though aliens who stayed in the U.S. for more than thirty days were supposed to be registered and fingerprinted, in practice these requirements were often ignored. Now, compliance will be stricter. For most visitors, however, there will be little obvious change. They might have to fill out an extra form, or get fingerprinted to get a visa, or maybe answer an extra question or two at the border. The actual tracking made possible by the VISIT system will not be obvious to the visitor, unless he or she *overstays*.

Q **What if I'm from Iraq? What differences will I see?**

A Since you are from Iraq, the answer is quite different. Aliens from Iraq, Iran, Sudan, and Libya are required to be photographed and fingerprinted when they come into the United States. Then thirty days later, they should appear at a BCIS office to show evidence of where they are living and whether they are in school or if they are working. In addition, aliens were always supposed to report their change of address within ten days. Now it appears this rule will actually be enforced.

Aliens from Iraq, Iran, Sudan, Libya, and some other *listed* countries are also subject to *Special Registration* where they have to provide even more details about their activities in the United States. Special registrants also have to *check out* and report when they leave the United States. The check out must be made only at certain designated ports of entry regardless of where the *special registrant* entered the country.

Q What if I'm not from one of the listed countries?

A You can still be subject to some of the same procedures. For example, U.S. consulates have the right to require a Form DS-157 *Supplemental Nonimmigration Application* from any visa applicant, not just those from listed countries. Nonimmigrants who stay in the United States more than thirty days, must report any change of address on Form AR-11 within ten days of moving. Also, the government can and does change the designations and require nationals from different countries to be registered.

AS A TOURIST

Q What is a tourist visa?

A A *tourist visa* is permission to enter the United States temporarily for pleasure. It is commonly referred to as a B-2 Visa.

Q How do I get a visitor's visa to come to the U.S.?

Visiting the United States

A You apply for a visitor's visa at the U.S. consulate in your home country using Form DS-156 *Application for a Nonimmigrant Visa*. The U.S. consulate can normally make a decision about your visa and issue it to you. However, you should know that after 9/11, the visa issuance process is now greatly influenced and controlled by the Department of Homeland Security which can make the process longer and more complicated than in the past.

Q Is there any way I can get into the U.S. without a visa?

A Yes. The *Visa Waiver Program* (VWP) was started as a temporary program that has now apparently become permanent. Although the U.S. government has been revisiting the question of whether the program should continue, for now, it continues to be a very popular way for the citizens of some countries to visit the United States. It allows citizens from certain countries to enter the United States just on their home country's passport.

Q Can I use the Visa Waiver Program from my country?

A It depends on your country. There are twenty-seven countries currently allowed to participate in the *Visa Waiver Program*. Those countries are:

Andorra, Australia, Austria, Belgium, Brunei, Denmark, France, Finland, Germany, Iceland, Ireland, Italy, Japan, Liechtenstein, Luxembourg, Monaco, the Netherlands, New Zealand, Norway, Portugal, San Marino, Singapore, Slovenia, Spain, Sweden, Switzerland, and the United Kingdom.

Q What is an MRP?

A A *Machine Readable Passport*. A machine readable passport serves the same function as a paper passport. The U.S. government is requiring a machine readable format for passports because of security concerns. This type of passport has your personal information entered on the data page just like a paper version would. However, it's set up so it can be processed electronically. Like many things, there are international standards for how this information has to be arranged including the size of the passport and photograph, and arrangement of data fields.

Q I want to visit the United States as a tourist. How do I know whether or not my country issues a passport the U.S. will accept?

A You should call the nearest U.S. consulate. In general, if your country has a U.S. embassy or consulate, you can be reasonably sure that the United States accepts your passport as an acceptable travel document. Be careful though, this does not mean that you can get a visa to the United States.

Visiting the United States

Q I have heard I will have to be fingerprinted and my eyes will need to be scanned if I want to enter the United States. Is that true?

A Not necessarily. Fingerprints are routinely required for many immigration forms and procedures, but not yet for every visa. In the near future, you may have to give the United States government other *biometric* information that can be read by machine as well. (Biometric information is information about you that is very difficult to forge such as your fingerprint or retina pattern.)

Q Why are the standards for passports becoming so much stricter?

A The U.S. government has two concerns with passports. The first is that passports are being stolen and used by people with harmful intentions to enter the United States. The second concern is the U.S. government doesn't always or accurately know who has entered and exited the United States.

Q Can my country stop participating in the Visa Waiver Program?

A Your country could choose to opt out of the *Visa Waiver Program*. However, what usually happens is that the U.S. government decides to drop a country from the program. The

Visa Waiver Program greatly simplifies travel between the U.S. and participating countries. Participating countries are reluctant to lose these benefits. The United States bases its list of countries, in part, on reciprocity. In other words, the other country must also allow U.S. citizens to enter without a visa.

Q: I am from Uruguay. I have heard I can no longer use the Visa Waiver Program to go see my uncle in Miami, is that true?

A: Yes it is, and it's not just Miami. If you are a first time visitor, you can be expected to produce a visa to enter the U.S. Those in the U.S. government who decide whether to certify a country for participation in the *Visa Waiver Program*, look very carefully at overstay rates for that country. An *overstay* is a person who had a visa to enter the U.S. for a limited time and purpose, but stayed in the United States after the visa expired. Since Uruguay has recently had a lot of economic turmoil, a number of citizens from Uruguay were overstaying their visas. While the number was not high, the government found the trend concerning. So the Attorney General and Secretary of State consulted each other as required by U.S. law. They determined that Uruguay would no longer be included in the Visa Waiver Program. As a practical matter, this means citizens of Uruguay now need to go to the U.S. embassy to apply for visas.

Visiting the United States

Q What do I do if I am from a country that participated in the Visa Waiver Program but that was dropped from the program while I was in the U.S.?

A You can still be in the United States lawfully. You must, however, leave at the time that appears on your I-94 form.

Q What is an I-94 form?

A Your *I-94* is the piece of paper that you received when you entered the United States. It shows the date on which you entered the United States. By comparing the date of entry with the length of time authorized by your visa, the BCIS can determine if you are currently in status or in *overstay* status.

Q I am visiting the United States as a tourist on a visa waiver. If I want to go to Canada for a day, do I travel back on a new visa waiver?

A No. If you leave the United States for a neighboring country you can come back to the United States by showing the BCIS personnel your *I-94 card*. You may use your I-94 to reenter the United States from the countries of Canada, Mexico, and the neighboring islands. You may come back to the United States during the time frame during which you were admitted to the U.S. under the *Visa Waiver Program*. However, you should be prepared for the fact that you will be inspected and you will have to talk to an immigration officer.

Q What exactly is *waived* under the Visa Waiver Program?

A You should know that the Visa Waiver Program does much that its name implies—it waives the requirement of applying for and getting a *B-1/B-2 Visa* before you travel to the United States. There are still significant limits. You still must be traveling to the United States for one of the purposes proper for a B-1/B-2 Visa. This means, you must be coming to the United States temporarily for *business* or *pleasure*. You are also still subject to exclusion from the United States, for example, if you have a criminal conviction.

Q This Visa Waiver Program sounds like a great idea. Can I use it if I live in the United States as a permanent resident alien and want to travel to one of the listed countries?

A No. You must be a citizen of the United States to take advantage of the reciprocity offered by the *Visa Waiver Program* in other countries. Permanent residence in the United States is not enough.

Q I understand I must be a citizen of a country that participates in the Visa Waiver Program to take advantage of it. Are there other requirements?

A Yes, the *Visa Waiver Program* functions much like a tourist or business visa. It is designed for short stays for the purposes of conducting business or coming for pleasure. Therefore, you must have a passport from your own country. After October 1, 2003, your passport must be a *machine readable passport*. Although you can enter the U.S. at land crossing points in the U.S. and Mexico, if you come to the U.S. by boat or plane, you must enter on a carrier that has a relationship with the United States government. One of the concerns that the United States government has with visitors is how they are going to get back home, especially if denied entry for some reason, so you must present evidence of a round trip ticket back home.

Q What documents do I need to present if I travel on the Visa Waiver Program?

A Primarily you need your passport, but you should have other documents available that prove you are coming temporarily for pleasure to the United States. A round trip airline ticket, hotel reservation confirmations, travel itinerary and are all useful in proving this. When you get to the U.S., you fill out and sign a *Visa Waiver Arrival Departure Record*. This is also known as your Form I-94W. It is going to be increasingly important in the future to show that, as a traveler, you entered the United States properly. It is also important to be able to show that you left the United States within the allotted time.

Q I am traveling to the United States on the Visa Waiver Program on business. I might get a job offer while I am here. Could I get a visa to take the job while I am in the United States?

A No. In order to take a job in the United States, you have to adjust your status. In general, you are not allowed to adjust your status if you entered on the *Visa Waiver Program*.

Q How does participating in the Visa Waiver Program affect my immigration rights?

A You should know that if you sign the *I-94W*, you waive the right to appeal or review an immigration official's determination about whether you are admissible or deportable.

Q Does every airline participate in the Visa Waiver Program?

A No. You should check carefully to make sure the airline or steamship line you plan on traveling with participates in the *Visa Waiver Program*. Most do, but some do not.

Q Can I stay as long as I want on a visitor visa?

A No. A visa is permission to enter the United States for a certain amount of time and for a definite purpose in a certain visa category. Tourists and temporary visitors for pleasure are limited to ninety days if they travel on the Visa Waiver Program and a maximum of six months if they travel on a B-2 Visa. Also, although these are the maximum time periods allowed, the BCIS border inspector can set a different maximum time limit based on what you plan to do in the United States. If you tell the inspector you have come to the United States to visit Disney World for one week, he or she can put this on your *I-94 arrival card*. You would then have to leave the United States at the end of the week.

Q Couldn't I just keep coming back into the U.S. as long as I left before my ninety days were up?

A This was rumored to be a common and successful strategy in the days before 9/11. This is now a really bad idea for many reasons. First, you risk being barred from entering the U.S. if you lie about having *immigrant intent*. Immigrant intent means you really intend to come to the U.S. to live permanently. It's fine to enter the U.S. on a tourist visa and it's fine to enter the U.S. with the intention of staying. It is most definitely NOT OK to come to the U.S. on a tourist visa with the intention of stay-

U.S. Immigration and Citizenship Q&A

ing. This is a red flag and could cause you much trouble down the road. You should not do this because if you are caught, you could be subject to removal and barred from coming back to the U.S.

Q If I file immigration forms, will the BCIS computers know that I have filed a certain form?

A No. If you've filed a form that you want to be able to prove to the BCIS that you have filed, bring your *receipt of filing* with you when you travel.

Q Can I use the Visa Waiver Program if I drive into the U.S. from Canada or Mexico?

A Yes, you may. The *Visa Waiver Program* can be used at land ports as well. You have to pay the entry fee the U.S. government collects. It's currently six dollars. You still must be a citizen of a participating country and have a valid passport from that country, but you do not need to have round trip tickets on an airline or steamship line that participates in the program. You do have to sign the I-94W. It is your arrival and departure form. Whether you drive in or fly in, you must show the BCIS people that you have enough money to pay your own way while in the U.S. The last requirement is that you must be able to show the BCIS you are not *inadmissible*.

50

Visiting the United States

Q Are there things I can't do if I come into the United States on the Visa Waiver Program as a tourist?

A Yes, you can only do what a person traveling as a *tourist* can do. You may not use the visa for things that indicate a more permanent connection with the United States. For example, you can marry while here on the Visa Waiver Program, but you could not start the process of becoming a permanent resident alien of the United States. Also, you cannot use the Visa Waiver Program to study. Students are required to obtain a different visa. Working is also not allowed under the Visa Waiver Program.

Q Can I extend my stay in the United States if I enter on the Visa Waiver Program?

A No. If you enter the United States on the Visa Wavier Program, you can stay in the United States for ninety days or less. You cannot extend your status (stay longer than ninety days). You cannot change to another visa status.

Q Where do I get an I-94W? From the U.S. consulate or embassy? And how much does it cost?

A You get the *Nonimmigrant Visa Waiver Arrival-Departure Record* Form I-94W from airline and travel agents and at ports of entry at land borders. You do not get it from the BCIS or

American embassies or consulates. The form itself is free of cost, but the fee to have it issued at the border is currently $6.00.

Q **What do I do if I lose my *Arrival-Departure Record* while I am in the United States?**

A Well, like many things, the I-94 and the I-94W are cheap to acquire, but expensive to replace. They currently cost six dollars when you enter the United States and $100 to replace. So please be careful with the card. You must have them to prove that you have exited the U.S. within your allotted time.

Q **I live in a country that participates in the Visa Waiver Program. My son is working in the United States. Are there reasons why I might need to apply for a visa, even though my home country participates in the visa waiver program?**

A Yes there are. The Visa Waiver Program has some limits. If you want to work or go to school while you're visiting your son, the Visa Waiver Program would not work for you. Also, if you want to stay with your son for more than ninety days, you should apply at the U.S. consulate in your home country for a *B-2 Visa* that can allow up to a six-month visit.

Q Is the tourist visa just for use as a tourist or can I do other things?

A It is mostly for tourism. Most people who come to the United States on a B-2 are tourists. However, the visa is designed for temporary visits for *pleasure* and there are many other things for which the visa can be used. For example, aliens traveling for their health to secure *medical treatment* can use the B-2. Aliens who come for *social visits* to relatives or friends use this visa. Aliens who come to *nonbusiness* conventions, conferences, or convocations of fraternal social or service groups also may use this visa. An alien who comes to the U.S. for an *amateur sports event* such as a cricket contest might also travel using this.

Q Can my fiancée use the B-2 Visa to come to the United States so that we can officially get engaged and she can meet my family? This is definitely a visit for pleasure.

A Yes, this visa may be used for becoming engaged or meeting parents or planned weddings. However, there's a catch. Fiancées usually travel on the *K Visa*, which allows the person to get married in the U.S. and stay to adjust their status. The B-2 Visa does not. This visa only allows the person to come to the U.S. for a limited time and then leave.

Q What other situations use the B-2 Visa?

A If you are a member of the military *and* an alien *and* you are going to become a U.S. citizen, you or your family may be able to use the B-2 Visa to come into the United States. However, as a dependent, you cannot use this option to come into the United States while your spouse does a tour of duty outside of the United States.

Q What if I got married to a U.S. citizen in my home country, but I have never lived in the U.S.? We live in a third country and I don't ever expect to come to the U.S., but my husband wants to be able to go see his family in U.S. Can I use a B-2 Visa?

A Yes, you may enter the U.S. on a B-2 Visa with your spouse or you may join him in the U.S. However, the key here is that this must be a temporary visit. You must show that you have a residence in your home country that you have no intention of abandoning it.

Q Do I have to go into the consulate for an interview for a simple tourist visa?

A As of August 1, 2003, everybody will need to go to a U.S. embassy or consulate for interviews. Exceptions to personal interviews are very rare. It is uncertain if visa processing personnel and departments will get any more money from the government. So, there may be exceptions to this for tourist visas for certain nationalities at posts where there is a very low incidence of visa fraud.

Q **My true love in life is cooking. I do not wish to become a professional cook, but it has always been my heart's desire to travel to New Mexico and learn how to prepare authentic Southwestern U.S. cuisine. Could I do this on a B-2 Visa?**

A Perhaps. If you are an alien destined to a *vocational* or *recreational school*, you may travel on a B-2 Visa. However, you will need to make it clear that this is not a professional or vocational school, but instead one for hobbyists. If you can't make this clear, the consular official should ask the BCIS to classify the program and decide if you need a Form I-20, which is the school *certificate of eligibility*.

Q **I am a lawful permanent resident alien. I used to live in the U.S. but I've been traveling for my job, and have lived outside the U.S. for more than a year. I know my Green Card's not good anymore, but is there a way I can still get to the U.S.?**

A Yes, there is. As a lawful permanent resident alien, you generally may not use your Green Card if you have been out of the U.S. for more than a year. You would need to have requested advance travel documents in order to reenter the U.S. However, as long as you have continued paying U.S. taxes, have kept your permanent residence, and have maintained your home in the U.S., you may get a nonimmigrant visa without giving up your Green Card.

Q Can the consulate official write things in my visa?

A Yes. Consulate officials often will make notes on the visa issued that might be helpful to BCIS personnel. They aren't supposed to write things that would be negative to your interests.

ON BUSINESS

Q I want to come to the United States on business. Is there a visa for me?

A Yes. The B-1 business visitor visa is one of the most common visas issued. A B-1 Visa allows you to come to the United States temporarily on business.

Q How do I obtain a B-1 Visa?

A You apply for a B-1 Visa at the U.S. consulate in your home country using Form DS-156 *Application for a Nonimmigrant Visa*. An approved visa means a U.S. consular officer has reviewed your application and decided that you are legally admissible to the U.S. To find out where the nearest U.S. consulate is, you can use the Department of State website to locate it at **www.state.gov**.

Q I know from friends that there are caps on most U.S. visas. Are there only so many people who can come to the U.S. on B-1 Visas?

A No. Some visa categories have limits of people who can use them. The B-1 Visa does not have a numerical cap.

Q Are there things I can't do in the U.S. while here on a business visa?

A Actually, there are many things you cannot do while you are in the United States on a B-1 Visa. The big no-no is to get paid in the United States for any work you do. This visa is for temporary business visits during which you are being paid by your foreign company or some other source of funding *outside* of the United States. You may not, for example, work as an employee for a U.S.-based company while on this visa. Another prohibited activity is to be a full-time student.

Q What do I have to do to be eligible for the B-1 Visa?

A The only requirements for this visa are that (1) you have a residence in a foreign country that you have no intention of abandoning and (2) that you are visiting the United States temporarily for business.

Q If I meet the requirements, do I automatically get the B-1 Visa?

A No. The consular officer must determine based on the information in your application that you are lawfully admissible to the U.S. To be lawfully admissible means you are not *excludible*. Whether or not you are excludible has nothing to do with whether you meet the basic requirements for the B-1 Visa. People are found to be excludible for many reasons. Excludibility means that there are problems with you or your background such that you will not be allowed to enter the U.S. These problems could be crimes, moral issues, or health issues. For example, tuberculosis, which is contagious, would be a very clear example of a bar that would make you excludible. In such cases, you will not get the B-1 Visa, even if you are otherwise qualified.

Visiting the United States

Q My company is sending me to New York for a conference. They do not know that I am planning in the future to quit and move to the United States. Can I tell the consular officer I am contemplating staying in the U.S. permanently?

A You should never lie to a consular officer. If you are planning on this business trip to stay in the United States, you do not qualify for the B-1 Visa. If, on the other hand, your plans to move to the U.S. are way off in the future and you have not fully developed the intent to immigrate to the United States, you should not discuss your tentative plans with the consular officer. U.S. law presumes that everybody who applies for a visa wants to come and live here permanently. The law makes the applicant prove they really just want to enter the U.S., do their business, and go home. This is usually accomplished by showing the consular officer that you are coming for legitimate *temporary* business such as the conference you are attending, and that you intend to return home after your temporary business is concluded.

Q What documents do I need to apply for a B-1 Visa?

A The B-1 Visa does not require much in the way of documentation. You will need to fill out the application on Form DS-156 *Application for a Nonimmigrant Visa*. A visa goes into your passport so you'll need to have a current passport from your country as well. You also need a current picture of yourself that meets very strict guidelines. Call the U.S. consulate or go to their website at **www.state.gov** to make sure of the requirements for the picture. Requirements for pictures have recently changed. Depending on the consulate and your particular circumstances, the consular officer may also require supporting documentation, like bank account information, to show the consular official you have the cash to cover the trip to the U.S. and to get you home and/or evidence of a round trip airline ticket. Also, if you are a man between the ages of 16 and 45, you have to fill out a new Form DS-157 *Supplemental Nonimmigrant Visa Information*. This is a supplemental form which requires biographical information. It can be downloaded from the State Department website as well.

Q I entered the United States on a B-1 Visa. What happens to me if I work while I have a B-1 Visa?

A That depends on what you mean by work. The B-1 is a business visa and you can work for your company back home, for example, making sales calls and taking orders. But, payment you received must be sourced outside of the United States with very few exceptions. If you are here on a B-1 Visa and work illegally, by getting paid by a U.S. based company for your services, for example, it can be very bad for you. People who violate conditions of their visa are subject to being deported and can be excluded from coming to the United States in the future.

Visiting the United States

Q What happens if I overstay on my B-1 Visa?

A It depends on how long you overstay. Once you stay past the expiration of your allotted time, you are *unlawfully present* in the United States—assuming you have not been paroled. If you stay for more than the 180 days allowed on your B-1 Visa, but leave the U.S. before one year is up, you may not return to the United States for three years. If you are an alien who is unlawfully present in the United States for more than one year, you may not reenter the United States for a period of ten years.

Q Is a B-1 Visa just for attending business meetings or visiting customers?

A No. The B-1 is an extremely versatile visa. You can do many different business activities. For example, you could go to a convention or a trade show. You might give a lecture or conduct a seminar. If you are a writer, you might do research at a college. If you are an athlete, you could compete in a sporting event as long as you were not paid directly. You may even compete for a prize as long as you do not get paid directly. If you are an employee of a foreign subsidiary of a U.S. company, you could come for training into the U.S. as long as you are paid by the foreign subsidiary and not the U.S. office.

Q I need to travel on business to the United States. Can I bring my spouse with me on the B-1 Visa?

A No. Some visas allow you to bring your spouse, but the B-1 is not one of them. Your spouse needs to apply in his or her own name for the type of visa that fits the purpose of his or her visit. For example, if your spouse is accompanying you, just to do sightseeing, he or she should apply for a B-2 tourist visa.

Q Can I come to the U.S. on a B-1 Visa as a volunteer?

A Yes. You must be in a *volunteer service program* and not be paid a salary. You may receive an allowance. A voluntary service program is organized and undertaken by a recognized charitable organization. You may not sell things for the organization or solicit donations.

Q I am on the board of an agricultural trading corporation in Illinois. Can I use a B-1 Visa to come to board meetings?

A Yes. If you are a member of a Board of Directors of a U.S. corporation you may come to the U.S. on this visa.

Visiting the United States

Q I am a cook. I have worked for the head of a U.S. company for a long time in Paris. She is now being transferred back to the United States. Can I go with her using a B-1 Visa?

A Maybe. The B-1 Visa can be used if you are the *domestic employee* of a U.S. employee residing abroad and you wish to follow that employee back to the U.S. You have to have been working for the U.S. employee before they get transferred. This is a nonimmigrant visa, so you will also need to show you have a residence abroad you will be maintaining. You need to demonstrate, at least, one year of experience as the cook. You will also need to show an original contract.

Your employer must also meet some requirements. He or she must show they are often transferred from one international location to another. They must also be your sole employer, furnish you free room and board and pay for your round trip airfare. The wages must be set at the prevailing rate and the contract must require the employer to give two weeks notice of termination. You, as the cook, are not required to give more than two weeks notice.

Q I own a cricket team. I want to bring some players into the U.S. for a tournament. They are not professionals and won't be paid although there will be a purse that they could win. Can they use the B-1 Visa?

A Yes. Athletes can come into the U.S. for these kind of events. They have to be coming to compete against another team. Additionally, the team itself has to be located in the foreign country.

Q I want to come to a trade show in the U.S. Could I use a B-1 Visa?

A Yes, but it depends on your individual circumstances. If you're coming to take orders for an olive oil company, you could certainly do that on a B-1 Visa. If you're coming to help plan or set up the show, that too might be possible, but this is usually determined one case at-a-time.

Q My cousin is a free lance photographer. She is not a U.S. citizen. She takes pictures of buildings and sells them to magazines that cover architectural subjects. She would like to come to Chicago to take pictures of all of the Frank Lloyd Wright buildings in Illinois. Could she do that?

A Yes, she could. Still life photographers may travel into the U.S. on a B-1 Visa in order to take pictures. However, she may not be paid by a U.S. company as their employee hired to take pictures. Instead, she should take the pictures in the U.S. and negotiate the sale here. But she should deliver the pictures after her return home, and she might also be wise to take payment there as well.

Q My uncle is a podiatrist and would like to come to the U.S. to watch a new surgical technique. Would that be permissible as long as he didn't do the patient care?

A Yes, as long as he isn't paid by a U.S. employer, pays his own way, and doesn't do any care, it should be a permissible use of the B-1 Visa.

PERMISSIBLE ACTIVITIES

Q Can I work a little on the side to make money while I'm here as a tourist?

A No. Working in the U.S. requires a visa in a category in which you are authorized to work. The tourist visa does not allow you to work. If the BCIS found out that you've worked in the tourist category, you would be in serious trouble. You would, also, find it very difficult to come back into the United States.

Q What would happen to me if I came to the U.S. on a B-1 Visa and I tried to get a regular job at the local supermarket?

A It's not likely you could get a job because a U.S. employer who is savvy to employment laws is going to require you to fill out the I-9 form because everyone in the United States, including U.S. citizens, must now provide evidence that proves they are *legally eligible to work* in the U.S. You could make it through the interview, but once they hired you, you would need to fill out the form. If you did somehow get the job, it would be a misuse of your B-1 Visa status, and you could be deported and excluded from future visits to the United States.

Q What if I decide to work under the table for cash?

A Here's the risk—you cannot work for wages paid from a *U.S. employer* during your time in the United States on a B Visa. It does not matter whether the payments are regular salary payments or under the table cash. So if you're caught, you can be deported and excluded from coming back to the United States.

Q I really need to raise cash. I'm here as a tourist on break from being a student in my home country. My friend works as a bartender in a rundown bar in a bad part of town. The owner pays everybody with a regular check, but you can only cash it at the bar. He does not report his employees to the government for tax purposes. My friend told me as long as I just work for cash I'm not really working for immigration purposes so it's ok on my visitor visa. Is that true?

A. No. This is a bad idea for any number of reasons. It's a bad idea for your immigration status because visitors are not allowed to work, period. It does not matter if its cash, check, or *special* check. Also, even though the owner finds it convenient to pay everybody with bogus checks right now, it could all change if his accountant scares him into complying with federal and state withholding requirements. In that case, the best result for you is for him to fire you, the worst case would be that he reports you to the BCIS / Bureau of Immigration and Customs Enforcement (BICE) as an illegal worker.

Q. I have always dreamed of buying a farm in the United States. I am particularly fascinated with how easily I can buy property in the United States. Is this something I can do on a visitor's visa?

A. Yes. This is a proper use of a B-1/B-2 visitor's visa. Also, you are right. Compared to some countries in the world, it is very easy for aliens to buy property in the United States. If you were a lawful permanent resident, you can just buy a farm much like a U.S. citizen would. You'll potentially have tax problems different from those of a citizen purchaser, but the purchase can be made easily.

Q: I travel to the United States frequently on business. I want to buy a condo here because I come here so often. I have been advised, by my brother, that I cannot own property in the U.S. as an alien. Is that correct?

A: No. Your brother is mistaken. There is no prohibition on foreigners owning property in the United States, although there are sometimes registration requirements. However, your brother does have a point. As a business visitor on a B-1 Visa, you are not supposed to be an immigrant intending to live in the United States. If your frequent, but lawful trips arouse the curiosity of a BCIS inspector, you may have some explaining to do. Buying property here while visiting on a nonimmigrant visa could indicate to them that you have *immigrant intent*.

Q: I want to drive while I am visiting the U.S. Can I do that legally?

A: Yes. You must be lawfully admitted to the United States, and you must have *a valid driver's license* from your home country. You must obey the traffic laws of the states you intend to drive in (including drinking and driving rules). This also includes the insurance requirements for the state. If your visit will last for more than thirty days, you should check with the state driver's license authorities as to whether or not you need to get a State driving license. Some states require you to get a temporary license if you spend more than a certain amount of time driving in the state.

Visiting the United States

Q Can I drive in the United States if I am an illegal alien?

A Illegal aliens do not have a legal right to drive in the United States. You can also only drive on your foreign license for the first year. You also may not legally drive if you overstay your visitor visa.

Q I am here legally as a visitor. How long can I drive in the U.S. on my foreign license?

A It depends on the state where you are living. Normally, you can drive up to one year on your foreign driver's license. After your first year is up, if you are still in the U.S. and you want to drive, you will have to obtain a state driver's license.

Q What happens if I am arrested and convicted of DUI (driving under the influence) or DWI (driving while intoxicated) while I am visiting the U.S.?

A If you are driving only on your country's license or if you also have an *international driving permit* or *Inter-American driving permit*, different rules apply. U.S. authorities generally do not have the right to take away your foreign driver's license, however, you may still end up loosing your privileges to drive in the United States if you violate U.S. law by getting convicted of DUI.

U.S. Immigration and Citizenship Q&A

Q My cousin does a lot of gambling. He's afraid the government won't let him take his winnings out of our home country. He brought $20,000 in cash into the United States on his latest visit and asked me to invest the money here for him. Is that OK?

A No. You might call what you're doing a favor, unfortunately the federal authorities might call it *money laundering*. Large sums of cash—particularly in excess of $10,000—are often problematic. Money laundering is one of the things that will definitely get you into trouble, since the U.S. views money laundering as one of the clear reasons to prevent an alien from coming to the United States. People who live in countries with shaky economies often use the United States as a shelter. However, it might be better to give your cousin a list of banks and tell him to wire the money directly into a U.S. *Dollar Account*. Aside from money laundering, your cousin has an immigration problem as well because one of the questions on the entry form at the U.S. border is "[Are you] carrying currency or monetary instruments over $10,000 U.S.?" If your cousin answered "no" he has lied on his entry form which could form the basis of criminal charges against your cousin and lead to deportation or exclusion.

Q I'm spending the summer in the United States on a B-2 Visa. Most of my friends are citizens and are politically active. They are part of a voting registration push for Latinos on their college campus. I speak English well and have been telling people I am a naturalized citizen so that I can take part in the political debates without being dismissed

Visiting the United States

as just a foreigner. Now they want me to register to vote. Could I get into trouble doing this?

A Not only can you get into trouble, you can get into a *lot* of trouble. It is a federal crime to impersonate a U.S. citizen. The most common way this can come up is if you try to register to vote under false pretenses. As a visitor, you can do many things in the United States. You can drive and own many kinds of property. You may **not** vote. Only U.S. citizens are allowed to vote. If you commit a crime while in the United States on a visitor visa, you may be subject to deportation and exclusion from future visits.

Q I am here as a visitor on a B-1 Visa. I want to form a corporation to do business in the U.S. Can I do this?

A Yes. A B-1 business visitor visa is appropriate for coming to the United States to form a corporation or otherwise take steps to set up a U.S. business for your foreign business activities in the United States. Discuss your plans with an accountant or attorney because there are special requirements for certain kinds of U.S. corporations.

Q My family and I want to sail while we're in the U.S. Can I buy a boat?

A Yes, as a visitor on a B-2 Visa you may buy a pleasure boat.

U.S. Immigration and Citizenship Q&A

Q Can I come to the U.S. on business in the B-1 category and also see the sights until it is time for me to go home?

A Yes. You will still have to leave when the time runs out, but you can also tour the U.S. while you are here on business. Most visitor visas are issued as B-1/B-2 that allows both *business* and *personal* activities during your visit.

Q What happens to me if I over stay in the U.S. while I am visiting on a B-1/B-2 Visa?

A If you over stay, you may be removed from the United States and/or you may be barred from entering the United States depending on the length of your *overstay*.

Q My cousin said he used to overstay all the time. He claims to have done this off and on for the whole ten-year period of his B Visa. Can I do this?

A It would be a bad idea to assume this attitude after 9/11. The U.S. government is spending millions of dollars and thousands of hours to get an *entry-exit system* to track people like your cousin and all visitors to the United States. Overstays, even short ones, can revoke your visa.

Q **What should I do if I overstay?**

A Be prepared to be questioned extensively if and when you try to return to the United States, and possibly be prepared to not be admitted. In that event, you could try to get the Secretary of Homeland Security to determine that *extraordinary circumstances* relating to the interests of the United States required that you be admitted. This is unlikely. As a practical matter, the easiest thing to do is probably to reapply for a new tourist visa.

Q **How do people generally get into trouble with B Visas?**

A The biggest challenge with having a B Visa is that if it's approved it can be good for ten years. This causes some travelers to begin to look at it as the equivalent of a *Green Card*. They come to the U.S. every year, off and on, and buy property and start spending the holidays here. None of these things are a problem by themselves. The challenge is that with the implementation of the U.S. VISIT system, the government is going to know when the individual alien has entered and left the U.S. and how often. If the visitor is spending too much time in the United States, BCIS will assume he or she has *immigrant intent* and will deny entry on a B-1/B-2 Visa.

Q How does the BCIS know how long visitors stay in the United States?

A One of the reasons the U.S. government is pushing U.S. VISIT so hard is that the exit-entry system is combined with the *machine readable visa* and passport requirement and scanned in *biometric* data. The data is scanned upon entry and upon exit. Thus, U.S. authorities should be able to easily and quickly identify (with a degree of certainty not presently possible) the person and decide exactly how long he or she have stayed.

Q Why is it such a big deal if I start to live in the U.S. on a B Visa?

A Living in the United States on a B-1/B-2 Visa means you're out of your valid status and may lead the BCIS to assume you have *immigrant intent*. Some visas allow you to have a *dual intent*. This means you can simultaneously plan on being an immigrant and living in the U.S. permanently and being a nonimmigrant who intends to depart the U.S. This visa is not one of them. If the BCIS or the U.S. consulate determines you have immigrant intent, there are a whole list of nonimmigrant visas that you will not be able to get—including the B-1/B-2 you already have.

Q I'm not in status. What can happen to me?

A You can be removed or excluded. Here's the practical point, before 9/11 the U.S. government had a general idea of what was going on with immigration. Now they are under profound and constant pressure to track visitors accurately and fully. So now if you overstay, there's an increased likelihood that the government will both know it and act on it. Before 9/11, unless you were unlucky or filed paperwork with the then INS without knowing you were out of status, your chances of being unnoticed were much greater.

Q My family and I are visiting Florida this summer. We have heard how dangerous it is, especially for people from Germany like us. I've noticed that a lot of U.S. citizens here have guns. Can I buy a gun to protect us as well?

A No. In general, nonimmigrant visitors to the U.S. may not possess firearms or ammunition. There are a few exceptions. For example, if you were a sportsman coming here to hunt or a member of a foreign country's law enforcement establishment who was here on official business that might be sufficient.

STAYING IN THE UNITED STATES

Q My brother came on a B-2 Visa as a tourist. Now he has decided he really likes it here and he wants to stay. What does he need to do to be able to stay in the United States?

A Your brother entered the United States on a nonimmigrant visa *with nonimmigrant intent.* Now he wants to change his status to that of an immigrant, since he has now decided he wants to live here on a more or less permanent basis. In order to remain in the United States, he needs to change his *visa category* to one that will allow him to stay in the United States permanently. This process is called *adjustment of status.* Your brother came to the United States on a B-2 tourist visa. This visa allows adjustment of status.

Q What is required to adjust status to an immigrant visa?

A The first requirement is to be inspected and admitted lawfully into the United States. You must also be in legal status. In order to adjust status to that of an immigrant, one must:
- make an application for adjustment;
- be eligible to receive an immigrant visa and be admissible to the United States for permanent residence; and,
- an immigrant visa must be immediately available.

Visiting the United States

This is the hard part, because you need to have either a job or a family relationship that will allow you to get an immigrant visa immediately.

Q Is there any sure way to adjust from a B-1/B-2 Visa to an immigrant visa?

A The most direct path for adjusting your status from a B-Visa holder to a permanent resident alien, is to be the beneficiary of an available *immediate relative visa*. Of course, for you to have this, you would have to be the *spouse, parent,* or *unmarried child* of a U.S. citizen.

Q My sister got a large number of parking tickets while she was a tourist in Chicago. Will this be a problem for her if she wants to adjust her status and stay in the United States?

A Probably not for immigration purposes. Although she would be in trouble if she had committed a crime while in the United States, parking tickets do not, by themselves, cause immigration problems.

Q Are there any visitor visa categories that I *cannot* get an extension for?

Yes, there are several visa categories that the BCIS will not allow to have an extension. For example, if you came to the United States without a visa under the *Visa Waiver Program*. In addition, you cannot get an extension if:
- you are a crewman of a boat or plane;
- you are just transiting through the United States; or,
- you came into the United States as a fiancé/ée of a U.S. citizen or dependent of a fiancé/ée.

FOR MEDICAL TREATMENT

Q My fiancée's cousin is very ill. She would like to come to the Untied States for medical treatment. Is there anything that can be done to allow her to come here for treatment?

A Yes. She might qualify to come to the U.S. for humanitarian reasons. However, this process still involves getting a visa unless your cousin is from a country that qualifies for the Visa Waiver program. Usually the visa applied for is the B-1/B-2 Visa. The B Visa allows people to visit the U.S. on a temporary basis for business, pleasure, or medical treatment.

Visiting the United States

Q I need to get medical care in the United States, but my country does not qualify for the Visa Waiver Program. What do I need to do to get the proper visa?

A Even though you are traveling for medical reasons, you will still need to go through the entire nonimmigrant visa process. You will need to fill out Form DS-156 *Application for a Nonimmigrant Visa* and any necessary supporting documents and apply for the visa at the nearest U.S. consulate.

Q What information will I need about my medical condition if I want to get treated in the United States?

A You will need detailed explanations and evaluations from your local medical treatment team that clearly show why you need to go to the United States for treatment.

Q Do I need papers from the U.S. hospital before I can get a visa for medical treatment in the United States?

A This is not an absolute requirement, but it is best if you can show documents from a U.S. hospital or treatment center that show why the treatment needs to be done in the United States. This is particularly needed for treatments that are long or expensive. The documents from the U.S. hospital should outline the length of the treatment and the cost. You should be prepared to show how you will pay for the treatment.

U.S. Immigration and Citizenship Q&A

Q Why is it that the U.S. consulate is so interested in my ability to pay for medical treatment? Doesn't the United States have health care?

A There are two reasons that the consular officer is concerned about payment. First, he or she wants to make certain that you will not work in the United States to pay your medical bills. Secondly, he or she wants to make sure that you do not run up large bills at a hospital that you cannot pay. The U.S. does have a health care system that requires public hospitals and doctors to treat patients and stabilize them regardless of the patient's ability to pay. The consulate is trying to avoid a situation where a U.S. doctor would give you a letter that said he or she would need an office visit with you to make a diagnosis. Then, after your arrival in the United States, the doctor would send you to a hospital. The hospital would then be required by law to treat you. If you could not pay the bill, the hospital would be forced to look to the monies put up by local charities for local indigents or use taxpayer money.

Q Can I come to the United States to be treated for any kind of illness?

A No. If your illness makes you excludible from the United States, you will not be able to come unless you get a waiver. Illnesses that can make you excludible include HIV (AIDS) and tuberculosis.

3.

Working in the United States

Coming to the United States to work or study—as an artist, nurse, scientist, engineer, journalist, teacher, college student, or as almost anything you can imagine—is one of the more common reasons families visit and live temporarily in the United States. A lot of people think that getting a "work permit" to work in the United States for one or two years is almost impossible. In fact, the law is quite liberal and open in this regard. As long as you have the right kind of job offer, occupation, or sponsorship, you can almost certainly get a temporary work visa.

How can you or a family member get one of these visas? What happens to you, the family? Can you come with your family member? Can you work in the United States if you come here? Can you go to school while your family member works? How long can you stay? These are some of the questions answered in this chapter.

Before reading the questions to find your situation, you might want to know what kind of temporary visas are available for people who want to work in the United States. In general, visas are available to people who have the right kind of job offer from a U.S. company, hospital, or organization (H Visas); to employees of foreign companies that are being transferred to the same company in the United States (L Visas); to certain kinds of investors and business people (E Visas); to individuals attending training or exchange programs (J, M, Q Visas);

to recognized artists, scientists, teachers, business executives, and athletes (O, P Visas); to religious workers (R Visas); to professionals from Canada and Mexico (TN Visas); and, to students (F Visas), although students can only work under very limited circumstances. These visas allow the principal visa holder to bring his or her spouse and minor children to the United States.

There are differences in what you have to do and what you have to have in order to get one of these temporary work visas, and there are differences in the treatment of family members of each of these visa holders.

The following questions and answers, taken from real-life situations, will help you identify these differences and see exactly how your situation might be handled. For a quick guide to the requirements for each of these visas, see Appendix A.

GETTING STARTED

Q My husband and I do not live in the United States. An American company wants to hire him to work for two years in Chicago on an engineering project. Can he get a visa for this? Can I go with him?

A Yes. There is a special type of nonimmigrant visa that allows foreign workers to come to the United States to work temporarily for a U.S. employer. The visa is called an *H Visa*. It was allowed by U.S. lawmakers to help the U.S. economy. It

Working in the United States

does this, by making it possible for companies, hospitals, farmers, etc. to hire foreign workers. The need for the foreign worker must be *immediate* and *temporary*. Your situation meets these requirements, so ask the U.S. company to start the application process. Your husband is being hired as an engineer. That is what the BCIS calls a *specialty occupation* and qualifies him for an H-1B Visa. You can get an H-4 Visa and go with him.

Q A company in Detroit wants to offer my wife a job. I am very happy because otherwise she and I would have to go back to our home country. Does it make a difference what position she will have? If she gets a visa for the job, can I stay in the United States too?

A Yes, it makes a big difference. All jobs are not equal in the eyes of the immigration service. In other words, if you want to use a job offer as the way to get a visa to stay in the United States, the job must be the right one and your wife must qualify for it. The law only allows foreigners in certain job categories to get a work visa based on the work they will temporarily perform in the United States. If your wife qualifies, you will be able to get a *dependent visa* and also stay in the United States.

Q What kinds of jobs qualify for temporary work visas?

A The main visa used for purposes of temporary work—the H Visa—allows for the following types of temporary workers (positions):

- registered nurses;
- workers in so-called *specialty occupations*, which is a job that requires at least a college degree (bachelor's degree);
- recognized artists, entertainers, fashion models, and athletes;
- seasonal farm workers and other seasonal or *peak load* temporary workers;
- participants in special education programs for handicapped children; and,
- participants in some other types of training programs.

Q Are there any limits on the number of temporary work visas available?

A Yes. The number of H-1B Visas, probably the best known *temporary* work visa for specialty workers, is *capped* at 195,000 total visas per year. In 2004, this number is set to be reduced to 65,000. The other categories are limited as well. Another type of temporary work visa—the L-1 Visa—for managers and executives being transferred by foreign companies to the United States—is not capped.

Q I have an H-1B Visa. What happens when I reach the maximum six year limit?

Working in the United States

A If you want to get another H-1B Visa, you will have to leave the United States and stay away for one year. Then you can apply for another H-1B Visa. You may *not* apply for an extension, however, if you qualify for a different type of visa or immigration status, you can seek to *adjust* your status.

Q My husband has been working for around three years in the United States on an H-1B Visa. Things were a bit slow at work, so he and I went back to our home country to spend time with our family. His U.S. company now wants to extend his visa. Can we do this from here?

A No. You must be *physically present* in the United States when the petition for extension is filed. The BCIS position is that if you are not in the United States, you are not *in status*. Therefore, you have no status to extend.

Q I have approached a lot of companies trying to get a job in the United States. As soon as they find out I am from Slovenia, they stop talking to me and say that I'll never get the right visa. Can I do anything about this?

A Yes. Try to find out if the companies you are talking to are concerned about the dangers of hiring *illegal* workers. Since employer sanctions were added to the immigration laws by the *Immigration Reform and Control Act of 1986*, a lot of companies have stopped hiring foreign workers to avoid being in a situation where they might have to pay a fine. If you think this might be happening in your case, make sure to discuss this issue at the beginning of any interview or contact with the company. Let them know that you are in the United States legally and have not, and will not accept any illegal employment. Remind them that you would be qualifying for the proper work visa on the basis of the job they are offering, combined with your qualifications. If the petition for this visa is approved, there is absolutely no danger that they would be subject to any fines or penalties for hiring you.

Q My husband is applying for a work visa. How does the H work visa processing work?

A Your husband's company prepares and files *a Labor Condition Application* on Form ETA-9035 with the State Workforce or Employment Agency/Department of Labor. The Department of Labor/State Workforce Agency must certify that it is *necessary to hire a foreign worker* for the job. In this application, the company must show:

- that your husband's wages will be at or more than the average for your occupation;
- that his job will not have negative effect on U.S. workers doing similar work; and,
- that no labor dispute exists at the plant where he will work.

A copy of the Labor Condition Application must also be posted at the company. The company then takes the approved form from the Department of Labor and attaches it to Form I-129. It sends Form I-129 with the H supplement and the Labor Condition Application (all together called the *petition*) to the BCIS Service Center responsible for the region where the work will be performed. The BCIS must examine your credentials and the job offer to make sure your *husband* and the husband's *position qualify*. The BCIS will send a notice of approval when it approves your petition. Because you are not in the United States, you will take the BCIS approval notice to the U.S. consulate along with a completed Form DS-156 *Application for Nonimmigrant Visa*. If all requirements are met, the consular officer stamps the H-1B Visa in your passport.

Q: It is taking us weeks and weeks to get all our documents together to apply for a work visa. How long will it take the government to process it?

A: If you are applying for an H-1B Visa for specialty occupations, you have two processing times to consider. First, the Department of Labor must certify *the Labor Condition Application*. This takes one to two months depending on the state you are in. Then, the BCIS must process and approve the *petition*. This can take another three to four months depending on the BCIS Service Center you send it to and the case load at the time.

Q: Is there any way I can speed up my work visa application (an H-1B)?

A: Yes. The BCIS offers *premium processing* for an extra payment of $1,000. This can reduce the processing time to as little as fifteen days.

Q I work at a hospital in Detroit as a nurse. My husband and I have applied to become permanent residents of the United States. We need to go home for about four weeks to take care of some family business. My hospital has no problem with letting me have the time off. Do we need special permission to go home and then be able return?

A You can travel home and then back to the United States on your current temporary work visa. As a registered nurse, you are working in the United States on an H-1C Visa. This visa has certain advantages over some other temporary work visas. One of these advantages is that you do not need *special permission* to travel out of the United States and still maintain your status. You only need to have your valid H-1C Visa and take with you the original *receipt notice* for your *adjustment of status application* (you received this on Form I-797).

Q I am working as a nurse in Phoenix and my wife is taking care of our children. We have applied for the Green Card. Can my wife start working before we get the Green Card?

A Yes. Based on your application for adjustment of status to permanent residents, you can apply for an *Employment Authorization Document*. Once approved, your wife can work.

Working in the United States

Q We have both been working in health care in the U.S. We have applied for the Green Card and have also received our Employment Authorization Documents. My wife is thinking about changing jobs to work for a different hospital. Is there any problem with this?

A Yes and no. There is no real problem because she is authorized to do it. But, there are consequences. Your wife has been working on a H-1C Visa, for temporary, nonimmigrant workers. That visa only authorizes her to work at the job covered by the visa. It also means that she is classified as a nonimmigrant. She has now applied for permanent residency and has received employment authorization based on the pending approval of her Green Card. So, she can work at another job.

But, by leaving the job she was approved for on the H-1C Visa and accepting another job, (*open market employment*) she gives up her nonimmigrant, temporary status. This could be a problem, if, for example, she needed to travel back to Mexico before her Green Card is issued. If she is not careful, such travel could lead to her losing the Green Card application. To avoid this possibility, your wife should either:

- not take a new job until after Green Card approval;
- take the job, but not travel outside of the United States before the Green Card approval; or,
- get advanced permission (advance parole) from the BCIS to travel outside the United States before she travels.

Q I have been working as an engineer at an American company in Boston. My wife has been living with me as my dependent on a dependent visa. My wife would like to work. Can she?

A No. You are working in the United States under a *specialty occupation* visa, an H-1B Visa. Your wife is entered as your spouse under a H-4 Visa. H-4 Visa holders may not work. Your wife would have to qualify and get approval for a work permit on her own.

Q My wife is a registered nurse working in Boston. We would like to move to Chicago to be near other family. Can my wife work in Chicago on her current visa?

A No. Your wife is working in the United States on the basis of a visa which the hospital in Boston sponsored for her, an H-1C Visa. The H-1C Visa only allows her to work in the employment that was covered and approved on the petition for the visa. If she can get the hospital in Chicago to file a petition on her behalf and it is approved, then she can change jobs and work in Chicago.

Q My wife is a nurse. A hospital in St. Louis wants to hire her. They have already filed the papers. There is so much work to do that she could start working now. The

Working in the United States

head nurse said if she just volunteers and doesn't get paid she can do it before she gets the visa and can get paid for it later. Is this true?

A No. If your wife works as a *volunteer* and then gets extra pay later because of it, she would be performing *unauthorized work*. This would violate her current status in which she is not allowed to work. If she works while on a visa that does not allow it, she can be permanently barred from adjusting her status to permanent resident in the future.

Q My husband just got a job with a large computer company in California. Can we bring our children to the United States? How long can we stay in California?

A Your husband will be coming to the United States on a *specialty occupation* visa, an H-1B Visa. This visa allows you as the spouse and the children to come with your husband on H-4 Visas. Normally, your visas will be limited to three years when you first come to the United States. You can extend them up to six years, if your husband continues to meet the requirements.

Q My family and I have been living in the United States for almost six years. I have an H-1B Visa and work for a multi-national oil company. I have been told that at the end of the six years, we will go home. Over the last six years, my family and I had to spend a lot of time at home for family rea-

91

sons. My employer was very generous in giving me time off. Will this time out of the country count towards the six year limit?

A No. You may be able to add the time you spent outside of the United States to the six year period and therefore stay longer. But, you must be able to prove that the time outside of the U.S. was *meaningfully interruptive* of your employment. Your employer would have to prove this to the BCIS. (In general, sick leave or leave to care for sick relatives would be accepted, but the burden of proof is on you.)

Q My husband's company is downsizing because of the economy. They said they will have to let him go. We came here two years ago because of this job and still have one year left on our visa. Can the company do this to him? Can we stay for the rest of the time on our visa?

A The company can terminate employees—even employees it has sponsored for H-1B Visas like your husband—as long as it complies with any labor laws that may apply. Also, once your husband is terminated, he will no longer have the right to work in the United States, because this right was only for the *specific* job he is doing now. This means, that you will not be able to stay in the United States once the employment ends, except for a ten-day grace period. If you do not wish to go back home right now, you should try to find another employer to petition for your husband or you.

Q A friend told me there is something called a *180-day rule*. What is it and can I make use of it with my company?

A The rule is for H-1B workers who have immigration petitions pending and who have filed for *adjustment of status* using Form I-485. Normally, H-1B Visa holders are tied to the company that petitioned for them and may not change jobs. But, an H-1B Visa holder who gets his or her status adjusted to that of a lawful permanent resident (LPR) can change jobs or take any job he or she wants. H-1B workers waiting for an adjustment of status to be approved would ordinarily not be able to change jobs even though they would be allowed to do so once their adjustment of status is approved. To protect these workers somewhat from the long processing times for adjustment of status, the so-called *180-day rule* has been adopted. The rule allows such workers to make their H-1B *portable* by being able to change employers if the BCIS does not make a decision on the adjustment of status application within 180 days.

In other words, if it has been more than 180 days from the time you filed Form I-485 and you have received a notice of approval from the BCIS, you can switch jobs and effectively stay in H-1B status.

Q I was working in a software company and was let go because we lost a big contract. The BCIS told me that my visa is no longer valid and I have to leave the U.S. I am here with my family (wife and two children) and flying back home on such short notice will be expensive. Is there anything I can do?

A Yes. Be aware that your *employer is responsible* to pay your transportation cost home, unless you made some other arrangement with the company. Contact the company's personnel office for assistance.

Q I am working for a large U.S. pharmaceutical company on an H-1B Visa and trying to plan ahead. My family would like to stay in America and the company would like to keep me. There is only about 1 ½ years left on my H-1B Visa. What can I do to stay longer?

A You are smart to plan ahead. As you know, the maximum period of admission for an H-1B Visa holder is six years. If your company really wants you permanently, it can apply for an immigration visa on your behalf. Your credentials would appear to qualify you for an EB-2 immigration visa. In support of the petition, you will need an approved *Labor Certification Application*. If you get your employer to file a labor certification application before your final year on the H-1B Visa starts, you may be in a position to extend your stay when your H-1B Visa expires. A relatively new law, passed in November, 2002, says that as long as your labor certification has been filed for 365 days when your H-1B Visa runs out, you can get an extension of your H-1B status until such time that a decision is made on your labor certification application. If your labor certification is approved before your H-1B

Working in the United States

status runs out, you can then apply for *adjustment to immigrant status*. You would keep your H-1B status until a decision is made on the immigrant petition.

Q I am reaching the end of my six-year stay on an H-1B Visa. During these six years, my company had me working over seas a lot of the time. Does this make any difference to the six-year maximum?

A Yes, it may. You can petition the BCIS to get back, or *recapture,* the days you were not in the United States. Make sure you have proof of your absence like airline tickets, employer records of your business travel, credit card purchases outside of the United States, etc. The days you recapture will be added to your six year maximum.

FOREIGN COMPANIES

Q My husband works as a manager for a Japanese company in Tokyo. Can his Japanese company send him to work for its office in San Francisco? Can I and the children go to San Francisco with him?

A Yes, your husband's company can send him to the United States. And, in fact, this is one of the easiest ways foreign

workers can come to work in the United States, as long as the requirements are met for the L-1 Visa. The requirements are:
- that the Japanese company has the proper relationship to the company in the United States;
- that your husband is a full time employee of the Japanese company and has been for at least one year during the past three years;
- that both the U.S. company and the foreign company must be doing business during the whole course of your husband's employment in the United States;
- that your husband is coming to the United States to work as a manager, executive, or in a position that requires specialized knowledge;
- that your husband has been working in this kind of position for the company in Japan; and,
- that your husband and you intend to leave the United States when your visa expires.

An L-1 Visa holder may bring his or her spouse and children to the United States, or the spouse and children may come later and join the *principal visa holder* in the United States.

Q I would really like to work in the U.S. to get experience. My company has a business in the U.S., but when I asked to work there, they told me I'd never get a visa. Is that right?

A No, it is not correct. There are visas available for foreign companies to send employees to the United States to work in their U.S. based business. This visa is called an L-1 Visa for *intracompany* transfers. But, the proper relationship must exist between the foreign company and its U.S. based business. The law states that the U.S. company must be the *same employer* or a *subsidiary* or *affiliate* thereof. The normal kinds of relationships that are easy for the BCIS to approve are:

- when the U.S. company is the exact same corporation as the foreign company (branch office);
- when one company owns the majority of the other company (parent-subsidiary relationship);
- when both the U.S. company and the foreign company are majority owned by a third company (affiliated companies); and,
- when the U.S. company is joint venture between a foreign company and another company.

Q I have been working for a large drug company in Switzerland for about seven months. I noticed on our company website that there is a job opening in our New Jersey office that I would be perfect for. It would be really interesting for my family to live in the United States for a while. Can my company transfer me to this job?

A Yes. To be eligible for an *intracompany transfer visa*, you normally must have at least one year of employment within the last three years with the foreign company. However, since 2002, there is an exception for employees of large companies like yours that have received pre-approved permission to transfer workers to the United States. For these companies, which have so-called *blanket petitions*, an employee must have been employed only six months within the last three years with the foreign firm. The six-month qualifying period only applies to

L Visa applications. It will not allow your company to petition for you to become a permanent resident, unless it first gets *labor certification approval*.

Q In one month, I will have been working for a company in Sweden for one year. They want to send me to their office in Minneapolis. I know these visa things take time. Can I apply now, so that I can have my visa ready when my one year is up?

A No. You must meet the one-year continuous employment requirement at the time your company files its application (petition) on your behalf.

Q I have been working well over one year for my company in Japan, but part of the time I was in the United States as a business visitor to help with some trade fairs and also as a tourist. My company now wants to send me to work in our subsidiary in the United States, but our personnel officer says that my employment is not continuous because of my stays in the United States. Is she right?

A No. When it receives the application from your employer, the BCIS will look to see if you have worked for the company for a *continuous* period of one year (six months for *blanket petitions*) within the last three years. As long as you are employed by the company, any time you may have spent in the United States does not interrupt the continuous nature of your employment, but it is added to the one-year (or six-month) requirement. Add the number of days you spent in the United States on business and as a tourist, and add that number to 365 (one year). This is the total number of days you must have worked for your company in Japan before it can send you to the United States.

Q How do I know what category I fit into for an L-1 Visa?

A What category you fit into can be a complex question. The law provides definitions, but there is certainly overlap and each situation is different.

In general, you are a *manager* if: you are in charge of the organization or a department; you supervise the work of others; you have the authority to hire and fire; and, you exercise discretion over your own day-to-day activities.

You are an *executive* if: you direct the management of the company or a major part of it; you establish goals and policies for the organization; you have wide decision making authority; and, you receive only general supervision from, for example, a board of directors.

A *specialty worker*, who for purposes of this visa is called a *specialized knowledge employee*, must have an advanced level of knowledge or expertise pertaining to the company's product, service, research, etc. and be a member of a *profession*, for example, architect, engineer, lawyer, physician, teachers, etc. For example, an executive secretary has been granted this status, but a teacher was not. A detailed description of your duties and background is important in identifying the right category.

Q I am working in India for a company as a senior software programmer. Because of problems in the U.S. economy, our U.S. subsidiary needs me. The company has always in the past sent workers on H-1B Visas, but these are getting harder to get and the workers are too expensive. Can the company send me on an L Visa?

A This is a tricky question, and one that is on the minds of U.S. politicians right now. A lot of U.S. companies have tried to replace expensive H-1B workers and U.S. national workers with low-cost L transferees because the L Visa does not require *labor certification*. Your company in India and your company in the United States have the proper relationship, but the L Visa was designed for top managers and specialized knowledge workers. The specialized knowledge workers must have *advanced knowledge* of the company's products, not just a skill like computer programming.

Q How long can I work in the United States if my company transfers me there?

A BCIS usually grants an initial period of three years. After three years, you can apply for an extension of stay. If an extension is approved, it is usually for a two-year period. The maximum stay (initial period plus all extensions) is five years for specialized knowledge workers and seven years for managers and executives.

Working in the United States

Q I am working on an L-1 Visa in a specialized knowledge category. I have to leave the U.S. next year because my five years are up. If my company promotes me to manager, can I stay seven years?

A Yes. Promotions within the qualifying categories are allowed. Be careful, however, you must be promoted and in your management job for a least six months before your five years are up, in order, to be able to get the full seven years. Your company should petition the BCIS to get approval at the time you are promoted.

Q My company applied for a company transfer visa for me. It was approved, but I was only allowed one year. Why? I am now in the United States and my year is almost up. What should I do? My wife and I want to stay and my company wants me to stay too.

A BCIS normally grants an initial period of three years, but can and does grant shorter periods in certain cases. In your case, your company did not make it clear in the original application (called the *petition*) that your services would be required for at least three years. You should now immediately have your company apply for an *extension of stay* using Form I-129. The application should contain a letter from the company that contains:
- your name;
- the purpose of the letter, i.e., request for extension of stay;
- your job title;

- an explanation that clearly sets forth the reasons your services are needed for an additional period of time; and,
- a request that the application be approved.

Q I am an Austrian working at my company's U.S. headquarters in San Jose. I am on an L-1 Visa and have been in the United States for six years. My visa will expire next year. What can I do?

A The maximum time you can stay in the United States on an L-1 Visa is seven years. This means that at the end of next year, you must either leave the United States or *adjust your status* to allow you to stay. Once you have reached the maximum stay under an L-1 Visa, you cannot come back to the United States (except for brief visits for business or as a tourist) until you have spent at least one year outside the United States.

If you are flexible, one possibility is for you to return to your parent company in Austria and work there outside of the United States for one year. Then have the company petition for another L-1 Visa. If you want to stay permanently in the United States, you can apply for adjustment of status to an employment-based immigration visa as a *business manager of exceptional ability*. One of the advantages of an L-1 Visa is that you can apply for a Green Card while working in the United States as a nonimmigrant.

Q I am an engineer working for a German-American company. For the last four years, I have been coming to the United States to work in our U.S. company but have been living in Germany. My company got a company transfer visa (L-1) for me, so that I would not have to worry about how long my visits to the United States might be. I have been told that my visa will run out next year after five years. But, I will still need to work in the United States on our projects. What can I do?

A You have at least two options. Because you live in Germany and only travel occasionally to the United States on almost a *commuter* like basis to work on projects, you qualify for an exception to the usual maximum five year period of stay. Have your employer file an I-129 form to apply for an *extension of stay* and provide proof that you reside primarily in Germany. A second alternative may be for you to give up your L-1 status and simply travel to the United States as a business visitor. In your case, this alternative would require some internal adjustments, because, as a business visitor, you could only be paid by and employed by the German company.

Q My family would like to live for a few years in the United States. I could work for my current employer because we have an office in New York. How exactly do I apply for a company transfer visa?

A You don't *apply*, your company *petitions* for you. You are called the *beneficiary*, because you get the benefit of being able to work in the United States. As you are currently working for your company outside of the United States, the application procedure works like this:

- your company fills out Form I-129, including an L-1 supplement and supporting letters, and sends it to the BCIS;
- the BCIS reviews the form and approves it;
- BCIS issues Form I-797 *Notice of Approval*, which shows that you are entitled to the visa;
- you prepare Form DS-156 *Application for Nonimmigrant Visa*;
- you take the DS-156 and the I-797 to the U.S. consulate in your country; and,
- the U.S. consulate issues the L-1 Visa and puts the visa in your passport.

Q I am the human resources person at a U.S. subsidiary of a German company. We transfer up to twenty employees each year from Germany to the United States. Does my company have to go through the whole visa application process each time?

A No. There is a special program called the *Blanket Petition Program* for companies like yours. Your company can qualify by filing Form I-129 and checking the box—*a blanket petition*—on the L Classification Supplement. Your company should list itself and its parent as qualifying organizations by showing that:

- the companies listed are engaged in commercial trade or services;
- your company is doing business in the United States and has had an office for more than one year;
- your company has three or more domestic and foreign branches, subsidiaries or affiliates; and,

➤ you have obtained approval for ten or more L Visa petitions in the last twelve months.

(There is an alternative to this last requirement. Show that you are a large company with more than 1000 employees in the United States and sales of at least $25 million.)

Each time you want to transfer an executive, manager, or specialized knowledge professional, all he or she has to do is to apply at the U.S. consulate. The only thing to watch out for is that you cannot use the blanket petition program for specialized knowledge workers if they are not professionals.

Q How long does it take to get an L-1 Visa?

A You can have your visa in as short as five weeks. The process at BCIS usually takes between four to six weeks, although the law says that a review and decision should be made within thirty days. Once you receive the approval from BCIS and take it to the U.S. consulate in your country, you can figure on about one week for consular processing, if your company has applied using a blanket application. If it is an individual application (that means your company has applied only for you, not others in your company), processing could take longer depending on the consulate. Even high-volume consulates process L-1 Visas quite quickly, no longer than, at the most, two to three weeks.

U.S. Immigration and Citizenship Q&A

Q I have heard a lot of stories about long waits for BCIS to process visa applications. I work for a large Japanese company as an executive and because of a change in our business situation I need to take over management of our U.S. subsidiary quickly. Our company has good political contacts in Washington, D.C. Should we try to get them to help speed up the process?

A Political intervention, for example, by a U.S. Senator or Member of Congress, can sometimes help in dealing with visa problems, but in your case there is an easier and more direct way to speed things up. The BCIS has a *premium processing service* for certain visas and the *intracompany transfer visa—the* L-1 Visa your company is applying for—is one of them. Have the company fill out Form I-907 and send it in with your application. The fee is currently $1000 in addition to the regular filing fee for the L-1 application. The *Premium Processing Services* guarantees that the BCIS will either approve, deny, or issue a notice for further information within fifteen days after receiving the application. You can even use this form to speed things up if your company has already sent in the petition.

Q My company got approval for me to be transferred to our U.S. office. I got a notice of this from the BCIS Service Center in Nebraska, but I lost it. I know I need it. What can I do?

A Get Form I-824 from the BCIS website at **www.bcis.gov**. Fill out the form checking the box in Part 2 that says "I am applying for a duplicate approval notice." Send the form and the fee (currently $140) to the Nebraska Service Center. (If you happen to have a copy of the original approval notice, you should send it with the form. It will speed up the process.)

Q We are a nonprofit social services organization in Lithuania with an office in New York. Can we send a Lithuanian national to manage our U.S. office?

A Yes, however, your organization must meet all the same requirements as a regular business. This means, among other things, that your organization in Lithuania and the organization in New York have real, common control, and the proper relationship. Also, as a nonprofit, your organization may *not* take advantage of *blanket petitions*, but must apply for each transfer on an individual basis.

Q My husband and I have been living in the U.S. for about two years. He was sent here by his company to do research at their U.S. product development center. So far I haven't wanted to work, but now a local gift store would like me to work there. Can I? Also, our son turns eighteen soon and would like to work. Can he?

A Since the beginning of 2002, the rules have changed to allow the spouses of L-1 Visa holders (managers and specialized knowledge workers like your husband) to work while in the United States. In fact, you have an advantage over your husband. His visa only allows him to work at the employment covered by the L-1 petition that is for his current company. You, on the other hand, can work wherever you want. You can even be self-employed. As an L-2 Visa holder, you only need to apply for an *Employment Authorization Document* (EAD). You will also need to show evidence of your husband's status and evidence that you are indeed his spouse. File Form I-765 with the BCIS Service Center responsible for the area where you live. Unfortunately, this new law does not extend to your son or other children. Children of an L-1 Visa holder are *not* allowed to work.

Q I have been working in New York for a U.K. publishing company. My wife stayed in the U.K. because she had a good job and could not work here. I have heard that there has been a change in the law that would allow her to work in the United States. Can I still apply for her to join me?

A Yes. You are in the United States on an E-1 Visa that allows you to work for a subsidiary of a U.K. company that is engaged in substantial trade between the United Kingdom and the United States. The E-1 Visa allows your spouse and children to either *accompany* you or *follow* you later to the United States. She is eligible for an E-2 Visa. Since the beginning of 2002, holders of E-2 Visas can also work in the United States.

Q My wife is applying for an *Employment Authorization Document* based on the fact that I am a manager of my company's subsidiary here. How long is her work permit valid?

A *Employment Authorization Documents* for the spouses of managers, specialized knowledge workers, treaty investors, or traders (L-2 and E-2 Visa holders) are valid for one year. They can be renewed for as long as the other spouse, the principal visa holder, stays in the proper status.

MANAGING YOUR OWN BUSINESS

Q It doesn't seem fair to me that big businesses can transfer executives to the United States, but a small business like ours can't. We need to start doing more business in the United States and I am the only one that can do it. I am Mexican, well-educated, and my wife and I own the business. I do not want to immigrate to the U.S. Can you help?

A Yes. Both large and small companies can use L-1 Visas to transfer managers and executives to the United States. Both large and small companies must meet the same requirements to do so. In your case, the facts are:
➢ you are the sole shareholder of the Mexican company, and the Mexican company owns 100% of the share of the U.S. company;

- you have been working as a full time employee of the Mexican company continuously for more than six months;
- you are clearly an executive of the Mexican company and are coming to the United States to be president of the U.S. subsidiary;
- your university and business schools degrees show that you are qualified for an executive position;
- you plan to return to Mexico once the business is running smoothly; and,
- both the Mexican company and the U.S. company will be doing business during the whole time you are in the United States and are financially able to do so.

So, all you need to do is have either the Mexican company or the U.S. company file Form I-129, the L supplement, and all supporting evidence on your behalf. Once it is approved by BCIS, you will get a Form I-797 that you can take to the U.S. consulate in Mexico City to get your L-1 Visa. Your wife can accompany you on an L-2 Visa.

Q My family (my wife, my mother, and myself) have a small consulting company in Europe. For a number of years, we have had a subsidiary in the United States that we used for tax purposes to sell our line of training materials. I wanted to transfer myself to the U.S. company to build it into a consulting office; not just a sales office. My application was denied. Why?

A You must provide enough information to convince the BCIS that the company would continue operating while you were running the U.S. office. You should have addressed this issue in the company support letter. The letter should have shown that because of the Austrian company's financial strength and management structure, it would have no trouble continuing to operate, to pay its staff, etc. for the period you needed to be in the United States. You also should have made it clear that your mother would continue to play a leading role in running the Austrian business, while you would be in the United States. (This sort of proof is more necessary with *family businesses* than with normal multi-national companies.)

Since you recently received the denial, you can file Form I-290B with the BCIS *Administrative Appeals Unit* to try to get a favorable decision. Make sure you check the box stating that you will be supplying evidence. Make sure you do so.

Q: I own a successful company and have established a subsidiary in Chicago that meets all the requirements for my son to be transferred there to begin to build it up. If I make my son the president of the U.S. subsidiary, can he automatically apply for the L-1 Visa as an executive or manager? If not, can he be sent in another category?

A: No. You must show that your son's *duties* are of an executive or managerial capacity. In your case, this may be difficult because your company in Chicago is small and just starting operations. One of the things the BCIS looks at is the size and organizational structure of the company. The better approach for you may be to have your son apply as a *specialized knowledge employee*. You do this by providing evidence that your son's transfer to the U.S. company is based on his specialized knowledge of your company's product, procedures and business operations in the company support letter that accompanies the L-1 petition. Since 9/11, the BCIS has been increasingly restrictive in what it will accept as proof of specialized knowledge. Therefore, in your petition, you will want to either show why a U.S. worker cannot be trained and/or point out the legal history of the specialized knowledge requirement so that the BCIS decision maker is aware that this requirement is not part of the law.

Q: I am owner and managing director of a mid-sized advertising agency. Can my company transfer my daughter to the United States to manage a new business?

A: Yes. The requirements are the same as for all L-1 intra-company transfers, but your company must submit additional evidence because you are starting a new business. Submit the evidence in the form of a *company support letter* with Form I-129. The additional evidence should include:
- evidence that the U.S. company has physical premises by showing, for example, a copy of a rental contract;
- that your daughter has been working for the U.K. company as a manager and will be a manager at the U.S. company;
- a financial plan and proof of financial resources to show that the U.S. office will be able to support your daughter (pay her salary, etc.) no later than one year after the petition is approved; and,
- that the U.K. company will continue to remain in operation for the whole time your daughter is in the United States.

Q My own company in Ireland petitioned for me to be transferred to our newly formed company in New York. Is there anything I have to do now? Anything to watch out for? My wife and daughter will be going with me.

A Yes. Once you receive Form I-797 *Notice of Approval* take it and copies of all supporting documents to the U.S. consulate in Dublin, along with Form DS-156 *Application for Nonimmigrant Visa*, photographs, and the processing fee (you should check with the consulate for the current fees). Your wife and daughter must also apply for their visas (L-2 Visas) on Form DS-156. (They are not automatically included on your application.)

Some consulates may require extra documentation like copies of your local tax returns. The consulate is not allowed to change the BCIS approval of your L-1 status, but it does have the power to deny you a visa, if there is any fraud. Because you are coming to the United States to manage a new office, your visa will be limited to a one year initial period. When the year is up, the BCIS will want proof that both the Irish company and the U.S. company are in operation.

Q What kind of documents will my family business need to have to support my transfer to my own U.S. company? I have heard that it is hard to get the BCIS to approve a transfer if you own both companies. Is there anything I can do to help my chances?

A As with every application (petition) for an intracompany transfer, you have to have documents about your foreign company, your U.S. company, and about you as the employee. The more detailed the documentation about your foreign company and the U.S. company, the stronger the application. A sampling of the documents we normally ask clients to obtain include:

➤ incorporation certificates;
➤ business permits;
➤ annual reports;
➤ detailed organizational charts;
➤ sample contracts and invoices showing larger orders;
➤ trade references;
➤ publicity received;
➤ recent financial statements; and,
➤ tax returns.

In addition, for the U.S. company, you should have a statement showing employee wages.

As an employee you should have:

➤ wage statements showing you as an employee of the foreign company;
➤ a resume;
➤ your job description and duties at the foreign company;
➤ your job description and duties at the U.S. company;
➤ any awards or publicity you received;
➤ your passport;
➤ your birth certificate; and,
➤ your I-94 form arrival record if you are already in the United States.

You will not need to submit all these documents with the petition, but you will need the information to be able to fill out the I-129 form and write a letter from the company in support of the petition.

You are right that it is *hard* to get approval, but this can be overcome by having the solid, detailed proof that your situation meets the requirements. In addition to the type of evidence and documents required in support of every L-1 petition, owners who are transferring themselves can strengthen their case by presenting evidence of *strong ties* to their native country and a clear intention to return there when the transfer assignment is finished. Evidence of large land holdings in your country, other business investment in your country, a house that you keep, strong family ties, etc. have helped others in your situation get their petitions approved.

Q: I am in the United States managing the U.S. subsidiary of my family business. My wife would like to help out in the office. Can I hire her?

A: Yes. You are in the United States as an *intracompany transferee* even though you transferred from your own family company. This means you have the same L-1 Visa as any other manager. One of the advantages of this visa is that your wife, as the holder of an L-2 Visa, can work. She can work for your company or for any other company. She should file Form I-765 with the BCIS Service Center responsible for your area to get her *Employment Authorization Document*. To anticipate your next question—unfortunately, your children do *not* qualify for this work permit, and your U.S. company cannot hire them.

Q My husband is part owner of a company that does a lot of business in the United States. We would like to spend a few years in the United States so that our children can experience what it is like to go to school there. Can we get a visa for this?

A Yes. You husband's company can send your husband to the United States as what is called a *treaty trader*. This visa, called an E-1 Visa, is a visa that allows companies that do a substantial amount of trade with the United States to send employees to work in the United States. The requirements for this visa are:
- the proper treaty must exist between your country and the United States;
- the company must be owned by nationals of your country;
- the employee sent to the United States must be a national of your country;
- the company must be engaged in a substantial amount of trade between your country and the United States;
- the trade must be principally between the United States and your country; and,
- the employee being sent to the United States must work there as an executive, manager or highly skilled employee.

If your husband's company meets all of the requirements, you and your children can get visas to come with your husband.

Q We have a small family business in Italy and are doing business with the United States. Our son works for us. Can we send him to work for us in United States?

A Perhaps. Your son could qualify for a *treaty trader* visa to work for your company in a management position in the United States. Italy has the proper treaty with the United States and your company is owned by your family who are all Italian citizens. The only issue in your case that needs to be better explained is what you mean by a *small* business. In order to get an E-1 Visa for your son, you will have to show that your company is doing *substantial trade* with the United States. The consular officer will look at the volume of trade, the number of transactions, and the continuous course of trade to determine if the trade you do with the United States is substantial. For example, a one-time sale to the United States of $1 million would not be considered substantial because a one-time sale is not continuous. But, a lesser amount could be substantial if the sales are regular and continuous throughout each year. You must also be prepared to show that your business with the United States is more than 50% of the company's international trade.

Q Our son is working for my uncle's company in the U.S. It's a good job, but he would like to get other experience. Can he change jobs?

A No. Your uncle sent your son to the United States on an E-1 Visa because your uncle's company does a lot of business in the United States. The E-1 Visa has many advantages, but one disadvantage—an E-1 Visa holder may not change jobs. In fact, if anything happens to change the qualifying basis, for example, your uncle stops doing business in the United States, your son would lose his status and would have to return home. If your

U.S. Immigration and Citizenship Q&A

son really wants to change jobs, he will have to find a way to qualify for another type of temporary work visa, such as finding another U.S. company to offer him a job and file the necessary petition to get him a work visa.

Q The company I work for in Ireland wants to send me to work in the United States because we do so much business there. The company told me I have to be Irish in order to get the visa. That's OK because I am Irish, but I want to take my wife with me and she is not Irish. Can I get a visa for her?

A Yes. The visa you qualify for is an E-1 temporary work visa that requires that you have the nationality of the country through which your company qualifies under the proper treaty. In your case, Irish. But, your spouse and children can be any nationality and they still qualify to go with you.

Q My company in Mexico City wants to send me to the United States to manage our business there. I understand there is more than one visa possible for this. Which visa would be best for me?

A Your company in Mexico conducts substantial trade in the United States and also has a subsidiary here. Without going into all the details, this means that your company could petition for either an E-1 treaty trader temporary work visa for you or for an L-1 intracompany transfer temporary work visa for

Working in the United States

you. Which is best for you depends on your plans. The E-1 Visa can be renewed indefinitely as long as you and your company maintain the same status. An L-1 Visa is limited to a maximum stay of five to seven years depending upon the job you are doing for your company.

Q My company sent me to Boston on an E-1 Visa. My wife came with me to Boston. Can she work?

A Yes. A new law passed at the beginning of 2002, allows spouses of E-1 Visa holders to work. And, unlike you, she is not limited to working for the company that sponsored your petition.

Q I own an import-export company and am in the United States on an E-1 Visa. I just noticed that it is about to expire. Do I have to go back to my country to have it renewed?

A No. The Visa Office of the U.S. Department of State will renew, or as they call it, *revalidate* your visa. There are some exceptions. You can only renew your visa if it is within sixty days of expiration. You cannot renew your E-1 or E-2 Visa at the Visa Office if you are from Cuba, Iran, Iraq, Libya, North Korea, Sudan or Syria. In these cases, you must renew your visa at a U.S. consulate abroad. Also, revalidation is not automatic. When you submit your E-1 or E-2 Visa to the Visa Office for revalidation, you must complete a new Form DS-156 *Application for a*

Nonimmigrant Visa and other supporting documents. If your application does not meet the Visa Office criteria or if something has changed that makes your application not clearly approvable, you will be asked to make a new visa application at a U.S. consulate abroad.

TEACHING, RESEARCH, SCHOOL, AND TRAINING PROGRAMS

Q Our son is interested in studying in the United States. What options does he have?

A There are a lot of options open to your son. Visas are available for students to study at colleges, universities, seminaries, conservatories, high schools, elementary schools, language schools, vocational schools, and flight aviation programs. If your son wants to pursue a formal degree, he can apply for a *student* visa (an *F* Visa). If he wants to pursue something less than a formal degree or a practical course of study, he can apply for an *exchange visitor* visa (a *J* Visa). If he were attending a vocational school program, he can apply for a *vocational student* visa (an *M* Visa).

In each case, your son will have to meet certain requirements. To begin with, these visas are temporary, nonimmigrant visas, so your son must have the intention of returning home after he completes his course of study. Also, your son must be able to demonstrate sufficient financial resources to support himself during the course of study, although sometimes it is also possible to supplement his income by working. And, finally, all of these visas require a sponsor. (In most cases, the sponsor will be the school that your son is attending.)

Q **Our daughter has been offered a summer internship at a U.S. company. What does she have to do to take advantage of this?**

A Your daughter should apply for an *exchange visitor visa* (J-1). She must do this at a U.S. consulate outside of the United States. The basic steps in the process are:
- the company, an *Exchange Visitor Program sponsor*, applies for approval to the U.S. Department of State (DOS) for your daughter's specific training program;
- when approved, the DOS issues a *Certificate of Eligibility*, sends a copy to your daughter, and, usually, notifies the U.S. consulate;
- your daughter fills out Form DS-156, the standard nonimmigrant visa form; and,
- your daughter takes the Form DS-156 to the U.S. consulate along with the Certificate of Eligibility, her passport, a photograph of her, and the appropriate fee (fees can vary depending on nationality so check the U.S. consulate to find out what the fee is).

The consular officer will review the documents and interview your daughter and then stamp the J-1 Visa in her passport. This will allow her to officially participate in the training program and receive a *stipend* from the U.S. company.

Q Our son has been in touch with a company in California and would like to work there in the summer to get special training in medical technology and equipment design. The company wants to have him and can even pay him, but they have told him they can't sponsor him. Does he have any options?

A Yes. The company is probably not on the U.S. State Department's list of approved *Exchange Visitor Programs*. This is a requirement for the type of visa your son needs to train and be paid in the United States. The company has two alternatives if they want to help your son get his visa. One is for the company to get approved as the sponsor of an Exchange Visitor Program.

The alternative is for the company to sponsor your son through an *umbrella program* that arranges for the transfer of exchange visitors for practical training with different U.S. employers. Two organizations that have obtained the necessary approvals from the Department of State are the *American Council on International Personnel* (212-688-2473) and the *Association for International Practical Training, Inc.* (301-997-2200). You might also check with the chamber of commerce in the country where you live as their U.S. branches have sometimes obtained approval to serve as program sponsors.

Q I teach at a college in Austria and have been offered the chance to teach for one year (and maybe more) at a university in Minnesota. May I take my family with me?

A Yes. You would be coming to the United States on an *exchange visitor visa* (J-1). That visa allows you to bring your spouse and children on J-2 Visas. The J-1 Visa for a college professor allows you to stay up to three years at the U.S. college.

Q My wife has been studying at the University of Illinois and has finished her doctorate degree. She would like to get some experience in her area of study. Does she have to do this at the University of Illinois because they sponsored her J-1 Visa?

A No. She is eligible to receive up to three years of *relevant practical training*. The training does not have to be with her original sponsor (University of Illinois). *Practical Training Program* participants do not have to get Department of State or BCIS approval. They simply need an approval letter from a designated exchange program officer that they will file with their Practical Training Program application.

Q My husband was on a government program that allowed him to teach high school in the United States for one year. I went with him and it was a wonderful experience. We just returned home and I found out that I could get sponsored for a job as a nurse in the United States. Can I go back to take the job?

U.S. Immigration and Citizenship Q&A

A No. Your husband as the *principal* J-1 Visa holder is subject to the *2-year return rule*, because his program was paid for by the Swedish government. As his spouse, you were in the United States on a J-2 Visa. J-2 Visa holders are subject to the same 2-year requirement as your husband, unless you can get a waiver. There are five ways to get a waiver of the 2-year rule:

- get a *no-objection* letter from the government that financed your status, (although this waiver is not generally available for medical residents or interns);
- get an *interested government agency* to file a request with the U.S. Department of State to waive the 2-year requirement, both the Department of State and the BCIS must approve the request for it to be valid;
- prove that if you return to your home country you will be *persecuted* because of your race, religion, or political opinions;
- prove that your spouse or child would suffer *exceptional hardship* if you returned to your home country; and,
- if you are a medical doctor prove you are going to be working full time at a health care facility *serving an area with a shortage* of medical professionals.

Q I am from Asia and am doing a medical residency in Boston. My husband came with me to Boston. Can he work while we live here?

A Yes. You are in the United States on an *exchange visitor visa* (J-1), which is one of the few nonimmigrant visas that allow your dependents to work. Your husband will need to get

BCIS approval. You must show that his income will not be used to support you. For him to get approval he should file Form I-765 *Application for Employment Authorization* with the BCIS along with a copy of your *Certificate of Eligibility for Exchange Visitor status*. You should also attach a written statement showing that your husband's employment is not necessary to support you.

Q **My wife has completed her medical residency and her hospital would like her to work there as a staff physician. Can she stay in the United States to do this?**

A No. Certain classes of exchange visitors are required to return to their country of last residency for a period of two years after the end of their exchange visitor status. During this two-year, period these individuals are not eligible to apply for employment status or immigration status in the United States. This so-called *2-Year rule* applies to:
- individuals who obtained their exchange visitor status through programs financed by the government (either their home country government or the U.S. government);
- individuals who are trained in an occupational specialty that is in short supply in their home country; and,
- individuals who have received medical training in the United States as interns or residents.

You wife did her medical residency in the United States and therefore is automatically subject to the 2-year rule. (You might be able to get a waiver of the 2-year rule if you can show that the job you have been offered as a medical doctor is at a health care facility serving an area with a *shortage* of medical professionals.)

Q My husband is a medical intern in Boston. When my husband started his internship, he was told he would have to go back to India for at least two years when he finished. Is there any way we can stay in the United States?

A Yes. Generally, exceptions to the *2-year rule* are not available for medical doctors. But, in July, 2003, the Department of Health and Human Services announced that *Exchange Visitor Program* applications (the J-1 Visa your husband has) are now available to request a waiver of the two-year foreign residency requirement. This is available for physicians with J-1 Visas who agree to deliver health care services for three years in primary care or mental *health professional shortage areas* (HPSAs) or *medically underserved areas* or *populations* (MUA/Ps).

Q My husband and I have been in the United States three years doing research at the University of Illinois. Our program was sponsored by our government. Our visa is now running out and we were told we have to return to our home country. Is there any way we can stay in the U.S.? What if one of us gets a job offer?

A You have a few ways to extend your stay. Your program sponsor, the university, can approve a six-month extension. The Department of State can extend your stay up to three years beyond the initial three years. To do that, there are two waiver possibilities appropriate to your situation:

- get your government to issue a *no-objection* letter stating that even though it funded your exchange visit it will not object to you getting a waiver of the *2-year rule* or
- get an *interested government agency* to request a waiver of the *2-year* for you.

Q **Which agencies are available as interested government agencies for purposes of the J-1 2-year rule waiver?**

A Some agencies that have served as interested government agencies include:
- Department of Agriculture;
- Department of Commerce;
- Department of Defense;
- Department of Energy;
- Department of Health and Human Services;
- Department of Housing and Urban Development;
- Department of Interior;
- Department of Transportation;
- Department of Veteran Affairs;
- Environmental Protection Agency;
- National Endowment for the Arts;
- NASA;
- National Science Foundation; and,
- Smithsonian Institution.

Q When my wife and I came to the United States, my wife was the principal visa holder and I was her dependent. We are now at the end of our visa stay and she wants to go back home. Can I apply for a waiver of the *2-year rule* and stay in the U.S.?

A No. The *accompanying* spouse or children of an exchange visitor may not file an *independent waiver petition*.

Q My husband has been teaching in California under a program sponsored by our government. His three years are up and now we were told we have to go back to our home country. We would like to stay longer so that our children can finish school. Is there any way to do this? We have looked into getting a waiver of the *2-year rule*, but don't think we can qualify.

A You have options. The *2-year rule* is designed to prevent exchange visitors who were sponsored by their governments from changing to a work visa (H or L status) or adjusting their status to permanent residency until they have spent two years in their home country. However, the 2-year rule does not prevent you from changing to some other visa categories. For example, you could return to your home country and immediately return to the United States on a B-1 visitor visa. Alternatively, and for you a more realistic idea, might be to obtain student status (an F-1 Visa) or if your employer is willing to sponsor you, a visa for education professionals with extraordinary ability (an O-1 Visa). The advantage to you of the F-1 and O-1 Visas is that you do not

Working in the United States

have to apply for them from your home country. You do have to apply for these visas outside of the United States, but you may be able to do this at a U.S. consulate in Canada or Mexico.

Q My husband will be finishing his residency as a doctor in Chicago. We want to continue to live in the United States, but we have to spend two years at home first. My husband is thinking about applying for a waiver of the *2-year rule*. In the meantime, my mother, who is a U.S. permanent resident, wants to file an immigration petition for us. What should we do first?

A Both. You can apply for a waiver of the 2-year rule and an immigration petition at the same time. In fact, in your case, you should do so. If the waiver and the immigration petition are both granted, you will be able to change your status without leaving the United States. If the immigration petition is granted, but the waiver is not, you will have to return to your country for two years, but then you would be eligible to apply for an immigration visa.

Q Our son is attending a two-year education program as an Exchange Visitor at a large state university in Michigan. Can he work?

A Yes, there are two possible ways he can work while completing his educational program. One is if he can get a *stipend* for academic training that is directly related to his major field of study. The other is to get *on-campus* employment. This is only possible when it is permitted by the terms of the exchange visitor program your son is in and if he meets certain other requirements (for example, good academic standing, limits on the number of hours worked, etc.).

Q My wife and I have been teaching in the U.S. for the last year. Now our visa has run out and we have to go back home. Our status expires this week. We would like to take two weeks to drive from coast to coast before leaving. Can we do this?

A It's OK to take your vacation. J-1 Visa holders have a *grace period* of thirty days after their status expires to leave the United States. The grace period is generally allowed for things like packing and getting organized to depart.

Q Our son is attending flight training school in Florida. He has just been told the school will no longer be able to accept foreign students. What should he do?

A Your son should immediately find a new flight school that is SEVIS approved and enroll in that school no later than the next semester, quarter, or other academic term. SEVIS stands for *Student Exchange Visitor Information System*. SEVIS is an Internet-based system providing the government, educational institutions, and exchange programs to exchange and share information about foreign students and exchange visitors. SEVIS applies to *vocational students* (M Visas), as well as to *academic students* (F Visas), and *Exchange Visitor Programs* (J Visas).

Q My husband is attending a vocational program for airline mechanics. We will be in the United States for two years. I would like to start at the university while I am here. Can I?

A No. Not unless you change your status. The spouse of a vocational student visa holder (M-1 Visa) is not allowed to engage in full time study, and the child or children may only engage in full-time study if the study is in an elementary or high school. If you are accepted at a university, you can apply for your own student visa (F-1), but you must meet all the requirements.

Q We are an ethnic dance troupe from Hungary. Six Flags Over Mid-America wants to hire us. Can we get a visa for this? If so can we bring our spouses?

A Yes and no. You may be able to qualify for a Q Visa for *temporary cultural exchanges*. Six Flags would have to file a petition on your behalf with the BCIS. It must also provide a program of practical training, employment, and the sharing of the history, culture, and traditions of your country. Six Flags must show that it will pay you the same wages as U.S. workers. The visa is limited to a maximum of fifteen months. This is not an easy visa to get, but for well-known theme parks like Six Flags or Disney World, it usually works. A Q Visa does *not* allow you to bring your spouse or children with you.

DOMESTIC AND AGRICULTURAL WORKERS

Q A fruit grower in southern California wants to hire me and some of my friends to pick fruit next season. Is this legal?

A Yes, as long as the grower follows the right procedures. The grower must get two copies of application Form ETA-750 from the Department of Labor and file one with the Department of Labor regional office and the other with the state employment service agency for the state in which work is sought. The application must be submitted at least sixty days before you start work and must be approved by the Department of Labor twenty days before the starting work date. If approved, the employer pays a base fee of $100, plus $10 for each position certified, up to a maximum of $1000.

Q Can I bring my wife and children with me if I come to work on a farm in the United States?

A Yes. U.S. immigration law allows you to bring your spouse and minor children if you are coming to the United States on an H-2A Visa to work temporarily on a farm.

Q What do I have to do if I get a job as a domestic worker or agricultural worker?

A You will generally only have to take all the papers you receive from your future employer and the BCIS and apply for a nonimmigrant visa at the U.S. consulate in your country. You do this like any other nonimmigrant with Form DS-156 *Application for a Nonimmigrant Visa*.

Q I may have the chance to work on a farm in the United States. Can the farmer pay me whatever he wants?

A No. If you get a visa for temporary farm work (an H-2A Visa), the farmer must pay you, at least, as much as offered to U.S. workers for the same job. This sounds easy, but in practice this has been interpreted to mean that the farmer must pay you the higher of:
- the industry's prevailing wage in the relevant labor market;
- the state or federal minimum wage; or,
- the *adverse effect wage rate* (AEWR), which is basically last year's average hourly wage for agricultural and livestock workers determined by the Department of Agriculture.

U.S. Immigration and Citizenship Q&A

Q I have just gotten a job picking fruit in southern Illinois. I will leave for Illinois next month. I have heard that I will live in a camp on the farm. Do I have to pay for that?

A No. If your employer is bringing you to the United States on an H-2A Visa as a temporary agricultural worker, he or she must provide housing for you unless you are a commuter worker. The farmer must also provide transportation from the camp to your place of work, three meals a day, or make kitchen facilities available to you, any tools you need to do your work, and workers' compensation insurance.

Q How can I get a visa as a maid? I have worked for American and other foreign families and would like to do it the United States.

A You must first find a family to sponsor you. The family will then file a petition on your behalf with the BCIS. They will also need to get *labor certification* from the Department of Labor to prove that there are not enough U.S. workers in their region to do your kind of job. Once the petition is approved, you apply for an H-2A nonimmigrant visa at the U.S. consulate in your country.

Q I have a job as a maid. I am in America on a H-2A Visa. How long can I stay?

A An H-2A Visa is normally valid for one year. You may be able to get one year extensions up to a maximum of three years. After three years, you must leave the United States for at least six months before you can resume any H-2A employment.

4.

Immigrating Based on Employment

Almost everyone knows that if they marry a U.S. citizen or have a relative in the United States, they have a chance at getting a Green Card. However, there are other ways to immigrate to the United States. The "Immigration and Nationality Act" provides a yearly minimum of 140,000 immigration visas for individuals who qualify based on their jobs or professional activities.

Employment-based immigrant visas are available to a wide variety of individuals. The law has set forth five categories of individuals who can get these visas. Each category is called a "preference," because if you have a job or engage in the activities of that category, you have preference over some other applicants for immigration to the United States.

The first preference is for persons of extraordinary ability in the arts, science, business, education, or athletics, as well as outstanding professors and researchers and multinational business managers. The second preference is for professionals holding advanced degrees and persons of exceptional ability in the arts, sciences, or business. The third preference is for skilled workers and professionals holding at least a bachelor's degree. The fourth preference is for religious workers and certain other special immigrants. The fifth preference is for investors who create jobs in the United States.

Most, but not all, of these visas require a sponsor. The sponsor is usually the company, university, or institution you are or will be working for. The process of getting one of these visas is complicated, but, if you and your sponsor qualify, the chances are very good that you will get the visa. There is often no waiting time for these visas like there is for family-based immigration visas.

WORKING PERMANENTLY IN THE UNITED STATES

Q I have been working for a U.S. company for around three years on a temporary visa. I heard that it is possible for the company to sponsor me for a Green Card. How does this work?

A If you have the right kind of qualifications, your employment can form the basis to get a Green Card. Your employer will have to petition for you by sending Form I-140 *Immigrant Petition for Alien Worker* to the BCIS. The petition must show that you are either an *employee of extraordinary ability*, an *executive* or *manager*, a *professional*, or someone who has *exceptional ability*. If approved, you can apply for an immigrant visa at the U.S. consulate in your home country. Or, as you are already in the United States, you can apply for adjustment of status using Form I-485.

Q I have been working for my company in the United States on an H-1B Visa in a very specialized area of industrial research. Can my company sponsor me for a Green Card?

A Yes, your company will be able to use the evidence of your educational background and exceptional ability as evidence to support a petition to sponsor you.

Q What kind of evidence do I or my company need in order to get an immigrant visa as someone with exceptional ability?

A Your company must get *Labor Certification Approval* for your job to show that there is, basically, a shortage of U.S. workers who can do what you can do and, therefore, that your presence in the United States will benefit the U.S. economy. You will need to provide proof of your educational background to show that you have at least the equivalent of a U.S. bachelors degree. You must also demonstrate your *exceptional ability* by showing that you have at least ten years of experience in your specialized field, that you have any necessary professional licenses or qualifications, that you have earned a high salary for your work, and that you have received recognition for your accomplishments in your field.

Q If my company refuses to sponsor me for a Green Card, is there any way I can do it on my own? I do not have family in the United States.

A Yes. It is not easy, but if you are considered an alien with *extraordinary ability* in the sciences, arts, education, business, or athletics, you may be able to apply for your own Green Card. This is sometimes called the *superstar visa* because film stars and Nobel prize winners have used it to immigrate to the United States. Although they are very hard to get, you do not necessarily need to be a Nobel prize winner to get one. What you do need to prove, however, is that in your particular field you have reached the top and have received international acclaim that has been extensively documented.

Q May my foreign employer sponsor me for a Green Card in the United States?

A Yes, as long at it has a subsidiary or affiliate in the United States and you are coming to the United States to work in a management or executive capacity for that same company. You also must have been employed by the foreign company full time for at least one year during the three-year period right before you will enter the United States. In practice, the standards for this visa are quite high. You normally must be a top executive in a large multinational company to qualify, but there are many examples of executives in smaller companies getting this visa, so you should review your own personal situation in detail to see if you might meet the requirements.

Q I have been working on an H-1B Visa. My company recently filed a Form I-140 *Immigrant Petition for Alien Worker* on my behalf. I've heard something about concurrent filings. What is that?

A What you have heard about is the ability, under an interim rule of the BCIS issued on July 1, 2002, of *beneficiaries* of immigrant petitions (that is you as the person who is getting the visa) to file Form I-485 *Petition to Request Permanent Residence or Adjust Status* at the same time. The rule applies to employment-based immigrant visas like yours in the EB-1, EB-2 and EB-3 categories.

Q What advantages does concurrent filing of Forms I-140 *Immigrant Petition for Alien Worker* and I-485 *Petition to Request Permanent Residence or Adjust Status* have?

A A *concurrent filing* could have many benefits depending on your current visa and family status, including:
- possible overall shorter processing time to get your Green Card;
- interim work permits and travel permission (advance parole) benefits available to each family member;
- keeping you in status based on your Form I-485 filing if your temporary visa status will soon expire; and,
- relief from an obligation to maintain or renew temporary visa status, such as H-1B or L classification.

Q Are there any risks to concurrent filing of Forms I-140 and I-485?

A Yes. The main risk is a financial one because you must support your adjustment of status application on Form I-485 with medical exams, evidence, filing fees, etc. If your immigrant petition is denied, you will have spent all that money for nothing. Another risk is that the adjustment of status application could be approved too quickly. This could have a negative impact on your family members abroad who could no longer join you as *nonimmigrants* on your current visa.

Q My U.S. employer has sponsored me for an immigration visa. Now it looks like the company may downsize. Will I lose the possibility of getting the immigration visa if I am let go?

A Not necessarily. It will depend on where you are in the process. If you have already received BCIS approval and have filed your Form I-485 for adjustment of status, you are pretty safe. A new rule under the *American Competitiveness in the 21st Century Act,* allows you to change employers 180 days after filing your Form I-485 if the BCIS has not made a decision on your case. This means that if you are laid off, you can get a new job and keep your immigrant petition.

Q If I change jobs before the BCIS approves my adjustment of status, does my new employer have to then sponsor my immigrant visa?

A No. As long as your job is in the same or similar occupational status, you can adjust your status using your existing Form I-485.

Q I have a U.S. company that is willing to sponsor me for an immigration visa based on my education, experience, and value to the company. My only problem is that I did not complete my degree at one school, and, although my degree is a master's degree, it did not take as long as in the United States. My company is concerned that I will not be able to prove I have the equivalent of a U.S. degree. What can I do?

A Proving that the beneficiary of an employment-based immigrant petition (Form I-140) has the U.S. equivalent of a foreign degree has always been a problem. Under the employment-based second preference that you are applying for (EB-2), you must establish that you have an *advanced degree*. Under U.S. immigration law, an advanced degree means any United States academic or professional degree or a *foreign equivalent degree* above that of a baccalaureate degree. A United States baccalaureate degree or a foreign equivalent degree followed by at least five years of progressive experience in the specialty shall be considered the equivalent of a master's degree. BCIS officers have been interpreting the regulation to mean only a foreign equivalent of United States baccalaureate degree would qualify you under the employment-based second preference. Thus, if you only had a three-year foreign degree combined with a diploma, BCIS officers reject such credentials even though they constituted the equivalent of a U.S. degree.

Q: I never actually finished university, but I have so much experience that I know I have at least the equivalent of a degree. Can I use this combination of work and university experience to qualify for an immigrant visa where I need a college degree?

A: No. Even if the BCIS has adopted a more generous view of accepting a foreign equivalent degree through multiple education programs, there is still no acceptance of establishing a foreign equivalent degree based on only work experience or a combination of education and work experience. While such a combination may be permissible to establish a foreign degree equivalent for H-1B Visa purposes, an alien beneficiary can only establish a foreign degree equivalency under an EB-2 or EB-3 petition through education.

Q: How can I be sure that my foreign degree and experience will be recognized by the BCIS in my petition?

A: Normally, if you follow the directions on Form I-140 *Immigrant Petition for Alien Worker*, and enclose the recommended documents, like your university academic record and letters from your company, your degree and experience will be recognized. If any of these documents is in a language other than English, you will have to provide translations. There are commercial services that will translate your documents and prepare foreign credential evaluations for you in order to show educational equivalence. One such service is the *American Evaluation and Translation Service* on the Internet at www.aetsinternational.com.

AS A TEACHER, RESEARCHER, ARTIST, OR OTHER CREATIVE OCCUPATION

Q I have been teaching at a university in the Midwest for around five years. My university would like me to stay permanently in a tenured position. My family would also like to stay in America. I have heard that if you don't have a family member to sponsor you, you need to be a business executive or scientist to get a Green Card. Is that true?

A No. It is true that business executive and scientists can use their employment as a way to get a Green Card, but you can do the same thing. Employment-based, permanent residence visas are usually referred to as EB Visas and cover a broad range of employment activities including business executives, scientists, researchers, scholars, university professors, athletes, artists, musicians, actors, lawyers, accountants, skilled workers, and unskilled workers. As a university professor, you clearly belong to a profession for which visas are available. Moreover, because you are already working for a U.S. university, you have already demonstrated that you have the type of skills that qualify you to work in the United States. If your university is willing to sponsor a petition for an EB Visa on your behalf, you should have no trouble getting your Green Card.

Q: **My wife is teaching at a state university in the southeastern part of the United States. We would like to stay in the United States. What does the university have to do to get us a Green Card?**

A: The basic steps to obtain permanent residency based on your wife's teaching position are:

- the university files a *Labor Certification Application* with the Department of Labor;
- the Department of Labor approves the Labor Certification Application;
- the university prepares Form I-140 *Immigrant Petition for Alien Worker*;
- the university supports the petition by enclosing Form I-140, the approved Labor Certification, a letter supporting the petition, documentation showing the university's ability to pay the salary stated in the petition, documentation that shows your wife meets the job requirements, and has the education and experience required by this visa category; and,
- the university files Form I-140 and all supporting documentation with the BCIS service center that is responsible for the place where your wife will be employed and pays the filing fee (currently $135).

Immigrating Based on Employment

Once the petition is approved, you can either apply at the U.S. consulate in your home country or, because you are already lawfully admitted to the United States, you can simply file for adjustment of status using Form I-485.

Q: Can I get an immigration visa based on part-time employment at a U.S. university?

A: No. The BCIS requires the university to show it will employ you in a tenured-track, permanent position. Part-time or temporary employment will not be enough.

Q: I am getting an immigration visa as a researcher with a major university. Does it make any difference on how my position is funded?

A: It might. The EB-1B Visa requires your position to be permanent. In some cases, the BCIS will not consider positions that are funded with grants to be permanent positions because the position might be eliminated when the grant money runs out. Normally, however, it is sufficient if the university clearly states that the position is permanent and checks the appropriate box in Part 6 of Form I-140.

**Q: I am putting together the documents I need to support my immigrant visa petition as a researcher. A lot of my research work was done for companies in my home country and the company made me sign a secrecy agreement. Can I use this research to support my application?

A Not directly. The EB-1B Visa requires that you document your accomplishments. You can do this by showing that your research has added to the body of knowledge in your field. Obviously, research done for one specific company, so-called *proprietary research* and research that you are required by agreement to keep secret, cannot meet this requirement. You may, however, be able to use your work at the companies indirectly if, for example, you can get leading experts in your field to write articles about what you were doing. You will have to review your secrecy agreement carefully to see if this will be possible.

Q A university in California petitioned for me to immigrate to work as a professor. The application was denied. What should I do?

A You can file an appeal with the *Administrative Appeals Unit* using Form I-290. Unfortunately, the track record for appeals of decisions on outstanding professors and researchers (EB-1 Visas) is not good. Almost all BCIS decisions on these visas are upheld. A better strategy might be to reapply for the visa. We would particularly recommend this approach if you have had more publications, received additional awards, or received additional international recognition while you were waiting for the decision on your visa application. You would, of course, include these new accomplishments in the new petition as well as address the reasons for the first denial. It may simply be that you did not present your evidence in the most convincing way. You should also survey your family situation to see if you might qualify for an immigration based on a family member or if your spouse could qualify for an immigration visa based on employment. (If your home country is not on the list that qualifies for the diversity visa—Green Card lottery—this is not an option for you.)

DUE TO INVESTMENTS OR FAMILY BUSINESS

Q What is the $1,000,000 visa?

A What you refer to as the *million dollar visa,* is actually an immigration visa available to individuals who invest money and create jobs in the United States. One of the requirements of the visa is that the investment must be $1,000,000 invested in a qualifying business over a two-year period. There are exceptions for investment in a rural area or an area that has high unemployment. If the investment is being made in one of these areas, the amount required is reduced to $500,000.

Q My family and I have decided that our future should be in America and we are willing to invest all our money to make this dream happen. How do we go about getting an investor visa?

A The procedure starts with you identifying an appropriate commercial business investment. This may be either a new, original business, or an existing business in which your investment will result in a restructuring into a new business or an existing business that will be expanded by at least 140% by your investment. You must then demonstrate that you are in the active process of investing at least $1 million in the business (or $500,000 if you are located in a rural area or an area with high unemployment). Finally, you must show that the business will create at least ten full-time jobs for qualified individuals over a two year period. If the business is a *troubled* business, you must maintain the number of existing employees at the same level for at least two years. You must also show that you will be engaged in the management of the business either as a manager, corporate officer, or director.

Once you are prepared to meet these requirements, you will fill out Form I-526 and forward it to the BCIS service center responsible for the area where your business is to be located. Once your petition is approved, you can obtain *conditional resident status* by filing Form I-485 *Adjustment of Status,* if you are already legally present in the United States, or by applying for the appropriate immigrant visa at the U.S. consulate in your home country. Then you can move to the United States.

Q Do I automatically get a Green Card if I invest $1 million dollars in the United States?

A No. You first obtain an immigrant visa that grants you *conditional resident status*. After two years in this status, you can apply for a Green Card by removing the conditions attached to your residency and becoming a permanent resident alien. You do this by filing Form I-829 *Petition by Entrepreneur to Remove Conditions*. In the petition, you must show that you have established the business you said you were going to establish.

Q How can we prove we have fulfilled the conditions of our investment so that we can get our Green Card?

A When you file Form I-829 *Petition by Entrepreneur to Remove Conditions*, you must provide five types of evidence:
- evidence that you started your business (for example a business license or Articles of Incorporation);
- evidence that you actually transferred the required amount of capital to the business;
- evidence that the capital invested was lawfully obtained (like tax returns);
- evidence that ten full time jobs are created (like tax records or payroll slips); and,
- evidence that you are actively engaged in the management of the business (like being named a corporate officer in the corporate records).

Q My family consists of my wife, two daughters, ages 15 and 18, and my son, age 20, who is married. We are starting a new business in South Carolina with an investment of $1,000,000. We want to immigrate to the U.S. as a family. Can we?

A No. Not all of you. The EB-5 employment creation immigration visa allows your spouse and your *unmarried* children to accompany you. You son is married and, therefore, does not qualify under this visa.

Q We are part of a large family in our home country with a very successful business. We are thinking of immigrating to the United States by starting a business there. What happens if the business we start does not succeed?

A When you come to the United States on an investor visa—an EB-5 employment creation immigration visa—you are placed in the status of a *conditional resident* for two years. In order to get your Green Card at the end of two years, you have to show that your business is still running and employing enough people. If you can't show this, you will have to leave or find another basis for immigrant status.

The potential problem for you is that during the time you are in the United States as a conditional resident, you will be liable for U.S. income tax on your world wide income. This will include all the income from your investments in your home country and elsewhere. This means that if your U.S. business does not succeed you will not only have a business failure, but also, potentially, two years of tax payments—and, at the end, no Green Card.

Q My husband and I got our Green Cards about four years ago and have now started our own medical software business. My husband wants to hire his brother who is still in our home country to be our chief software development officer and also get him a Green Card. Can he do this?

A Yes. Your husband's brother may be able to qualify for an immigration visa based on his impressive academic credentials and experience in the medical software industry. This would be an employment-based immigration visa and would require that your husband's brother have a job offer and labor certification. Another fairly new requirement, that you should be aware of, is the need to file an *Affidavit of Support* (Form I-864) for your husband's brother. This would be necessary in your case because:

- your husband owns more than 5% of the company that will petitioning for his brother's visa;
- your husband is related to his brother; and,
- your husband's brother is immigrating to the United States, not entering on a temporary visa.

Q What is an *Affidavit of Support* and how does it work for small business owners like me?

A The *Affidavit of Support* (Form I-864) is required by the BCIS to show that an intending immigrant has adequate means of financial support. Becoming a *public charge* became a new ground of inadmissibility with the passage of the *Illegal Immigration Reform and Immigrant Responsibility Act of 1996*, so the BCIS wants to ensure that immigrants will have enough money to support themselves and their families. For most employment-based immigration visas, the Affidavit of Support will not be required because the immigrant is coming to work at a job that the BCIS can see will provide support. But, in those cases where the immigrant is coming to work for a relative or for a company owned by a relative, the BCIS wants some additional assurance that the immigrant will indeed be paid. It does this by requiring the relative whose company is filing the petition to enter into a contract with the immigrant and the federal, state, and local government that might give any public benefits to the immigrant. The contract is in the form of the Affidavit of Support in which the sponsoring relative promises to pay back any agency that provides means-tested public benefits to the sponsored immigrant and to notify the BCIS if the sponsored immigrant changes addresses.

As you can see, this is quite a bit of responsibility. In practice, for example, if you sponsor your brother to work for you and he applies for food stamps, Medicaid, or some other public benefit, you would be responsible to pay back the agency that issued the food stamps. This might not seem like much of a risk at a time when your business is going well and you can pay your brother a good salary, but the obligation extends for a long time and it is always difficult to predict the future success of any business. Your obligation of sponsorship continues indefinitely until your brother either:

- dies;
- leaves the U.S. permanently;
- becomes a U.S. citizen; or,
- gets forty employment quarters under Social Security.

5.

Immigrating Based on Family

Do you want to get a Green Card? Do you already have one? This chapter discusses some of the most common ways you can get a Green Card with the focus on family-based immigration. You can also qualify for a Green Card based on your employment or business and those Green Cards are covered in Chapter 4.

We start the chapter with a discussion of what a lawful permanent resident is and what a permanent resident must do to maintain his or her status. Many lawful permanent residents are not aware that spending more than a year outside the United States puts them at great risk of losing their Green Card. Sometimes, even infrequent trips outside the United States can result in losing the Green Card.

Then, we talk about when and how legal permanent aliens can bring their relatives to the United States. This opportunity is available for spouses, minor children, and unmarried sons and daughters of lawful permanent residents. These relationships create what immigration law calls a "family-sponsored preference." The number of these visas is limited by preference and by country. They are also more limited than the preferences available to U.S. citizens sponsoring immigrant visas.

Because marriage forms one of the most common bases of family-based immigration for lawful permanent residents, we include Q&As on the "Marriage Fraud Act" and "conditional immigrant status." Under these rules, a marriage that lasts less than two years may result in the loss of immigration status.

The last few years, have also brought changes to family-based immigration. "The Legal Immigration Family Equity Act of 2000" (LIFE) has made it possible for some families that have been waiting a long time for their visas to be reunited in the United States. LIFE also has created a new V Visa for spouses to travel to the United States as non-immigrants even though a petition for immigrant status has been filed for them.

LAWFUL PERMANENT RESIDENTS

Q I am from Jamaica, and I have lots of friends who now live in the United States. Many of them are now *permanent resident aliens*. What does that mean? Are they now Americans or are they still Jamaicans?

A For purposes of U.S. immigration law, they are still Jamaican citizens. However, they are now also, *lawful permanent residents*. A lawful permanent resident (also known as a permanent resident alien) is a foreign national who has been granted the privilege of permanently living and working in the United States.

Q My relatives in the United States say my husband and I should come there to live with them. As a family, we have agreed to immigrate to the United States. How do we get started?

A The first issue to tackle is to determine whether you and your family members *qualify* to immigrate to the United States. You cannot simply file an application for yourselves to come to the United States. Rather, someone (a family member) or someplace (an employer) must *petition* or *sponsor* you to immigrate. If your relatives here in the United States want to petition for you and your family members to come, you must first determine the *status* of your relatives here in the United States (citizens or permanent resident aliens). Next, you must determine whether the family connection they have with you is one that will *support* a petition for permanent residency on the behalf of you and your family members.

Q If my family member in the United States is a permanent resident alien, can he or she petition for me to come to the United States to live and work as a permanent resident alien myself?

A It depends on your family relationship. The first hurdle that you cleared is that your family member here in the United States is a permanent resident alien. The good news is that permanent resident aliens can sponsor certain of their relatives to also come to United States as permanent resident aliens.

However, the next hurdle is to determine what the family relationship is between the two of you. Spouses *always* qualify, children *sometimes*, but brothers and sisters *do not*.

Q My mother is the permanent resident alien in the United States who wants to sponsor me to come and live with her. Is this a family connection that will support a petition for permanent residency?

A Maybe. Permanent resident aliens may file a petition for their spouses and for their unmarried children under 21 years old, as well as their unmarried sons and daughters over 21 years old. If you fall into one of the two above categories, then your mother would be able to sponsor you to come to the United States.

Q What is the difference between who a United States citizen may sponsor to come to the United States and who a lawful permanent resident may sponsor?

A A United States citizen may sponsor a *spouse*; his or her *children* under the age of 21; his or her unmarried sons or daughters over the age os 21; as well as, married children or sons and daughters of any age; his or her *parents* (if the citizen is 21 years or older); and, his or her siblings. Whereas, a permanent resident alien may only sponsor a *spouse* or his or her *unmarried children* (either under or over the age of 21).

Q Aside from the distinctions between who a citizen may sponsor and who a permanent resident alien may sponsor, are there any other differences between the two categories that I should know about?

A Yes. In addition to the distinction between citizens and permanent resident aliens, there is a further distinction even within each of these categories. As we know, citizens of the United States may petition for their spouses, children, parents, and siblings to come to the United States to live. However, not each of these family members of citizens are on equal ground with each other. For example, spouses, unmarried children under the age of 21, and parents are considered *immediate relatives* of the United States citizen. As such, a petition to bring these relatives to the United States to live is processed ahead of all other family-based petitions (including those for any family member of a permanent resident alien) because it is not subject to numerical limitations.

Further, unmarried sons and daughters over the age of 21, married children (of any age), and siblings of United States citizens fall into what is called *preferences*. This means that these family members can be sponsored by their United States citizen relative, but the processing time for their applications will be longer than those filed for immediate relatives because these categories are subject to numerical limitations.

Finally, the immigration laws create further distinctions between the spouse, unmarried children under the age of 21, and unmarried children over the age of 21 for a permanent resident alien.

Q I am a permanent resident and my cousin who lives in another country wants to come live with me. How can I start the process of bringing my cousin over?

A Unfortunately, your *cousin* will not be able to come to the United States to live with you simply based on your petition. Pursuant to the immigration laws and the family-based preferences, you may not sponsor your cousin to come to the United States because he or she is not a family member listed in the *Immigration and Nationality Act* who can obtain any immigration benefit from permanent resident aliens (or from citizens for that matter).

Q My best friend from my home country is now in the United States for three months on business. He constantly calls me to tell me how great the United States is and how much I would like it. I have decided that I would like to join my friend in the United States to live and work. What does he need to do to sponsor me?

A Actually, there is nothing he can do to sponsor you. Since your friend is neither a United States citizen nor a permanent resident alien, he does not have the authority to sponsor anyone to come to the United States to live and work.

Immigrating Based on Family

Q My coworker was a permanent resident alien, who then naturalized to become a United States Citizen. She has filed a petition to sponsor her brother to immigrate to the United States. I told her of my plans to also file a petition for my brother to come to the United States to live and work. My coworker, however, says I won't be able to sponsor my brother because I am a lawful permanent resident. Is she right?

A Yes, she is correct. As a *citizen* of the United States, your coworker may sponsor several of her family members to immigrate to the United States. The family members that a citizen may sponsor include:

- a spouse or child under the age of 21;
- unmarried children under the age of 21;
- unmarried sons or daughters over the age of 21;
- a married son or daughter of any age;
- siblings, if the United States citizen is at least 21 years old; and,
- parents if the United States citizen is at least 21 years old.

On the other hand, you, as a permanent resident alien, do not get as much generosity. A *permanent resident alien* may only sponsor the following family members to immigrate to the United States:

- a spouse;
- unmarried sons or daughters over the age of 21; but not,
- brothers or sisters.

U.S. Immigration and Citizenship Q&A

Q My brother has been a lawful permanent resident for approximately six years now. He had a child out-of-wedlock with his girlfriend in our home country. They have now gotten married and wish to bring their daughter to the United States to live with them. Can they do this?

A Yes they can. Since your brother is a permanent resident alien, he may bring his unmarried daughter, who is under the age of 21, to the United States to live with them. An important factor to note is that your brother and his wife were married before the child turned 18 years old, thereby *legitimating* the child. Your brother will need to submit a copy of his Green Card, a copy of the child's birth certificate, and his marriage certificate.

Q My best friend is a permanent resident alien and has recently married her boyfriend from Germany. She is fairly confident that she can petition for him as her new spouse to come to the United States to live. However, he has a small child from a previous relationship who he is raising. Can my friend also petition for her new stepchild to come and live in the United States?

A In this case, yes. Your friend may file a petition for both her spouse and her stepchild to come to the United States to live. It is important to note that if the stepchild had been 18 years old or older, your friend would not be able to file a petition for her stepchild to come to the United States. The marriage that creates the stepparent-stepchild relationship must have taken place *before* the child's 18th birthday.

Immigrating Based on Family

Q I am a permanent resident alien. Once I have determined that I am eligible to sponsor my wife to come to the United States, what is the next step I need to take to bring her here?

A You must next file Form I-130 *Petition for Alien Relative* with the BCIS. Along with the form, you must also submit documentation that verifies your status as a permanent resident alien (such as your Green Card); a copy of your marriage certificate; two Green Card style photographs of each of you; and Form G-325A for each of you.

Q Two months ago, I submitted to the BCIS my Form I-130 to petition for my brother to immigrate to the United States. I know it's only been two months, but we are anxious to be reunited. How much longer will we have to wait before he can come live with me?

A The filing of the application is just the first step of the process. Your brother must now wait for an immigrant visa number to become available. How long he must wait depends on the *preference category* and the *country of your brother's nationality*. He can get a good idea of how much longer he has to wait by consulting the *Visa Bulletin* and looking for the numbers for his home country. The Visa Bulletin will tell him what year is being processed for visa issuance for a particular country. Usually, the numbers indicate that those applications filing for this year probably have to wait for a number of years before an immigrant visa will be issued. Brothers of U.S. citizens, which is what your brother is, are in the fourth preference category and generally the wait is quite long.

Q My uncle is a lawful permanent resident. He recently filed a Form I-130 petition for his wife so she could join him here in the United States. The petition has been approved, but he hasn't heard anything more. What is the next step in the process?

A Waiting. Once the State Department determines when an immigrant number becomes available, your aunt and uncle will be notified by the BCIS that a visa is available. Your aunt will then be instructed to go to the U.S. consulate servicing her area to complete the processing of her application and to pick up her visa.

Q My wife picked up her visa from the United States consulate in our home country and is on a plane on her way to join me here in the United States. Can we now relax, secure in the knowledge that she is a permanent resident alien?

A Not yet. There are still a few steps that must be completed. Once your wife comes to the United States, she may file Form I-485 to *adjust status*. You will both be scheduled for an adjustment interview, and, at that time, she will either be granted adjustment or she will be denied. If she is granted adjustment, she will get a stamp in her foreign passport and a Green Card in the mail.

Q My brother has recently filed an *adjustment of status* application. He realizes that it may be awhile before the application is approved, but, meanwhile, he is afraid that his bills will begin to mount up. His friend has offered to get him a job, but my brother is afraid to work before the adjustment is completed. Should he be afraid?

A Your brother will be able to apply for a *work permit* while his adjustment application is pending. Your brother can use Form I-765 to apply for an *Employment Authorization Document* (EAD) that shows his right to accept employment. If your brother's adjustment application is approved, he will not need an EAD because his Green Card will serve as his proof to accept employment.

Q My brother, who lives with me in our home country, says that his wife, who is a United States citizen, is going to apply for a Green Card for him so they can live together in the U.S. I know sort of what it is, but what exactly is a Green Card? Is it green?

A The term *Green Card* refers to the plastic card issued by the United States government that identifies the cardholder as a lawful permanent resident alien. The official name for the card is the *Alien Registration Receipt Card*. The name "Green Card" came about because years ago when the card was first issued, it was actually green in color. However, more recent versions of the card are not green, but white or pink. Yet, still, the term "Green Card" was so widely used that the name has stuck. Almost everyone knows what you are talking about when you refer it as a Green Card.

Q I have just been issued a Green Card from the Bureau of Citizenship and Immigration Services. I see that the card has my name on it, but what does all the other information mean?

A This card serves as *proof* that you are a permanent resident alien in the United States and that you are authorized to work. You should carry this card with you at all times. In the front, the top of the card says "Resident Alien" and has your full name as well as a picture of you. The front of the card also has your fingerprint that was taken during the process of applying for your permanent residency. Finally, there is an eight-digit number that is preceded by the letter "A". This is commonly referred to as your A *number*. This number is your personal identifier. Anytime you are in contact with the BCIS or other government agencies, they will likely ask you for your A number. The back of the card also has lots of identifying information about you, including the date you were admitted to the United States. The various numbers of the back of the card are internal codes used by the BCIS to further identify you and your status.

Q Do you keep one Green Card for life?

A No. Up until the late 1980s, permanent resident aliens usually got one Green Card that lasted for life or until the alien applied for naturalization. Now, Green Cards are valid for a period of ten years, at which time they expire and must be renewed.

Q My brother is a permanent resident alien who has been in the United States for almost nine years now. Although he is not concerned about it, I know that his Green Card will probably expire soon. Will someone from BCIS send him a reminder letter to renew it, like what is done for a driver's license?

A No. Your brother is wholly responsible for knowing when his Green Card is due to expire and when he needs to start filing the necessary form to get the renewal done.

Q My Green Card does not expire until next year, but I want to be sure to renew it in time, so there is no gap between the time it expires and the time I get a new one. What do I need to do to renew my Green Card?

A The first step is to fill out BCIS Form I-90 *Application to Replace Alien Registration Card*. You can get this form by downloading it from the BCIS website, or you may call the BCIS

Forms Center at 800-870-3676 and order the form through the official Forms Line.

Q My sister knew that her Green Card was due to expire last year, but she did not do anything about getting it renewed. Her friend told her that she is basically an unlawful immigrant now, and that if the BCIS finds out that her Green Card expired, she will be deported. Is this true?

A No. Although it is important for your sister to renew her Green Card in a timely manner, she is not now an *illegal alien* and is not subject to deportation for an expired Green Card. Your sister can still file Form I-90 to request a replacement alien registration card. However, your sister will likely be subject to long delays in having her application processed. If your sister had filed for renewal in a timely manner (before the expiration date), she would certainly have a shorter waiting period to get her new Green Card.

Q My neighbor did not file a timely application to have her Green Card renewed, and now she needs to travel back to her home country to take care of family business. Is it OK for her to travel with her expired Green Card and just explain to the border authorities that her new Green Card is coming in the mail?

Immigrating Based on Family

A Absolutely not. By leaving the United States with an expired Green Card, your neighbor is likely to face problems when she tries to reenter the United States. If your neighbor has filed her Form I-90 *Application for a Replacement Card*, she can go to her local district office where she filed the Form I-90 and get a stamp in her passport which supplies proof of her status as a lawful permanent resident.

Q Now that I am a permanent resident alien, are there special rules that I have to follow?

A Yes. A permanent resident alien has the *privilege* of working and living in the United States. That said, in order to maintain his or her status as a lawful permanent resident, the individual must follow the laws that granted that status in the first place. For example, a permanent resident alien must obey the laws of the United States. Engaging in criminal activity can severely jeopardize his or her right to remain in the United States.

Q Are there any rules that a permanent resident alien must follow that a U.S. citizen does not have to follow?

A Yes. A United States citizen has the right to vote. A permanent resident alien does **not** have the right to vote. Even worse, if a permanent resident alien does vote and later tries to apply for naturalization, he or she will not be allowed to naturalize and will likely face deportation. Further, a permanent resident alien is required to adhere to *specific residency requirements*; whereas a United States citizen may enter and leave the United States or even live outside the United States at his or her own preference.

Q: After being out of the United States for more than a year to care for my sick mother, what can I show to help my case and keep my Green Card?

A: The more of the following, the better:

- family ties to the United States—such as where your children live, your brothers and sisters, etc.;
- property holdings in the United States—like a house, a rented apartment, bank accounts;
- business ties in the United States—like a business you or your family owns, a job that you can return to;
- compliance with all United States tax laws, including filing tax returns while you are out of the country; and/or,
- possession of a social security number.

You should also be prepared to show details of your mother's illness, like doctor's reports, that support the idea that you always thought your stay would be short. It will also help to show why no one else was available to care for your mother and why you were not able to bring your mother to the United States to care for her there. If, after carefully evaluating all these facts, you think you might be able to demonstrate the proper intent, fill out Form DS-117 *Application to Determine Returning Resident Status* and apply at the United States consulate in your country.

Q These residency issues seem pretty serious. What are the consequences of me not strictly adhering to the residency rules?

A Unfortunately, the consequences can be rather harsh. As a permanent resident alien, you must always be mindful of the amount of time you spend outside of the United States. Remember it is a PRIVILEGE to be allowed to live and work in the United States. It's best not to give the United States government any reason to think that you don't appreciate that privilege. To that end, here is what you need to be aware of—if you leave the United States for more than six months without first getting *advance permission*, there is a chance that the United States government will interpret this behavior to mean that you no longer wish to be a permanent resident alien, thereby *abandoning your residency*. Further, should you decide to apply for naturalization, you will have to answer very detailed questions about the number of days you have spent outside the United States.

FAMILY-BASED PREFERENCES

Q I am a United States citizen and would like to bring my brother to the United States to live permanently. I believe my brother won't have to wait long since I am a citizen, but my friend says he will have to wait for a visa to be available. Who is right?

A Your friend is correct. Even though you are a United States citizen, the family members that you can sponsor to immigrate to the United States fall into *two separate categories*. Spouses and children of United States citizens are considered *immediate relatives* and will not have to wait for a visa number to become available before they can immigrate. Whereas, siblings of United States citizens are not immediate relatives. Their visas are subject to *numerical limitations* and, therefore, must wait until a visa is available to them before they can immigrate to the United States.

Q I am a nurse. I was able to get a Green Card that allowed my husband to join me in the United States. Because of his job, he could not do this right away. In the meantime, I have become a naturalized U.S. citizen. My husband is now able to move to the United States. Can he still come under my original visa since his name is already on it?

A No. Because you are now a U.S. citizen, you must file an *immediate relative petition* for your husband.

Q My father is a lawful permanent resident and has petitioned for me to come live with him in the United States. At first, I was very excited about this, but then he told me that it would probably be many years before I would actually be able to come. Is he correct?

Immigrating Based on Family

A Your father is indeed correct. Although he may rightfully sponsor a petition for you to come and live with him, you still must go through the process of obtaining a visa to enter the United States. This is where the long, long wait begins. You are in the *second preference family category*, which is subject to numerical limitation. Since there are many people who have filed petitions in the second preference category to have their family members immigrate to the United States, each one of these applications are received and processed in *chronological order*. There are many *beneficiaries* in line ahead of you and that is part of the reason for the long wait.

Q My neighbor and I got into an argument over the status of my son who is married. I specifically recall that, as a United States citizen, my spouse and my children are my immediate relatives. However, my neighbor says that my son is not considered an immediate relative. How can this be?

A While you are partially correct in your understanding of family relationships as defined by the *Immigration and Nationality Act* (INA), in this case, your neighbor is technically right. Here's how it works: family members of United States citizens and lawful permanent residents are placed in different categories depending on what the family relationship is. In your case, while it is true that spouses are immediate relatives for immigration purposes, not all children are immediate relatives. In fact, because your son is *married*, he is not considered an immediate relative.

Q As a United States citizen, I know that my spouse is an immediate relative for immigration purposes. Who else is considered my immediate relative?

A As a United States citizen, for immigration purposes, the definition of an *immediate relative* includes the following people:
- your spouse;
- your unmarried children under the age of 21; and,
- your parents.

Q The classification of who constitutes an immediate relative of a United States citizen leaves out a lot of my family members. Can you explain how my other family members are classified?

A Since you are a United States citizen, there are a couple of different classifications you should be aware of. If you file a petition for your relative to come to live and work in the United States, and your relative is not an immediate relative, his or her immigration visa will be subject to numerical limitations. For example, your married sons or daughters are *third preference* relatives, and your brothers or sisters are *fourth preference* relatives.

Q What exactly are these family based preferences and what relatives do they cover?

A People who want to immigrate to the United States are divided into categories based on a preference system. This means that some relationships are *preferred* over others in the number of immigrant visas available each year. *Immediate relatives* of a United States *citizen* are at the top of the pile in their own category, because they are not subject to numerical limitations. If a United States citizen is the sponsor of an alien relative, there are additional preference categories. For example, if the foreign relative is an unmarried child who is **over** the age of 21, the relative is considered to be in the FIRST PREFERENCE category. Further, if the foreign relative is a married son or daughter, that relative is considered to be in the THIRD PREFERENCE category. Finally, if the foreign relative is the brother or sister of the United States citizen, that relative is considered to be in the FOURTH (and last) PREFERENCE category.

Q Do any of these preference categories apply to lawful permanent residents or are they only applicable to United States citizens?

A Family members of *lawful permanent residents* are also categorized by the family-based preference system. If a lawful permanent resident is the sponsor of an alien relative, there are two preference categories, both in the SECOND PREFERENCE. For example, if the foreign relative is the *spouse* or *unmarried child under the age of 21*, the relative is considered to be in the PREFERENCE CATEGORY 2A. Further, if the foreign relative is the *unmarried child over the age of 21*, the relative is considered to be in the PREFERENCE CATEGORY 2B.

U.S. Immigration and Citizenship Q & A

Q My husband is a Green Card holder. My son and I are planning to go to the United States next month. We are both approved under my husband's visa. It has been almost a year since my husband got his Green Card with the permission to bring us to the United States. Will this be a problem? Also, my son, who is 18, does not want to live with his father and has already said he will go and live with his uncle as soon as he gets to the United States. Will he lose his visa this way?

A You and your son can both get visas to the United States as family members *following to join* the principal visa holder. U.S. immigration law sets no statutory time period within which you and your son have to follow your husband to the United States. Furthermore, there is no requirement that the following-to-join spouse or child live with the *principal visa holder* in the United States.

Q My grandson says that he was researching the topic of family preferences, but that he could not determine which family preference category he would fit into. Could it be that he does not know whether to look in the family-preference list for citizens versus the family preference list for lawful permanent residents?

A Actually, it does not matter which list your grandson looks at, he will not find a preference category for *grandchildren*. In fact, there are a number of people who are not eligible to immigrate to the United States based on a family petition filed by a United States citizen or a lawful permanent resident. Included on this list are *cousins*, *nieces* and *nephews*, *godchildren*, *close family friends*, and some others.

Q **What factors determine how long a foreign relative will have to wait before he or she will immigrate to the United States once a petition has been filed on their behalf?**

A The first factor to consider is who the sponsor of the petition is. If the sponsor of the petition is a United States citizen and the foreign relative is an immediate relative, the waiting time between when the petition was filed and when the foreign relative will actually be able to immigrate is governed only by the actual processing time it takes to issue the visa. Whereas, if the foreign relative is not an immediate relative, the next factor to consider is what preference category the foreign relative is in. Depending on which preference category the foreign relative is in, the wait could be from two years to fourteen years before a visa number will be available for the relative to immigrate.

Q **My coworker, who is a United States citizen, filed a petition to bring her sister here to the United States to live with her. They have received notification that the petition has been processed and approved and that they will be notified when a visa number become available. Is there any way for my coworker to determine approximately how long her sister will have to wait for a visa number?**

U.S. Immigration and Citizenship Q&A

A Yes. On the approval notice your coworker's sister received, there is a date which indicates what date the petition was filed for her. This is also known as a *priority date*. Each month the Department of State publishes and makes available a document called a *Visa Bulletin* that shows the month and year of the visa petition they are currently working on. By comparing her priority date with the date in the Visa Bulletin, your coworker's sister will be able to approximate how long she will have to wait for a visa number. The Visa Bulletin can be obtained by accessing the State Department website at **http:// travel.state .gov/visa_bulletin.html**, through an immigration attorney or immigration social services organizations.

Q My friend told me that even though I may not think I qualify to adjust my status in the United States, I should check with a lawyer to see if any of the provisions of the new LIFE Act might apply to me. What is the LIFE Act?

A In December, 2000, President Clinton signed into law an immigration legislative package called the *Legal Immigration Family Equity Act (LIFE Act)*. This new law allows for certain categories of individuals to remain in the United States while their petitions for adjustment of status are being processed, despite the fact that they have violated their immigration status. Among other things, the Act also allows certain categories of individuals to come to the United States to be with their family members while their immigrant visa petitions are pending.

Q I am the daughter of a lawful permanent resident. My mother filed a petition for me to come to the United States to live with her and the petition was approved. However, I have been waiting for a few years already for a visa number and it looks like it could take a few more years. Will the new V Visa created by the LIFE Act help me?

A Yes. The new V Visa will help you as long as you meet the following requirements.
- Your mother must have filed the immigration petition for you on or before December 21, 2000.
- You must have been unmarried and under the age of 21 at the time.
- You must have been waiting three years since the petition was filed and either:
  - no decision has been made;
  - your petition was approved, but there are no visa numbers available yet; or,
  - your adjustment of status application/immigrant visa application is pending.

ENGAGEMENTS TO BE MARRIED

Q My American boyfriend of four years has finally asked me to marry him. We have been seeing each other by doing short visits both in America and in Greece, however, now that we are engaged, I need to be in the United States for an extended period of time in order to plan the wedding. How can I come to the U.S. for longer than the two to three weeks I usually spend there?

A If you have been traveling to the United States on a B-1/B-2 Visa, you may certainly continue to do that and request that your visa be issued for three or four months or however long (up to six months) you think you need to plan the wedding.

Q I am from South America and I met a United States citizen here while he was on vacation. We hit it off very well and have decided that we want to stay in touch. I suggested that he sponsor me to come and live in the United States for about six months to see if we wanted to move forward with the relationship. What does he need to do to sponsor me to come to the United States to live?

A Although United States citizens may sponsor their *fiancés* to come and live in the United States, they may not sponsor their *girlfriends*. In your case, you could apply for a B-1/B-2 Visa and come to the United States to see him for a couple of months and then decide whether the two of you wish to continue the relationship, but you would have to convince immigration authorities that you had the *intent to return* home.

Q I am a lawful permanent resident. My girlfriend from Romania and I just got engaged. We have decided that we don't want to have a long engagement, but want to get married as soon as possible. If I fly to Romania tomorrow so that we can elope, can I bring my new bride back to the United States with me on the plane when I leave?

A No. Because she is now the spouse of a lawful permanent resident, she falls into the PREFERENCE 2A category and must remain in Romania until a visa number becomes available for her.

Q I am a U.S. citizen. I was traveling in Mexico, when I met and fell in love with my fiancée. I want her to come and live with me as soon as possible. What do I need to do?

A If your fiancée is not a United States citizen and you are going to be married in the United States, the first step is for you to file a petition with the BCIS on behalf of your fiancée so that she can travel to the United States to get married. You must file Form I-129F *Petition for Alien Fiancé(e)*, along with supporting documents.

Q My brother is in the process of petitioning for his fiancée to come to the United States so they can get married. He told me that he was relieved to find out that all he had to do was fill out the two-page I-129F form and then his fiancée would soon be joining him in the United States. This seems surprisingly simple to me. Is that really all he has to do?

U.S. Immigration and Citizenship Q&A

A. Not by a long shot. In addition to filing Form I-129F, your brother must also submit many important documents to the BCIS. First, your brother must provide proof that he is a United States citizen. This can be shown with his birth certificate, his U.S. passport, a Certificate of Naturalization, or a Certificate of Citizenship. Next, your brother and his fiancée must submit Form G-325A *Biographic Data Sheets*. This form must be filled out in quadruplicate by both your brother and his fiancée. Further, they both must submit one color photograph of themselves taken within thirty days of filing the application. Also, if either of them have been married before, they must submit copies of their divorce decree, death certificate, etc. Finally, if either your brother or his fiancée are subject to age restrictions (younger than 16 years old), they must submit proof of permission to marry.

Q. My neighbor has been a lawful permanent resident for four years. Her boyfriend from her home country recently proposed and they are engaged to be married. She is eagerly gathering the documents she needs to petition for her fiancé to come to the United States so they can get married. Is the list of required documents the same for her as it is for a United States citizen?

A. No. There is no required list of documents for your neighbor to gather because she is not eligible to file a Form I-129F *Petition for Alien Fiancé(e)*. Lawful permanent residents may not file petitions for fiancé visas. This petition is only available for United States citizens. Your neighbor will have to go home, get married, and then file a Form I-130 petition for the immigration of her spouse.

Q My brother is engaged to be married to a woman he has never met. It is the culture in our homeland that young men and young women wishing to get married allow the older members of the family to arrange the marriage. What should my brother do about the requirement of having to have met his fiancée in person in order to petition for a K-1 Visa for his new fiancée?

A The *in-person* meeting requirement for a K-1 Visa comes with a few key exceptions. This requirement can be waived if the couple can establish that an in-person meeting before the wedding would violate all their long-term customs or that the meeting would create an extreme hardship for the United States citizen.

Q My best friend successfully petitioned for her fiancé to come to the United States on a K-1 Visa. Although they originally planned on getting married in a couple of weeks at city hall, they are now contemplating having a more traditional wedding sometime in the Spring. Will the BCIS care about their specific wedding plans?

A Yes. Very much so. The K-1 Visa provides a wonderful opportunity for future spouses to be together as soon as possible. This visa also comes with a lot of strings attached. In this case, your friend and her fiancé need to be very careful about the timing of their actual wedding. One of the conditions of the K-1 Visa is that the couple must get married *within ninety days* of when the foreign fiancé arrives in the United States.

Q My sister is having a difficult time with her on-again/off-again fiancé. They became engaged recently, so she began the process of filing the fiancé petition to get her fiancé here so they could get married. He did, in fact, get a K-1 Visa and came to see my sister. Unfortunately, they did not get along too well and he wound up going back home before they could get married. Last week, he called my sister and said he wants to go forward with the wedding plans. My sister believes that since her fiancé has only been gone for three weeks, they can still rely on the K-1 Visa he got the first time he came into the United States. Is she correct?

A Unfortunately, no. Even if the original grant of ninety days has not elapsed, her fiancé will not be able to use his same visa to reenter the United States. This is true despite the fact that the purpose of him using the visa now, is to finish the process he started when he first came. Because your sister's fiancé left the United States before they were married, he will not be allowed back into the United States without obtaining a new visa.

Q My fiancé came to the United States last month so that we can be married. However, his mother has gotten ill back in his home land and he wants to go back to be with his family. Since we did not get married yet, I am a little nervous about him leaving the country. He assures me that his trip back home will be so short that he won't even be missed in the United States. Should I be worried anyway?

A Yes. In this post September 11, 2001 world of terrorism and security threats, the nations' borders are being watched closely. The better idea is for your fiancé to *request permission* to travel back to his home country before he leaves the United States. This advanced permission is called *advance parole*. If your fiancé leaves the United States without applying for advance parole, he will be considered to have abandoned his K-1 Visa status with the BCIS.

Q My son's fiancée is preparing to come to the United States so that she and my son can get married. She has a small child from a previous relationship. Will she be able to bring her child with her?

A Yes. If your son included the child on the Form I-129F application, then the child may travel with his mother to the United States. The son would be coming to the United States on a K-2 Visa.

Q Now that my fiancé is here in the United States with me and we have gotten married within the ninety-day period, we have filed for him to adjust his status to that of a lawful permanent resident. My husband wants to now go out and work. How long will it take for him to acquire permanent residency?

A Because of processing delays and backlogs beyond your control, your husband may not receive his Green Card for months yet. However, this does not affect his ability to go out and work. In fact, he is eligible to apply for a *work permit* while his adjustment application is pending. Your husband would need to file Form I-765 *Application for Employment Authorization Document*. Once he has adjusted to permanent resident status, he won't need a work permit, because his Green Card will serve as proof that he has the right to live and work in the United States.

Q My husband and I have been married for about two years now. I vaguely recall that when we were filling out his immigration papers two years ago, there was some other form we would have to turn in to the BCIS shortly before our second wedding anniversary. What form are we supposed to turn in?

A You are referring to Form I-751 *Petition to Remove the Conditions on Residence*. Specifically, both you and your husband must fill out and sign this form during the ninety days prior to your second wedding anniversary. Your husband is considered a *conditional permanent resident* during the first two years of the marriage. Once you file this form, the condition on his resident status will be lifted and his status will be that of a *lawful permanent resident*.

Q My brother and his wife were married for one year, then they separated and eventually filed for divorce. My brother is worried that since they never made it to their second wedding anniversary, the BCIS will revoke his conditional permanent residency. Should he be worried?

A Not necessarily. The BCIS recognizes that not all marriages succeed. Even bona fide marriages can fail before the couple makes it to their two-year anniversary. To that end, there is a procedure whereby your brother could request that he be allowed to file Form I-751 *Petition to Remove the Conditions on Residence* to remove conditions on his status *on his own* and to allow him to stay in the United States as a lawful permanent resident. In order to make use of this procedure, your brother must request a waiver of the requirement to file a joint petition. Your brother must file Form I-751 (with only his signature). He must also submit a copy of his Green Card; evidence that the marriage was entered into in good faith; and, a copy of his divorce decree.

U.S. Immigration and Citizenship Q&A

GREEN CARD LOTTERY

Q What exactly is the diversity lottery (or Green Card lottery) program. Why was it created?

A The diversity lottery program was created by Congress to promote diversity by offering the chance to acquire a Green Card to people in countries that do not normally immigrate to the United States in large numbers. Therefore, Congress created a new visa category called the DV-1 Visa and a new procedure for applying for the visa called the diversity visa lottery. However, it is a little misleading to call it a *Green Card Lottery*, because, even though applicants may initially be selected, not all will receive a Green Card.

Q My boss told me that when the visa lottery program first started there were 55,000 visas available to natives of countries that had low rates of immigration to the United States. Recently I heard that the number of available visas is only 50,000. Is this a sign that this program may be coming to an end?

A Not necessarily. As a result of changes to the law in 1997, 5,000 of the available 55,000 visas were *carved out* and re-allocated for use pursuant to the *Nicaraguan Adjustment and Central American Relief Act* (NACARA), amnesty-type legislation

Immigrating Based on Family

that allowed Cubans and Nicaraguans living in the United States to adjust status without returning home. The visa lottery program will continue to remain in effect until Congress decides to end it.

Q My daughter discovered that her friend cannot take advantage of the Green Card lottery because she is a native of the Philippines. What other countries are not allowed to participate? Who gets to make that decision?

A The list of countries that can and cannot participate in the diversity lottery may change from year to year. Each year, the United States Department of State looks at the total number of aliens that immigrate to the United States from each country in the world. If a country has sent a total of more than 50,000 immigrants to the United States in the previous five years, the natives of that country are not eligible to participate in the diversity lottery program. For *DV-2005*, the natives of the following countries are not eligible to participate in the Green Card lottery: Canada, China (main-land born), Columbia, Dominican Republic, El Salvador, Haiti, India, Jamaica, Mexico, Pakistan, Philippines, Russia (newly ineligible), South Korea, United Kingdom (except Northern Ireland) and its dependent territories, and Vietnam. Persons born in Hong Kong SAR, Macau SAR, and Taiwan are eligible.

Q My cousin from Yemen has expressed an interest in immigrating to the United States. Her parents told her she should apply for the Green Card lottery, but she is not sure if she meets all the requirements necessary. What are the eligibility requirements necessary to participate in the visa lottery program?

A The first issue your cousin should look at is whether she is a native of a country that is allowed to participate in the visa lottery program. At this time, Yemen is not one of the countries excluded from the program. It is on the list. Having cleared that hurdle, your cousin must now determine whether she meets the required educational or work experience requirement. All applicants must have a high school diploma or the equivalent (a twelve-year course of elementary and secondary education) or the applicant must have two years of work experience within the last five years.

Q My cousin won the Green Card lottery. He has been working for the last ten years so he could fulfill the work experience requirement. Does it matter what type of work he has been doing?

A Definitely. Your cousin must have been doing work that required at least two years of training. Until recently, the State Department looked to the *Dictionary of Occupational Titles* in order to determine whether an applicant's work experience met the requirements. However, since July 31, 2001, the State Department has been guided by O*Net Online, a website designed for the Department of Labor that makes occupational information accessible. It can be found at **http://online.onetcenter.org**. Applicants will also find a link to a Labor of Department list of qualifying occupations at the Consular Affairs website at **www.travel.state.gov**.

Q My parents are originally from Grenada, but they were visiting Canada for a short period of time and that is where I was born. I know that natives of Canada are not eligible to participate in the diversity lottery program, but I really consider myself to be Grenadine because this is where I grew up. Can I consider the country of my home as my native country for purposes of the diversity lottery program?

A In your case, yes. Usually, a *native* of a country is someone who was physically born in that country, not someone who just grew up in that country and is attached to it. That would make you a native of Canada. However, for the purposes of the diversity visa program, although you are a native of a country that is ineligible to participate in the program, since neither of your parents were born in Canada, nor did they reside there when you were born, you may claim the nativity of your parents' country of birth, Grenada.

Q What is the form that is used to enter the visa lottery program?

U.S. Immigration and Citizenship Q&A

A New procedures for applying have been established for the DV-2005 program. Entries for the DV-2005 Diversity Visa Lottery must be submitted between Saturday, November 1, 2003 and Tuesday December 30, 2003. For the first time, no paper entries will be accepted. The Department of State will only accept a completed *Electronic Diversity Visa (EDV) Entry Form* submitted electronically at **www.dvlottery.state.gov**. Also, for the first time, the Department of State will send DV lottery entrants an electronic confirmation notice upon receipt of a completed EDV Entry Form.

Q What information needs to be included on the new 2005 Electronic DIversity Visa (EDV) Entry Form?

A The new 2005 EDV Entry Form requests much of the same information that was requested by paper submission in past years, plus a few new questions. The new EDV form requests the following information:

➢ your name—last, then first then middle;
➢ your date of birth—day/month/year;
➢ your place of birth—city/town, district/county/province and country;
➢ your gender (newly added question);
➢ your marital status (newly added question);
➢ number of children you have under the age of 21 (newly added question);
➢ spouse and/or unmarried children under the age of 21 with names, dates of birth, and places of birth;
➢ your native country, if different from your country of birth;

- your current mailing address and telephone number (and e-mail address); and,
- your photograph.

Q If no mail is being accepted for the DV-2005 program, how does the State Department get a signed copy of the Electronic Diversity Visa (EDV) Entry Form and how does it get the photographs?

A As part of the new procedures, a signature is no longer required in conjunction with the petition. The photograph will have to be sent electronically with the EDV Entry Form.

Q Are there any special rules for electronically sending the photographs with the Electronic Diversity Visa (EDV) Entry Form?

A Yes, there are lots of rules. If all required photographs are not attached with the EDV Entry Form, the entry will be disqualified. Some of the rules regarding the photographs are as follows:
- the photo must be a recent one of the applicant, his or her spouse and each child, including adopted children and stepchildren who are unmarried and under the age of 21 (even if the child no longer resides with the applicant or will not immigrate with the applicant), unless the child is already a Legal Permanent Resident or a U.S. Citizen;

- group photos will not be accepted. Each family member must have a separate photograph. Therefore, each individual needs a computer file containing his or her digital photo;
- the digital photo can be produced either by taking a new digital photo or by scanning a photographic print with a digital scanner; and,
- the photographic image must be in the Joint Photographic Experts Group (JPEG) format.

Applicants should carefully check the Department of State instructions for further detailed information regarding the specificity of the photographic requirements.

Q My daughter has encouraged her friend to apply for the visa lottery program. My daughter says that since so many people will send in an application in hopes of winning a visa, her friend would benefit from sending in his application as soon as possible instead of waiting until November like everyone else. Is my daughter right?

A Absolutely not. The rules for applying for the lottery are fairly straightforward and strict. Typically the Department of State will announce the application period in late July or August with a submission date sometime in October. For the DV-2005 Program, the application period was announced in August, and the submission date is between November and December of 2003. Prior to the DV-2005 Program, applicants had thirty days between the time the applications could be sent in and the deadline for when the applications could be accepted. With the current DV-2005 Program, the application period has been extended to sixty days. Applications will only be accepted during the speci-

Immigrating Based on Family

fied time period. Any applications that are submitted either before or after the relevant time period will simply be rejected. Further, with the new electronic filing system set up for the DV-2005 Program, applicants will not be able to access the necessary form until November 1, 2003, when the application period begins.

Q My cousin has been trying to come to the United States for a long time. Once he heard about the diversity lottery program, he realized that it offered him his best opportunity to try to live in the United States. Since he views this opportunity as his best shot at immigrating, he thinks he can increase his odds of winning the lottery if he submits more than one application. Is this a good strategy?

A No. This is a very bad strategy. Each applicant is allowed to submit only one entry per year. If more than one entry is received by the diversity visa processing center, all applications for that person will be disqualified. Pursuant to the rules for the new DV-2005 Program, an electronic record will be permanently maintained by the Department of State.

Q My best friend's brother was recently notified that he was selected to participate in the diversity lottery. Does this mean he will soon be coming to live and work in the United States?

A Not exactly. The diversity lottery program provides the selected applicant with the opportunity to apply for permanent residency in the United States. The diversity lottery program allocates 50,000 visas per year, yet the State Department selects more than 50,000 applications. This is because a high number of the selected applicants will ultimately not complete the process or will be found ineligible for a Green Card.

Q My uncle has been notified that he has won the diversity lottery visa. How long will he have to wait before he can actually come to the United States?

A Successful applicants will be notified by mail and will be provided with further instructions. In order to actually receive a visa, your uncle must meet all the eligibility requirements of obtaining a visa. DV-2005 Visas will be issued between October 1, 2004 and September 30, 2005.

Q My cousin has been notified that he has been selected for the visa lottery program. The number that has been assigned to him is pretty low, so there is a good chance that he may actually get a visa. However, he has a criminal background that would ordinarily prevent him from obtaining a visa. Will he get a special break since he won the visa through the diversity lottery program?

A Not at all. Your cousin must still meet all requirements of *eligibility* in order to actually get the visa and receive a Green Card when he arrives in the United States. Once his criminal background issues are discovered, he will be disqualified from the visa lottery program unless he is eligible for a waiver. However, there are no special provisions for the waiver of any ground of visa ineligibility other than those ordinarily provided for in the *Immigration and Nationality Act*.

Q My father lives in Romania with his new wife and three small children. He entered the visa lottery program for the fourth year in a row and actually won. However, he feels that his luck is bittersweet because although he his happy to be able to immigrate to the United States, he is unhappy about having to leave his family behind. How soon can he bring his family to be with him in the United States?

A Assuming that he filled out the diversity application correctly, he may bring his family with him when he immigrates to the United States. If your father is ultimately given a Green Card, he will be allowed to bring his wife and any unmarried children under the age of 21 with him. However, strict deadlines for when they immigrate to the United States may pose a problem. He and his family members must get their visas and immigrate by the end of the fiscal year. Under no circumstances will visas be issued after this date, nor can his family members obtain diversity visas to follow to join him after this date. The safest course is for all family members to be prepared to immigrate as soon as the diversity visa is available.

Q My sister and her husband are both interested in participating in the visa lottery program. Can they submit one application for the both of them?

A Yes, they can, but they probably shouldn't. The better idea is for them to each submit their own applications. They will each have to list the other on the application as a spouse, so if either one wins the lottery, they both will be able to immigrate. This doubles their chances of winning the lottery without violating the rule against applicants submitting multiple applications.

Q My friend is eligible to participate in the visa lottery program, but she has already filed an application for a work visa. Is she precluded from filing for the diversity visa as well?

A Not at all. Your friend may still file an application for the diversity lottery program. Your friend may then choose to accept whichever visa is approved first or whichever visa best suits her needs.

Q My cousin is already here in the United States on a B-1/B-2 visitor visa. She just received notification that she won the Green Card lottery. Does she need to go back to her home country to pick up her diversity visa to come back to the United States?

A Not necessarily. So long as your cousin is in the United States in a valid immigration status (not in overstay), she may stay in the United States and apply for an adjustment of status (the adjustment of status must be completed by the end of the fiscal year).

6.

United States Citizenship

There are four ways to become a U.S. citizen. The first is the easiest and that is to be "born" in the United States or one of its territories. The second way is to be born outside of the United States to a "U.S. citizen parent." The third is by "naturalization." And the fourth is if "your parents naturalize before you turn 18."

In this chapter, we answer questions about how to acquire U.S. citizenship. We place particular emphasis on naturalization, because this is the route to citizenship used by lawful permanent residents. Naturalization requires certain prerequisites. These include: five years as a lawful permanent resident and a period of continuous residence in the United States. We also discuss the language test and U.S. history test requirements.

Naturalization also requires a past to be of good moral character and fairly free of criminal activity. These requirements can often be very close calls. We discuss some of the more common problems that people in modern society might face in trying to overcome a less than perfect background.

U.S. citizenship can be hard won. It can also be easily lost. Although the U.S. Supreme Court has greatly softened the rules regarding loss of citizenship over the years, it is still possible to lose this great privilege. If you take on the "nationality of another country," if you "serve in a foreign army," "work for a foreign government," or "commit treason" you can lose your citizenship.

Naturalized U.S. citizens can lose their citizenship for additional reasons and face the almost science-fiction sounding process of "denaturalization." This process can reach back into the past and take away citizenship.

QUALIFYING

Q Both of my parents have been living in the United States as permanent resident aliens for twelve years. I was born in the United States four years after my parents arrived here. Now, we would all like to become United States citizens, how do we get from our current status to citizenship?

A As a general rule, there are two ways in which a person can become a United States citizen—either by *birth* or by becoming *naturalized*. In your case, the very fact that you were physically born inside the United States automatically confers the status of citizenship on you. The second method of becoming a United States citizen is through the process of naturalization, whereby lawful permanent resident aliens (such as your parents) submit to the BCIS Form N-400 to apply to become naturalized.

Q My mother is from Jamaica and my father is from Belize. They both came to the United States many years ago and that is where I was born. Am I a citizen of Jamaica, a citizen of Belize, or a citizen of the United States?

A You are definitely a citizen of the United States. You acquired your citizenship by being born in the United States, regardless of the citizenship of your parents. However, you could also be a citizen of Jamaica and/or Belize, depending on the laws of citizenship of those countries and whether either of those countries recognizes *dual citizenship*.

Q My wife and I traveled to the United States on a B-2 visitor visa. We planned on vacationing in the United States for six weeks and then returning home. However, my wife, who was seven months pregnant, went into pre-mature labor and our son was born in the United States. We returned home three weeks later. Is our son a citizen of the United States even though he only stayed there for three weeks?

A Yes. Birth in the United States automatically confers citizenship on the person born here. This is a right guaranteed in the Fourteenth Amendment of the United States Constitution.

Q My friend from law school, who was born in Guam, insists that she is an American citizen by birth. I disagree. I believe she is perhaps eligible to apply for citizenship because Guam is a territory of the United States, but she is not automatically a citizen. Who is right?

A Your friend from Guam is correct. Individuals who were born in the United States, including Guam, the U.S. Virgin Islands, and Puerto Rico (unless they were born to a foreign diplomat) are United States citizens by birth. Their birth certificates are proof of their citizenship.

Q My husband, my son, and I have been permanent resident aliens in the United States for over six years now. Although my husband and I do not intend to apply for citizenship, our 14-year-old son has decided that he definitely wants to become a citizen and has stated that he intends to file an application for naturalization, with or without our approval. Is there anything we can do to stop him from applying for citizenship?

A Fortunately, you do not have to do anything to stop him at this point. The very fact that your son is only 14 years old makes him ineligible to become a naturalized citizen based on his own application. If you, as his parents, first became naturalized citizens, he could then apply for naturalization. However, since neither you nor your husband are inclined to become U.S. citizens at this point, your son will have to wait until he is 18 years old before he can file an application for naturalization on his own.

United States Citizenship

Q My husband is a United States citizen and I am a citizen of New Zealand. We have both been living in Korea for the last year because of his job requirement. When I was 8 1/2 months pregnant, I went back to my home country of New Zealand to give birth to our baby. Is there any chance that our son could be a United States citizen?

A Yes, so long as certain conditions have been met. Your U.S. citizen husband must have maintained a United States residence before your son was born. Your husband would have to show proof of United States residency by providing a copy of an apartment lease, ownership of property, or United States tax returns. Alternatively, if your U.S. citizen husband can show that he lived more than five years in the United States, at least two years of which were after his 14th birthday, your son can obtain U.S. citizenship.

Q My father is a U.S. citizen and I am a U.S. citizen, but was born in Germany and grew up there. I married a Turkish man and we lived together in Turkey for ten years. Two years ago, we had a daughter. She was born in Turkey and has Turkish citizenship. One year ago, we got divorced and I decided to come to the United States. Now I would like to bring my daughter and establish her U.S. citizenship. Can I do this?

A Yes. The general rule is that for you to be able to get citizenship for your daughter, you would have to show that you, yourself, were physically present in the United States for a period totaling not less than five years, at least two of which were after attaining the age of 14. You cannot do this because you grew up overseas. But, the law also provides that if your parent was a U.S. citizen and your parent met these *physical presence requirements*, your child can benefit from expedited naturalization as a U.S. citizen.

Q: My husband is a U.S. citizen, but I am not. While we were living outside the U.S., I gave birth to our daughter who is now one. How do we prove that she is a citizen when we get back to the United States?

A: There are certain procedures you must follow to obtain proof of your child's United States citizenship. First, you should go to the United States consulate in the country you are living and your husband must show proof of his United States citizenship. Next, you must provide a copy of your daughter's birth certificate to the consular officer. Finally, you must provide proof that your husband was a United States resident before the birth of your child. The consular officer will then give you a document that confirms the United States citizen status of your daughter, that can be used to get her a United States passport for travel back to the United States.

Q: I am a United States citizen and now divorced. My son was born outside the U.S. and we never tried to get U.S. citizenship for him. Now, my ex-wife is getting remarried. We would like to bring my five-year-old son back to the United States to live. Can we get U.S. citizenship for him?

A Yes. In fact, the law provides for expedited citizenship naturalization for alien children of U.S. citizens who are living outside the United States. Your son is under 18 and so appears to qualify as long as you, as the citizen parent, were physically present in the United States for a period not totaling less than five years, at least two of which were after attaining the age of 14.

Q My wife and I are U.S. citizens. We have just adopted a baby girl. Does our new daughter automatically become a U.S. citizen?

A Yes. Under the *Child Citizen Act*, effective February 21, 2001, most foreign-born children automatically become a U.S. citizen on the date they immigrate to the U.S. In the past, the adopted child held the citizenship of the foreign country where he or she was born until the child's application for citizenship was approved by the BCIS.

Q I am not a United States citizen or a permanent resident alien, but my mother is a United States citizen. My mother has always told me that I have the right to call myself a United States citizen, because she is a United States citizen. Is she right?

U.S. Immigration and Citizenship Q&A

According to a fairly new change in the law, you may qualify to be a United States citizen. If you were born outside the United States before May 24, 1934 to a United States citizen mother and a noncitizen father, you are now considered a United States citizen by birth, as long as your mother resided in the United States *before* your birth.

Q I am a United States citizen and my husband is a permanent resident alien. We have been married and living in the United States for about one and a half years. My husband wants to become a United States citizen as soon as possible. How soon can he apply for naturalization?

A As a general rule, permanent resident aliens must establish *five years of continuous residence* in the United States before they can apply for United States citizenship. Spouses of United States citizens (such as your husband), need only establish *three years of continuous residence* in the United States before applying. Because you have been married for less than two years, your husband is considered a *conditional resident alien*.

Q I have been a permanent resident alien who has lived in the United States for fourteen years. I recently moved from the West coast to the East coast. I am now in the process of applying for naturalization. Does it matter what state I am living in so long as I have met the requirement of five years of continuous residence in the United States?

A Yes. As an additional factor of the continuous residence requirement, you must also have been in the state in which you filed the application for at least three months prior to filing the application.

Q My father is a permanent resident alien who is applying for naturalization. His friend, who just became a naturalized citizen, told him that his application would most likely be denied because he travels outside of the United States too much. Can this be true?

A Yes. It can be true. Not only does your father have to meet the *continuous residency requirement*, he must also satisfy a *physical presence requirement*. This means your father must have been physically present in the United States for at least one half of the period of time required to establish continuous residence. For permanent resident aliens who have to establish a period of five years of continuous residence, they must also show that they were physically present in the United States for at least two and one half years. As such, your father would need to literally count the number of days he was absent from the United States versus the number of days he was present in the United States. Also, there are some groups that are exempted from this requirement under specific circumstances, as well as some groups that are allowed to count periods of time spent outside the United States toward meeting the physical presence requirement, because they are working for the U.S. government.

Q My brother is a conditional permanent resident alien who has been married to his United States citizen wife for one and a half years. They have been having some marital problems and are now separated. Shortly before the separation. They filed Form I-751 to remove the condition on his residency, and they also filed Form N-400 so he could apply for naturalization. Will the separation affect his chances of becoming a United States citizen?

A Possibly. The three-year residency requirement applicable to spouses of United States citizens (such as your brother) only applies if the couple has been living in *marital union* during the three-year period. Some adjudicators have interpreted this to mean that a legal divorce, a legal separation, or even possibly an informal separation serves to terminate the marital union. Your brother should be aware that most naturalization examiners have interpreted the concept of living in marital union to mean *actually residing together.*

Q My mother and I have been permanent resident aliens for seven years. Although we are grateful for the opportunities we have enjoyed in the United States, we both still feel very close to our home country and do not want to lose our citizenship there. Is there any legal requirement that we become United States citizens after a certain period of time as permanent resident aliens?

A Not at all. Although many permanent resident aliens seek to become naturalized citizens at the first opportunity they can, there is certainly no requirement to do so. You and your mother can choose to live as permanent resident aliens for an *indefinite* amount of time. However, it is important to keep in mind that there are many advantages that U.S. citizens enjoy that are not afforded to permanent resident aliens.

Q I have been in the United States for four years now. I enlisted in the United States Navy during the Gulf War and was honorably discharged from active duty at the end of the war. My friend, who was looking into becoming a United States citizen, informed me that there is no way for me to become a United States citizen, since I was never a permanent resident alien. Is she right?

A Your friend is partly right. Generally, all aliens must first be legal permanent residents before they can apply to be United States citizens. However, there is an exception to this rule—those aliens who have *served honorably in active duty during a time of war* need not be permanent resident aliens before they can apply for naturalization to become United States citizens.

Q My college roommate and I both joined the U.S. Armed Forces at the same time. I am a U.S. citizen by birth and he is a permanent resident alien. Although we did not fight in any specific wars during our two-year tour of duty, we were both deployed to areas of the world that had a high risk of conflict. Since he has only been a permanent resident alien for two and a half years, he is not yet eligible to apply for naturalization. Isn't there some way that the BCIS could bend the rules for this loyal soldier and allow him to naturalize sooner than the required five years?

A Even if the BCIS were inclined to take action to expedite the naturalization process for this young man, it has no specific authority to do so. That power rests solely with the President of the United States. The President can (and has) issued a *Presidential Executive Order* that would allow your roommate to naturalize in an expedited process.

Q I don't speak English fluently. Is this going to be a problem when I apply for naturalization?

A Possibly. The general requirement is that the applicant must be able to *read, write,* and *speak ordinary English.* Just because you don't speak English fluently does not automatically mean you will not be allowed to naturalize. Don't forget, the standard is that you be able to read, write and speak ordinary English.

Q My neighbor has been a resident alien for six years now. Fortunately, her son knows English and is able to translate for her. She is only 42 years old, so she does not qualify for the exemption of the reading and writing of

English for purposes of naturalization. Can she use her son as a translator to help her qualify for naturalization?

A Yes and no. Although her son may be able to translate for her so that she can understand the questions, she must still be able to speak, read, and write ordinary English. If she gets to the naturalization interview and is not able to demonstrate an ability to read, write, and speak ordinary English to the satisfaction of the naturalization officer, her application will likely be continued. The good news is that if she does not satisfy the English or government and history portion of the interview, she can be scheduled for another examination within ninety days of the initial naturalization interview (or at a date later than that if she requests it and signs a waiver of her right to a BCIS decision within 120 days).

Q My mother and father have each been legal permanent residents for twenty-five years. They are both in their mid-sixties and have recently decided to apply for naturalization. While their native language is English, they both have some trouble reading and writing due to their age. They are nervous about their ability to pass the English test requirement for naturalization. Is there any accommodation that can be made for them?

A Yes. There are several exceptions to the general rule that all applicants must demonstrate the ability to read, write, and speak ordinary English. These exceptions include the following people:

- those with a disability that makes them physically unable to comply with the requirement;
- those with a developmental disability or mental impairment;
- those who are over the age of fifty (on the date of filing the application) and who have lived in the United States as permanent resident aliens for at least twenty years; and,
- those who are over the age of fifty-five (on the date of filing the application) and who have lived in the United States as permanent resident aliens for at least fifteen years.

Your parents would seem to qualify for an exemption based on their age and number of years of living in the United States as permanent resident aliens.

Q **My parents are happy to hear that they are exempt from the English test. Can they assume that they are also exempt from taking the United States history exam as well?**

A Absolutely not. For most applicants, there is a list of about one hundred questions, of which the examiner will usually ask the applicant about ten questions. The applicant must answer at least seven questions correctly. However, your parents may fit into a small exception to the normal rule. If your parents are over sixty-five years old (on the date of filing the application) and have lived in the United States as lawful permanent resident aliens for at least twenty years, they will be allowed to take a simpler version of the United States history test. They will be asked approximately ten questions out of a possible twenty-five questions. They need to answer at least six questions correctly.

United States Citizenship

Q I am in the process of filing my application for naturalization. As I go through the form, I see there is a section on *good moral character*. I've always considered myself to be a decent person and all my friends say I have a kind heart. Is this enough to satisfy the requirement of good moral character?

A Not necessarily. Even if your friends consider you to be a kind person, you must be able to show that you have not been involved in prostitution, smuggling, bigamy, illegal gambling, or a whole host of other criminal and/or morally reprehensible behavior. Although the focus is on your behavior during your period of continuous residency (either three or five years), this does not prevent the BCIS from looking at your past behavior prior to the continuous residency requirement.

APPLYING

Q I have been a permanent resident alien for seven years. I am now interested in becoming a United States citizen. Should I call BCIS and tell them they can go ahead and change my status now?

A While that may seem like a reasonable way to go about it, there is much more to the process than that. Your first step should be to get the proper documents and forms needed to apply for naturalization. The main form you need to fill out is

U.S. Immigration and Citizenship Q&A

Form N-400 *Application for Naturalization*. It is a ten-page application that requires you to provide detailed information about yourself.

Q My brother was granted status as a permanent resident alien approximately one year ago. He is very eager to go to the next step and apply for naturalization. How soon can he begin the process?

A The application for naturalization may be filed with BCIS up to three months before he meets the residency requirements. That date is also, usually, three months before the five year anniversary of the date an alien became a permanent resident (for permanent resident aliens who are married to United States citizens, that date is three months before the three year anniversary of the date the alien became a permanent resident).

Q Although my brother has only been a permanent resident alien for approximately one year, he is eager to file an *Application for Naturalization*. He believes that given the long delays in processing applications, he can only benefit by filing his naturalization application early. Is this true?

A Your brother may wind up doing more harm than good by trying to file his naturalization application early. The BCIS examiner will almost certainly recognize that his application was filed sooner than three months before the anniversary

United States Citizenship

date of his status as permanent resident alien. He will, eventually, be informed that he is not yet eligible to apply for naturalization and will probably have to start the whole process over at the correct time.

Q My friend, who is a lawful permanent resident, now wants to apply for citizenship. Although he is blind and may have a difficult time getting through the naturalization process, he is afraid that asking the BCIS for special help may have a negative impact on his application. Should he be worried?

A Not at all. What your friend needs to do is to first determine whether he needs a disability waiver or whether he needs an accommodation. The fact that your friend is blind, suggests that what he needs is an accommodation. Part three of Form N-400 *Application for Naturalization*, specifically asks whether the applicant needs to request an accommodation based on a disability or impairment (such as being blind). Asking for an accommodation, will not affect your friend's eligibility for naturalization. The decision to grant an accommodation is made on a case-by-case basis, though the BCIS will make every effort to make reasonable accommodations.

Q My sister is in the process of applying for naturalization. Is Form N-400 *Application for Naturalization* the only document she needs to submit to BCIS to complete the application procedure?

A. Definitely not. In addition to Form N-400, your sister must also submit a copy of her Green Card (both front and back), two identical photographs, and any other documents that indicate that she is eligible to become a United States citizen. These other documents could include marriage certificates, divorce decrees, birth or death certificates, tax returns, or court documents related to child support or criminal matters. A good rule of thumb is that if you answer a question on the application that could be substantiated by additional documents, it is best to include those documents with the application, so there is no unnecessary delay in processing the application.

Q. My coworker is filling out her Form N-400 *Application for Naturalization* She has left some questions unanswered and has provided only a vague answer for other questions. Her plan is to fill in the details when she gets further along in the application process. Is this a good strategy?

A. This is a very bad strategy. The naturalization examiner at BCIS will be looking carefully at applications to ensure that they are completely and accurately filled out. If there are many obvious gaps in the information provided, the application will not be accepted as complete. Your coworker will probably end up wasting (not saving) a lot of time by not submitting a thoroughly filled out application.

Q My coworker has submitted her Form N-400 *Application for Naturalization* and it has been accepted for processing. However, because she answered many questions from memory and did not carefully fill out the application, she does not exactly remember what she wrote on the application. Will the BCIS examiner test her on the answers she put down on the application?

A Yes. At the interview, the BCIS examiner will place your coworker under oath and may ask her questions about her background, any documents she submitted with her application, and any questions from the application itself. Since your coworker was somewhat careless about filling out her application, any discrepancy between what she put on the application and what she says at the interview will be viewed as suspect and may cause delays in the processing of her application or even denial of her application.

Q My brother is completing his Form N-400 *Application for Naturalization* and has asked me to look for a couple of old photographs of him to submit with the application. Does it matter what he looks like or what he is wearing in the picture?

A Very much so. The requirements for the photographs are very specific and the processing of his application will be delayed if he does not comply with the requirements. First, he must submit two identical color photographs that show a frontal image of his face. Also, the photographs must be unmounted and printed on thin paper with a white background. The photographs must have been taken within thirty days of the submission of his Form N-400 *Application for Naturalization*. Also, your brother should print his name and his *alien number* lightly in pencil on the back of each photograph. Finally, your brother should not be wearing anything on his head (including caps, scarves, or headbands), unless he is required to wear a headdress by a religious order.

Q**My uncle has completed his Form N-400 *Application for Naturalization*, taken the required photographs, and gathered all of his supporting documents. I told him that I believed the BCIS is located in Washington D.C. and that is where he should mail his application packet. If this is not the correct office, will they forward it to the correct office?**

A No. Where your uncle should mail his application depends entirely on where he lives. Your uncle needs to find out where the applicable BCIS Service Center that serves his geographical area is located and mail his application packet to that address. If your uncle sends his application packet to the wrong BCIS office, it will most likely be returned to him, eventually. He will then have to re-send the application packet to the correct office, causing him great delay in the processing of his application.

Q My cousin has a complete Form N-400 application packet and knows where to mail it. After he submits the application, will he be billed for the appropriate fee?

A No. When your cousin submits his application package, he must include the necessary fees or the application will not be accepted. The current fee to file the Form N-400 application is $260. However, because application fees change from time to time, before filing any application it is wise for your cousin to call his local BCIS office or go online to the BCIS website at www.immigration.gov and check the Forms and Fees section to be sure you have the most up to date information on filing fees.

Q My coworker has filed her Form N-400 *Application for Naturalization*, has been fingerprinted, and is scheduled for her naturalization interview in two months. A family reunion in her home country has been planned in three weeks. Since she is so close to the end of the process, is it OK for her to travel out of the country until it is time for her interview?

A Yes. Although many naturalization applicants are wary to travel abroad until they have a naturalization certificate (or a U.S. passport) in their hands, legally your coworker may travel back home until her interview in two months. She does not have to be physically present in the United States from the time of filing until the time she is sworn in as a citizen. She may make departures from the United States so long as she does not break her period of continuous residence.

Q My boyfriend filed his *Application for Naturalization* about four months ago and just recently completed his fingerprint appointment. How much longer will he have to wait until he becomes naturalized? How can he check on the status of his application?

A Fortunately, your boyfriend is approximately halfway through the process of becoming a naturalized citizen. Your boyfriend may check on the status of his application by calling the BCIS Service Center where he filed his application, or he could go online to the BCIS website at **www.immigration.gov**.

Q My coworker received a letter requesting that she submit additional documents. Should she wait for the fingerprint appointment and just bring the new documents with her?

A No. It is not uncommon that the BCIS may need additional documents in order to have a complete file for each applicant. The immigration officers at the fingerprint facility will not accept additional documents that were requested. Their purpose is to process your fingerprints only. It is important that your coworker respond to any requests for documents in the correct manner. The letter your coworker received should inform her of exactly what documents are being requested and where she should send them. Your coworker should carefully follow the instructions and the timeline specified in the letter. Failure to do so, may significantly delay the processing of her application or may even result in the denial of her application due to her failure to respond to the request for additional documents.

Q My cousin received a letter from the BCIS informing her of the date, time, and place for her fingerprint appointment. Due to a scheduling conflict, she will not be able to make it to her appointment. Is there anything she can do about having to miss her appointment?

A Your cousin should immediately call the telephone number listed on her appointment letter and try and reschedule her appointment date. If this is not possible or if the appointment date is very near or has already passed (but is still within eighty-four days of the original appointment date), your cousin also has the option of appearing at the location listed in her letter on any Wednesday to take advantage of the walk-in service. The burden is on your cousin to try and reschedule or use to use the walk-in service. If your cousin simply ignores the letter and eighty-four days or more have elapsed since the date of her original appointment date, her application will be delayed or possibly be denied due to abandonment.

Q I just received a notice in the mail from the BCIS, letting me know the date, time, and place of my naturalization interview. Unfortunately, the date falls on a day when I will be out of town on vacation. Is there a walk-in day to appear for the interview like there is for the fingerprint appointment?

A No. If it is not possible for you to make it to the naturalization interview, you should immediately notify the office where your interview is scheduled. You should both call that office and send them a letter asking to have your interview rescheduled. You should know that rescheduling the interview will likely add several more months to your waiting period.

NOTE: If an emergency has come up and you cannot make it to your naturalization interview, you should immediately call the National Customer Service Center (NCSC) at 1-800-375-5283 to request rescheduling. Your request will then be passed on to your local office that will make the final decision on whether to reschedule your appointment.

Q My coworker, who recently moved, applied for naturalization approximately eight months ago and is scheduled to appear for her naturalization interview in 2 ½ months. Should she just wait until her interview to let the BCIS and the local office know she moved?

A Absolutely not. If the BCIS is unable to contact your coworker either by telephone or mail, they may think that she has abandoned her application and they will administratively close her file. It is likely that the BCIS will deny a naturalization application based on an applicant's failure to appear or reschedule a fingerprint appointment, a naturalization interview or an oath ceremony.

United States Citizenship

Q My brother has gone through the whole long naturalization process and completed the naturalization interview yesterday. He answered all questions correctly and was given a piece of paper that says he will be contacted in a few weeks. Should he now start watching his mailbox for when his naturalization certificate will come?

A Not quite. Your brother still has one more obligation to fulfill before he receives his naturalization certificate. Assuming that his application has been approved, your brother will receive in the mail a notice of the *Naturalization Oath Ceremony*. Your brother can choose to have the Oath Ceremony performed either by the BCIS or an eligible court. During the Oath Ceremony your brother must take an oath of allegiance to the United States. Your brother will receive his naturalization certificate at the end of the Oath Ceremony.

Q My company is eager to send me to a two-week training seminar out of the country. However, the date of my oath ceremony is scheduled for when I will be at the seminar. Should I tell my employer that I can't go to the seminar or should I tell the BCIS that I can't attend the Oath Ceremony?

A Applicants, who cannot attend their scheduled Oath Ceremony, should send a letter to the local office (with the original notice of Oath Ceremony that the BCIS sent you). In your letter, you should explain why you cannot attend the Oath Ceremony and request that you be rescheduled for a later date (after your seminar) or requesting that your appointment be expedited and that you be rescheduled for a sooner date (before your seminar). The BCIS may allow for an expedited naturalization ceremony when the applicant demonstrates sufficient cause, based on special circumstances such as: serious illness of the applicant or the applicant's immediate family; permanent disability which would prevent the applicant's personal appearance; developmental disability or advanced age; or, exigent circumstances relating to travel or employment.

Q I have completed the naturalization process and I have received my *certificate of naturalization*, however, at the oath ceremony, my Green Card was taken away. Should I fold up my certificate of naturalization and keep it in my purse or wallet so that I have evidence of my citizenship with me?

A You no longer need your Green Card because you are a U.S. citizen now. It is strongly encouraged that you obtain a U.S. passport as soon as possible after you receive your certificate of naturalization. In fact, many applicants go right from the oath ceremony to a post office to apply for their U.S. passport.

Q My fiancé recently received his *certificate of naturalization* and then we bought a house together and moved in. Sometime during the move my fiancé lost his certificate of naturalization. Can he go back to the BCIS and request a new copy?

A Your fiancé will not be able to get a new copy of his certificate of naturalization from the local BCIS office. Instead, your fiancé must file Form N-565 *Replacement Naturalization Citizenship Document*. Your fiancé should know that it could take as long as one year before he receives a replacement certificate.

Q My coworker completed her naturalization interview four weeks ago, and just today, she received in the mail a letter from the BCIS indicating that her application for naturalization has been denied. Should she call the local office to try and set up an appointment with the naturalization officer that originally interviewed her?

A No. Your coworker should file Form N-336 *Request for Hearing on a Decision for Naturalization* to request an administrative hearing with a different immigration officer. Your coworker has thirty days after the denial to request the hearing. Also, your coworker should include with Form N-336 a filing fee of $195 and any documents, written statements, or briefs that would tend to support her bid for naturalization. Finally, your coworker should know that her request for a hearing will be rejected if it is not filed within the 30-day deadline, and her application fee will not be returned. In most cases, your coworker will be scheduled for a hearing within 180-days of when she files the appeal.

DETERMINING FACTORS

Q I have just completed the naturalization process and have received my naturalization certificate. I have been encouraging my brother, who is a permanent resident alien, to also become naturalized. However, he is reluctant to file for naturalization because he has a criminal record. Is he right to be worried?

A Yes. Although a criminal record might not automatically disqualify your brother from naturalizing, he should definitely be aware of the effect his criminal history might have on his chances of becoming naturalized. If your brother has a criminal record due to traffic violations or other minor crimes, he may not be barred from becoming a citizen. If, however, his criminal background relates to serious criminal convictions, he may be barred from becoming a citizen altogether.

Further, the applicant for naturalization must fill out Form N-400 as *completely* and as *accurately* as possible. Lying during any part of the naturalization process shows a lack of good moral character.

Moreover, even if he has had his conviction *expunged*, it is very important to be honest with the BCIS at all times when it comes to issues of criminal history. Your brother should honestly answer all questions regarding *arrests* (even if they didn't lead to a conviction), *convictions* (even if they were expunged or occurred before he turned 18 years old), and any crimes *committed* (even if there was no arrest or jail time).

Q My aunt has been a permanent resident alien for seven years now and wants to apply for naturalization. However, two years ago, she filed a petition for her son to become a permanent resident alien. On that application, she indicated that he was not married, when, in fact, he was. Will the BCIS care about this transgression?

A Very much so. If the BCIS finds out that your aunt lied on the previous petition in order to get her son into the United States, her application for naturalization will likely be denied and her son may be deported. She might also face further sanctions from the BCIS.

Q As I was filling out my application for naturalization, I noticed that there were questions about whether I ever failed to file a federal income tax return or whether I currently owe any taxes that are overdue. While I have never failed to file a proper tax return, I do owe a large amount of federal income tax that is, in fact, overdue. If I decide not to reveal this information on my application or during any part of the naturalization process, will the BCIS contact the IRS to check up on me?

A The first thing you should realize is that it is a very bad idea to willfully lie or omit information during the naturalization process, because if your misrepresentation is eventually discovered, there is a good chance that your application may be denied because you showed a *lack of good moral character*, regardless of whether the underlying tax issue would have been enough to prohibit you from naturalizing. It would be to your advantage to truthfully answer all questions during the naturalization process, and then resolve your overdue tax payment issues BEFORE you submit your Form N-400 application.

GAINING AND LOSING NATURALIZATION

Q My mother was a permanent resident alien for fourteen years. She recently became a naturalized citizen, but she has lost her naturalization certificate. Unfortunately, my grandmother recently died and my mother would like to go and pay her last respects to her mother. Will the immigration officers have a record in their computer that my mother is now a citizen even though she does not have her naturalization certificate?

A If your mother obtained a U.S. passport before she lost her naturalization certificate, then she will not have a problem traveling in and out of the United States. Her U.S. passport will serve as official proof that she is a citizen and will afford her the freedom to travel.

Q My friend thinks I am wasting my time and my money by applying to become a United States citizen, because I already have all the benefits I'm going to get as a permanent resident alien. Is my friend right?

A Your friend is dead wrong. There are many additional rights, responsibilities, and privileges that come with becoming a United States citizen. Some of those privileges include: the *right to vote* and the *right to hold public office* (with the exception of the United States Presidency).

Q My father has been a permanent resident alien for over fourteen years now. He is contemplating the idea of applying for naturalization. However, he believes and has stated many times that no matter how long he lives in the United States, his first country is his birth country and he will always be loyal to it. Could this sentiment cause problems if he applies for naturalization?

A Possibly. Your father needs to be cautious about his strong sentiments for his birth country. Although grateful for the opportunities they enjoy in the United States, most aliens are reluctant and even opposed to relinquishing all ties to their heritage. It is a requirement of United States citizenship that your father give up prior *allegiance* to other countries. If your father does not feel that he can uphold this responsibility, then he should think twice about applying for naturalization. If he admits to, or is discovered by the naturalization officer that his allegiance is not to the United States, then his application for naturalization will be denied.

Q I completed my naturalization process last year and had been enjoying being a United States citizen until last week when I received a notice from the BCIS indicating that the government intended to reopen my naturalization case. I am now a citizen of the United States. Can the BCIS do this?

A Without a doubt, the BCIS or the government may, with good cause shown, file a petition to reopen naturalization proceedings. Even though one year has passed, if the government or the BCIS has evidence that you were not, in fact, eligible for naturalization, presented false information during the naturalization proceeding, or if you had been granted naturalization by mistake, you may still get your naturalization revoked. In fact, the government has up to *two years* after an alien has been naturalized to initiate revocation procedures.

Q My coworker has been a naturalized citizen for three years now, however, she has moved back to her home country to be with her family. Since she does not plan to come back to the United States, is there a way she can relinquish her U.S. citizenship?

A Yes. Your coworker can take the affirmative step of *renouncing* her American citizenship before an American diplomat or consular officer.

United States Citizenship

Q My son has been a naturalized citizen for four years. However, last year he went to Afghanistan and fought with a terrorist group against U.S. forces. Should our family be worried that he won't be accepted with open arms when he returns to the United States?

A Not only will your son not be welcomed with open arms, he most likely will no longer be considered a United States citizen. By serving in the armed forces of a foreign country engaged in hostilities against the United States, your son has committed an act of *treason* that would serve as a *good cause* to strip him of his United States citizenship.

7.

Bureau of Citizenship and Immigration Services

Every nonimmigrant, every immigrant, and every U.S. citizen who enters the United States deals with the new BCIS and its directorates. Every time you cross the border and talk to an immigration inspector you are dealing with the BCIS. This Chapter is for everyone.

The "Homeland Security Act of 2002" established the new Department of Homeland Security and its sub-agency the Bureau of Citizenship and Immigration Service (BCIS). The Immigration and Naturalization Service (INS) was abolished. The BCIS is now the lead government agency that you have to deal with when you have immigration problems; want to immigrate to the United States; need to extend your visit to the United States; or, want to adjust your status.

In this chapter, we answer questions regarding how to deal with the BCIS on ordinary matters and in emergency situations. We discuss how the BCIS and the new Bureau of Immigration and Customs Enforcement (BICE) tries to exclude people at the border and what to do if you are excluded. We also discuss one of the most difficult situations an alien in the United States can face—"removal"—and what to do if it happens to you.

CHANGES IN IMMIGRATION LAWS AND PROCEDURES

Q I need to get some information about bringing my brother to the United States to live with me. Is the INS still open for business?

A Not exactly. As of April 1, 2003, the agency known as the INS no longer exists. However, the duties and responsibilities of the former INS have been absorbed into a new organization called the Bureau of Citizenship and Immigration Services (BCIS).

Q What is the BCIS?

A In November, 2002, Congress passed the *Homeland Security Act* in response to the September 11, 2001 terrorist attacks. This Act created the *Department of Homeland Security* and did away with the INS. The functions of the former INS have been divided into two new agencies: the BCIS, in charge of *administering immigration and citizenship benefits* and the Bureau of Border Security (BBS), in charge of *enforcing the immigration laws* of the United States.

Bureau of Citizenship and Immigration Services

Q How is the Department of Homeland Security organized?

A The Department is divided into five interlocking Directorates:
- The Border and Transportation Security Directorate;
- The Science and Technology Directorate;
- The Information Analysis and Infrastructure Protection Directorate;
- The Management Directorate; and,
- The Emergency and Preparedness and Response Directorate.

Q What has changed in immigration laws since 9/11?

A In response to 9/11, the government of the United States passed many wide sweeping laws that were designed to take care of many national security concerns. The ones that require special attention for an immigrant are these three.
- The *Homeland Security Act*—This Act created the *Department of Homeland Security* and did away with the INS. The functions of the former INS have been divided into two new agencies: the BCIS, in charge of *administering immigration and citizenship benefits* and the Bureau of Border Security (BBS), in charge of *enforcing the immigration laws* of the United States.
- The *Enhanced Border Security Act*—This legislation was passed to increase the ability of the then INS, FBI, and State Department to prevent terrorists from entering the

United States. Before this legislation was enacted, commercial interests had pushed the INS to speed travelers through in less than forty-five minutes. This legislation removed that goal. It, also, put the pressure on to move more quickly so biometric information such as fingerprints and perhaps retinal scans could be gathered and used.

- The *U.S.A. Patriot Act* (Uniting and Strengthening America by Providing Appropriate Tools Required to Intercept and Obstruct Terrorism)—This is a very comprehensive Act with wide ranging effects. It does everything from barring money launderers to increasing overtime pay for border agents.

Q Are there other government agencies besides the BCIS that have a role in immigration?

A Yes. Some of the other key players are:

- *Transportation Security Administration* (TSA)—responsible for security of all airports;
- *Bureau of Immigration and Customs Enforcement* (BICE)—responsible for enforcement within the interior of the nation; and,
- *Bureau of Customs and Border Protection* (BCBP)—responsible for border inspections, border patrol, and agricultural quarantine.

Q My cousin would like to come to the United States to live and work. He said immigration was done through the Illinois State Department of Labor. Are there other government agencies that have a role in immigration?

A Your cousin must be applying for a visa that requires *labor certification*. Although he's correct that the Labor Departments of individual states have something to say about his work visa, the main immigration agencies are the Department of Homeland Security, Department of State, and Department of Health and Human Services.

Q My sister is trying to get her fiancé to the United States so they can start their lives together. Should she continue to send all paperwork and correspondence to the INS office she's been working with or is there a new office under the BCIS?

A Unless she is told differently by the office she is currently working with, she should continue to send all paperwork and correspondence to that office. It is very helpful to check the website periodically at **www.bcis.gov** for updates on where to send paperwork.

Q My family is in the horse racing business. I noticed that the agricultural inspectors I used to deal with to bring horses to this country are now part of Department of

U.S. Immigration and Citizenship Q&A

Homeland Security (DHS). Why did the government move part of the U.S. Department of Agriculture (USDA) to the DHS?

A The Department of Homeland Security has as its mission preventing terrorist attacks within the United States and reducing the vulnerability of the United States to terrorism. Every agency that had anything to do with people and property coming into the U.S. was moved into the new department. DHS is specifically concerned about threats to the food supply of the United States.

Q When my aunt came back into the United States from Mexico she said she heard that the Border Patrol was going to be phased out. Who actually will watch the border now?

A Many of the same people who made up the Border Patrol will work for the Bureau of Border Security. Much of their efforts are focused on Mexico and its border with the United States. Their job is to prevent illegal activity and to expel people they catch.

Q My cousin got into some trouble with immigration. He finally wound up being removed and sent back to our home country. We live in Chicago, but the BICE put him in a county jail in a small town 100 miles west of Chicago. Can they do this?

A Yes, the BICE can detain prisoners in county jails. Actually, if you are detained for an immigration related occurrence, there is a real possibility you will spend your time in a county jail because the BICE often contracts out the housing of detainees to local jails with open space.

Q My cousin is in law school. She says I can sue the BCIS if they lose my application. Can I take the BCIS to court if I don't like what they do?

A Yes, you can sue the BCIS. Depending on merits of your case, you might even be able to sue them successfully. There are also several other administrative procedures designed for you to appeal actions that the BCIS has taken. However one new development that might be helpful is that of the *ombudsman*. An ombudsman looks out for the interests of citizens in dealing with the government.

Q What exactly is the *Executive Office for Immigration Review (EOIR)* and will I ever have to deal with them?

A Generally, the United States administrative decisions—such as those made by the BCIS—can be reviewed either by the law courts or by administrative bodies, that have the ability to review the decisions. In the case of the *Executive Office for Immigration Review* (EOIR), it served that function at the INS, and it will continue to do so for the BCIS. The country is divided up into a group of courts and a Board of Immigration Appeals. However, the Board of Immigration Appeals handles most appeals you might make. The EOIR tends to handle a lot of *asylum* cases.

Q My grandfather does not have the hang of computers yet. How would he send a regular letter to the Department of Homeland Security?

A When he masters the Internet, he can go to their website at **www.dhs.gov** for their email address. In the meantime, he can use regular mail and send it to:
United States Department of Homeland Security
Washington, D.C. 20528

BEING EXCLUDED FROM ENTERING THE UNITED STATES

Q My father has filed a petition for me to come and live with him in the United States. We just got word from the consulate here that a visa has been approved for me to travel to the United States. Does this mean I don't have to worry about having any problems at the border since I have been pre-approved to enter the United States?

A No. Receiving a visa does not *pre-approve* you to enter the United States. Your visa will allow you to board an airplane in your country and travel to some destination in the United States. The visa is evidence that you meet the requirements for *admission* to the United States. However, once you get off the plane, you will still be subjected to a United States border inspector who will make a decision as to let you cross the border into the United States.

Q My father has never been to the United States before. Since he is not a lawful permanent resident or a United States citizen, will he be carefully inspected at the border?

A Partially. Your father will be subjected to an evaluation by immigration officials to determine whether he should be allowed to enter or stay in the United States. Immigration officials conduct these evaluations when individuals are *entering* the United States, when individuals apply for *adjustment of status*, and when lawful permanent residents (Green Card holders) leave the United States and then *reenter*.

Q My family came to the United States about six years ago. Now we are in the process of trying to petition for other family members in our home country to join us in the United States. Not all of our relatives are decent people. Do the United States immigration agencies have some way of determining who they should keep out of the country?

A Yes. When a foreign national first applies for a visa in their home country to come to the United States, the consular officer in that country will make an assessment of whether the person should be granted the right to travel to the United States. Further, when the individual presents him or herself at the United States border, a border inspector will make a careful evaluation to determine whether that person should be allowed to enter the United States. You do not have to be entirely *decent* to get into the United States, but if you are a *criminal*, a *terrorist*, or have certain *diseases*, you will not be admitted.

Q My cousin was stopped by United States immigration officials after arriving at the airport. Why?

A It could mean any number of things. However, since the subject matter here is admissibility, let's assume that your cousin was stopped by United States immigration officials in order to determine whether he was admissible to the United States. If this is the case, the border inspector will be looking at a number of factors, including (but not limited to): your cousin's passport, his visa and his luggage to determine whether the correct person has the correct documents and to ensure that he is entering the United States with the proper visa for his intended visit.

Q Is there any specific reason why a United States border inspector would prevent me from entering the United States even though I have a valid visa?

A Yes. Actually, there are many reasons why a United States border inspector might decide not to let you physically enter the United States, despite the fact that you were issued a visa in your home country. If the border inspector refuses you entry to the United States, that means he or she has found you to be *inadmissible*. There are approximately ten reasons why a border official would deny you entry to the United States. These are called *bars to admission*. The grounds that can bar you from admission are:
- health-related grounds;
- criminal and related grounds;
- security and related grounds;
- public charge grounds;
- labor certification;
- illegal entrant and immigration violator;
- documentation requirements;
- ineligible for citizenship;
- alien previously removed; and,
- miscellaneous.

Q If the border inspector determines that I am inadmissible, can I appeal the decision and still try to get into the United States?

A It depends. For some of the grounds of inadmissibility there are exceptions to the general rule and for some of the grounds of inadmissibility there are *waivers* to the general rule. Waivers and exceptions are complex issues. At this point, you would be well advised to talk to an immigration attorney.

Q Are health-related issues one of the grounds for making a person inadmissible to the United States?

A Not necessarily. If you were suffering from nothing more than a bad cold, this would not be the type of health issue that would render you inadmissible. A person is deemed inadmissible for health-related grounds such as:
- a communicable disease of public health significance (including HIV and tuberculosis);
- lack of certain required vaccinations;
- a physical or mental disorder with associated harmful behavior; or,
- drug abuse or addiction.

(There are waivers or exceptions that apply to most of these grounds.)

Q My brother has been a lawful permanent resident for four years. Unfortunately, he has had some problems with the law over the last few years. He was just recently arrested again for a criminal offense for which he has a court date next month. Is it OK for him to travel as long as he comes back in time for his court date?

A That all depends on what is in your brother's criminal history and what this new charge is about. As a general rule, there are many criminal grounds for exclusion, one of which could apply to your brother. The grounds of inadmissibility for criminal and related grounds are as follows:
- crimes involving moral turpitude;
- drug offenses whether in the United States or a foreign country;
- multiple criminal convictions;
- drug traffickers;
- prostitution and vice;
- conviction of a serious crime and assertion of diplomatic immunity from prosecution; and,
- violation of religious freedoms.

If your brother has multiple criminal convictions, he may be found inadmissible when he tries to reenter the United States and ultimately placed into removal proceedings. (If he is placed into removal proceedings, he may qualify for one of the waivers available for this category.)

Q My pen pal lives in another country and wants to travel to the United States in search of a better life and better financial opportunities. Unfortunately, she does not have any substantial savings. She believes that she would not be able to get a visa to come to the United States because of her financial situation, therefore, she has arranged to come to the United States by sneaking aboard a vessel that is traveling to United States shores. If she is caught, what will happen to her?

A First of all, your pen pal is quite right that she would have had a difficult time obtaining a visa given her financial situation. One of the grounds of inadmissibility to the United States is becoming a *public charge*. If the government does not feel confident that she would be able to financially support herself or secure a commitment from someone else to support her (an *Affidavit of Support*) she would likely not be allowed to enter the United States.

Regarding the issue of her being a *stowaway* on this vessel, if she is caught, she will be subjected to removal procedures and will be returned to her country. This ground of inadmissibility regards illegal entrants and immigration violators and includes:

- aliens in the United States without permission or parole;
- aliens who fail to attend a removal hearing;
- aliens who engage in misrepresentation;
- aliens who make a false claim to citizenship;
- stowaways;
- aliens who engage in smuggling;
- aliens who engage in document fraud; and,
- aliens who are student visa abusers.

There would be no exception or waiver available to her unless she was a *refugee* or *asylee*.

Q I am a lawful permanent resident from Mexico and I make several trips each year back to Mexico to see my family. I've never had any problem leaving or entering the United States. However, on my last trip back from Mexico, I was detained at the airport and after being questioned, my Green Card and passport were taken away. The immigration officer told me that I needed to appear at the local BCIS office where I live in order to clear up my status. What is going on?

A When an individual arrives in the United States, he or she must be inspected by a border inspector who will determine whether that person should be allowed in the United States whether that person is entering the United States in a proper category; and, what the appropriate length of stay is allowed to that person. This process is called a *primary inspection*. If all goes well and the individual's documents are in order, that person is said to have *cleared* inspection and will be allowed to enter the United States.

However, if the border inspector has questions, doubts, or reservations about the person's documents or intentions, that individual will be subjected to further scrutiny, such as *secondary inspection* or *deferred inspection*. In your case, the border inspector has found something about your status, Green Card, or passport that raises questions. The border inspector will now try to clear up the questions he or she has so that a final decision on your admissibility can be made.

Q What happens if the inspector still cannot make a decision about my entry?

A If the border inspector still cannot resolve the question of your status, you could be detained until such a decision can made, but more commonly you are then subjected to a process known as *deferred inspection*. This step is taken when the border inspector has determined that he or she does not have enough information at the time to make a final decision on your eligibility to enter the United States. Therefore, you are allowed to *physically enter* the United States. However, you have been *paroled* into the United States and are **not** considered to be *officially admitted* to the United States. You are then instructed to present yourself at your local immigration office where further investigation and questioning may take place.

Q What will happen at my deferred inspection appointment?

A The immigration officials are supposed to investigate your case within thirty days and make a decision on your admissibility when you come to your appointment. However, given the fact that since 9/11 the United States has placed a priority on issues of increased domestic security and has implemented higher levels of enforcement, your case may take longer than thirty days to investigate and resolve. If that is the case, then your appointment will be continued and you will be asked to return at a later date. Eventually, however, a decision will be made on your case. The documents you provided, coupled with the service's own investigation should prove that you are indeed admissible. At that point, your Green Card and passport will be returned to you and you will be free to continue on your way.

✏️**NOTE:** For further travel, you should carry with you all documents relative to this issue, so that should you be detained at the border again, you will be able to show that this matter has been resolved.

Q My cousin from Chilé was stopped at the border in Florida and not allowed to enter the United States. What options are available to him at this point?

A If your cousin was stopped at the border in Florida, this means the border inspector could have given him two options. Your cousin could withdraw his application for admission and get on the next plane back to Chilé. This is called *voluntary departure*. Your cousin could also have been placed into *removal proceedings*. If your cousin was placed into removal proceedings, he will then be scheduled for a hearing before an immigration judge.

Finally, in 1996, pursuant to the *Immigration Reform and Control Act*, a new procedure called *expedited removal* was introduced. Under this new procedure, it is possible that your cousin could have been removed from the United States without the chance to have his case heard by an immigration judge. Pursuant to this new addition to the law, border inspectors at ports of entry (POEs) to the United States have the authority to order an alien removed without any hearing:

- if the immigration official discovers that the individual tried to enter the United States by fraud or by misrepresentation;
- if the individual arrived without proper documentation or without any documentation; or,

➢ if the individual falsely claimed to be a lawful permanent resident or a United States citizen.

Q I believe that my cousin was subjected to an order of expedited removal. How long should he wait before trying to come to the United States?

A At a minimum, he will have to wait ten years before being eligible to come back to the United States. The punishment for an expedited removal is the same as that for a removal order that is handed down by an immigration judge. If your cousin attempts to come back to the United States and is removed again or subsequently, he will be barred from coming back to the United States for twenty years. Because he is facing such stiff penalties, he would be wise to consult with an immigration attorney before attempting his next entry.

Q My niece is a lawful permanent resident. She recently took a trip to Jamaica to visit her friends and family. When she came back to the United States, she presented a fake U.S. passport to the border inspector and stated that she was an American citizen. It was discovered that her passport was fake and she was denied entry into the United States. Is she now subject to an order of expedited removal proceedings because she falsely claimed to be a United States citizen?

A Usually that would indeed be the case. However, because she is a lawful permanent resident, she falls into a small class of individuals who are exempt from the expedited removal provisions. That group includes:
- aliens who are natives or citizens of a Western Hemisphere country that does not have full diplomatic relations with the United States if they arrive by aircraft (Cuban nationals);
- aliens who have been previously admitted as lawful permanent residents or refugees;
- aliens who have been granted asylum; and,
- unaccompanied minors (usually).

These individuals will be referred to an immigration judge for a hearing.

Q Are there any appeal options for aliens who are facing an order of expedited removal?

A Only two classes of aliens may take advantage of an appeal process. The first group consists of aliens who claim, under oath, to be lawful permanent residents, refugees, asylees, or United States citizens, but whose claim cannot be verified. These individuals can be ordered removed, but the case will be referred to an immigration law judge for review. The second group consists of aliens who are found not to have a credible fear of persecution or torture. If the individual requests an appeal of the credible fear decision, their case will be heard by an immigration judge. However, if the judge then determines that the alien does not have a credible fear of persecution or torture, that decision is final and the alien will be ordered removed.

Q My friend and I were coming to the United States together for a vacation. While my border inspection process went smoothly, my friend's did not. The border inspector determined that my friend was not admissible and my friend was ordered to be detained. What does all this mean for my friend?

A If the border inspector determined that your friend may be inadmissible, your friend is entitled to a hearing (except in certain cases) on his case before an immigration judge. However, such hearings may not be able to be scheduled right away. Therefore, the immigration service has placed your friend in a detention facility until he can be scheduled for a hearing before an immigration judge.

Q What is bond? How is it set? How much is it?

A The arresting officer will set a bond amount at the time of the arrest. The amount of the bond set depends on a number of factors, including: the seriousness of the immigration ground of removal, the length of time the person has been in the United States, any familial ties the person has in the United States, and the possibility of any relief from deportation, etc. If bond is posted, your friend will be released from custody.

Q Can my friend do anything if they refuse bond?

A Yes. If bond is not granted, your friend may appeal that decision to the Board of Immigration Appeals (BIA).

Q My brother was returning to the United States when he was detained at the border and placed into removal proceedings. We were able to bond him out of detention and are in the process of looking for a lawyer to represent him. What will happen to him now?

A After your brother was released from detention, he should have received a document called a *Notice to Appear*. This is the document that lets the alien know what the charges are. It is also called the *charging document*. Your brother will then have a hearing in front of an immigration judge to determine whether or not he should be removed. Your brother will be allowed to (and should) produce as much evidence in his favor as he can. If the immigration judge finds your brother to be removable, that decision can be appealed to the BIA.

U.S. Immigration and Citizenship Q&A

BEING REMOVED FROM THE UNITED STATES

Q I understand that an alien arriving in the United States can be turned back at the border for a number of reasons. What happens to those people who are already in the United States and then proceed to violate immigration laws? Is that what is called being *deported*?

A Prior to the *Immigration Reform and Control Act of 1996*, persons who came to the United States and were found to be excludable could be placed into *exclusion proceedings*. Those persons who were already in the United States who committed an immigration violation became subject to *deportation proceedings*. The term that now describes these procedures is called *removal proceedings*. This term represents the proceeding by which a person is expelled from the United States, whether it be at the border or from inside the border. Further, the *Immigration and Nationality Act* continues to distinguish between persons who are *inadmissible* and persons who are *deportable* (subject to removal).

Q My friend says that even if he were caught doing something illegal, he wouldn't get deported because he is a lawful permanent resident. Is he correct?

A The fact that he is a lawful permanent resident will not shield him from being removed if he violates certain immigration laws. (If he were a United States citizen, this answer would be quite different, as citizens are not subject to removal from the United States.)

Q **My father is engaged in some questionable activities. What are some of the other reasons that he could be removed from the United States?**

A Generally, there are six broad categories of removable offenses.
1. Immigration status violations:
    ➤ aliens who were inadmissible when they entered the United States or tried to adjust their status;
    ➤ aliens who worked without authorization;
    ➤ aliens who overstayed the time allowed on their visas;
    ➤ aliens who had their conditional residence status canceled;
    ➤ alien who engaged in alien smuggling; and,
    ➤ aliens who committed marriage fraud.
2. Crimes of moral turpitude:
    ➤ aliens who have been convicted of a crime involving mortal turpitude (morally offensive crime) within five years of him or her being admitted to the United States, where the maximum sentence of one year or more could be imposed;
    ➤ aliens who have been convicted of two or more crimes of moral turpitude;
    ➤ aliens who have been convicted of a controlled substance offense (except a single offense involving his or her own use of thirty grams or less of marijuana);

- aliens who have been convicted of an aggravated felony any time after he or she has been admitted to the United States;
- aliens who have been convicted of a firearms offense;
- aliens who have been convicted of domestic violence, stalking, or child abuse; and,
- aliens who are drug abusers or drug addicts.

3. Document fraud and false claims:
   - aliens who fail to register a change of address;
   - aliens who are convicted for crimes related to the use of false documents; and,
   - aliens who falsely claim to be citizens of the United States.

4. National security:
   - aliens who pose a threat to national security;
   - aliens who engage in terrorist activity;
   - aliens who engage in actions which could have potentially serious adverse foreign policy consequences for the United States; and,
   - aliens who have engaged in Nazi persecution of genocide.

5. Any alien who becomes a public charge within five years of entry into the United States, from a cause that did not arise after entry.

6. Aliens who have voted in violation of federal, state, or local law.

Q My friend was recently arrested, although he wouldn't tell me what the charge was. In any case, since he is not a United States citizen, he is worried that this arrest could lead to him being placed into removal proceedings. Is this correct?

A Arrests are not convictions, however, *if* his arrest leads to a conviction, it will depend on the actual crime that was committed as well as the possible punishment is imposed as to whether removal proceedings are possible.

Q My brother received a notice to appear for a removal hearing from the BICE. My brother is fairly irresponsible and didn't show up for the hearing. What is going to happen to him?

A It is likely that the immigration judge proceeded with the hearing despite your brother's absence. This could be very bad news indeed for your brother. If an alien does not show up for his or her removal hearing, the immigration judge will proceed with the case so long as there is sufficient information to indicate that the alien received proper notice of the hearing. The immigration judge could then enter an order of removal, *in absentia*, against the alien, since he or she is not present to offer evidence or information to refute the charges.

One of the unfortunate consequences of having an order of removal entered, in absentia, against an alien is that it is very difficult to reverse such an order. If an order of removal were entered against your brother, he would now have to show that he did not attend the hearing due to circumstances beyond his control. Your brother should immediately seek the help of an immigration attorney who can find out the disposition of that hearing and advise him on what his next step should be.

Q I received a notice from the BICE stating that I need to appear for a hearing in front of an immigration judge. My friends say I should get an attorney right away, however, I know that I haven't done anything wrong, so I don't want to incur the expense of hiring an attorney. What can I expect to happen at this hearing?

A At the hearing, the immigration judge will formally notify you of the charges against you, and at this time you must either admit to or deny the charges stated in the *Notice to Appear*. The immigration judge will also give you the opportunity to request some form of relief from removal.

At this point, the assistance of an immigration attorney would serve you well. The immigration judge will also allow you to present evidence to support your request for relief. If additional time is needed to prepare your case, you can request a continuance of the case to some date in the future.

Q I am an illegal alien who has been living in the United States for three years. Last month, the BICE caught up with me, and after going through a removal hearing, I was ordered to be removed from the United States. Winning an appeal seems like a long shot to me. Is there any other recourse available to me?

A Yes. Although you have been ordered to be removed because of your illegal presence in the United States, you still have the opportunity to determine whether you may be eligible for:

Bureau of Citizenship and Immigration Services

- any waivers of removability (deportability);
- asylum;
- adjustment of status to permanent residence;
- cancellation of removal;
- suspension of deportation (if placed into proceedings before April 1, 1997, or if a NACARA applicant);
- legalization and registry; or,
- voluntary departure.

Perhaps some or none of these avenues of relief are available to you, but you should look at each possibility carefully to determine whether you qualify.

Q My father's lawyer called me today to let me know that we have exhausted all avenues of appeal on his case for removal. Once my father leaves the United States, how long does he have to wait before he can try to get back in?

A People who are ordered removed from the United States are heavily penalized. Your father will be inadmissible to come back to the United States for ten years. However, there is a small exception to this rule, whereby your father can request that he not be officially removed from the United States. Instead, your father would ask the immigration judge to allow him to *voluntarily depart* from the United States, within a certain period of time and paying for his own fare.

U.S. Immigration and Citizenship Q&A

SPECIAL REGISTRATION

Q My daughter-in-law is a lawful permanent resident, but I don't think she had to participate in *Special Registration* when she came to the United States. What is Special Registration and why does the United States government require it now?

A *Special Registration* is a system developed by the United States in response to the terrorist attack of September 11, 2001. This new system was created pursuant to the *U.S.A. Patriot Act of 2002*. This system is designed to keep track of the numerous nonimmigrants who enter and exit the United States on a yearly basis, as well as some nonimmigrants who are already in the United States. This system applies mainly to nonimmigrant males (age 16 and older) from specific countries.

Q My neighbor from Pakistan says he must comply with the requirements of *Special Registration* because Pakistan is on the list of countries that must comply. What is this list and what countries are on it?

A The INS (now BCIS) announced the beginning of the Special Registration program on September 11, 2002. The first phase of the Special Registration system required selected individuals to be fingerprinted, photographed, and interviewed under oath at United States ports of entry. By November 6, 2002, the second phase began and the INS announced that citizens or nationals of Iran, Iraq, Libya, Sudan, and Syria were required to comply with the Special Registration system between November 15, 2002 and December 16, 2002. This was the beginning of the growing list of countries from which nationals and citizens would be subject to the requirements of Special Registration.

On November 22, 2002, the INS further announced that citizens or nationals of Afghanistan, Algeria, Bahrain, Eritrea, Lebanon, Morocco, North Korea, Oman, Qatar, Somalia, Tunisia, United Arab Emerites, and Yemen were also being added to the list, and needed to register between December 2, 2002 and January 10, 2003. On December 18, 2002, the INS made yet another announcement, stating that citizens or nationals of Pakistan and Saudi Arabia were being added to the list and needed to register between January 13, 2003 and February 21, 2003. Finally, the INS made one last announcement (for now) that citizens or nationals of Bangladesh, Egypt, Indonesia, Jordan, and Kuwait were being added to the list and needed to register between February 24, 2003 and March 28, 2003. As of that time, no further countries have been added to the list. There are currently 25 countries on the list. Additionally, foreign nationals, not just citizens, of these countries who are entering the United States are also subject to Special Registration.

Q As a lawful permanent resident of the United States for twelve years, I don't think it is right that I should be subjected to *Special Registration* just because I am originally from Qatar. Are there any exceptions to the general rule?

A Yes, you are exempt. Special Registration does not affect individuals who are:
- United States citizens;
- lawful permanent residents;
- refugees (in some cases);
- individuals who have been granted asylum (in some cases);
- diplomats and their dependents;
- individuals with diplomatic visas; and,
- representatives and employees from accredited international organizations.

Q My brother is from the United Arab Emerites, but he is also a citizen of France and lives in France. He is in the United States on business and will be here for approximately two months. Does he need to comply with *Special Registration* since he is a French citizen now?

A Yes he does. The fact that he has *dual citizenship* with France does not exempt him from the requirement to comply with Special Registration. The fact that he was born in the United Arab Emerites means that he is a citizen of a country that is on the list, therefore, he must comply with the requirements of Special Registration.

Q Is the *Special Registration* procedure any different for those individuals who are already in the United States and those who are at the border trying to enter?

A Yes. Those individuals who are subject to *Special Registration at a point of entry* will be photographed, fingerprinted, and questioned by an immigration official at the border. Further, if the individual stays in the United States for thirty days or more, he or she is required to report to his or her local BCIS office and register between thirty and forty days after his admission into the United States. At this meeting, the individual is required to bring:
- proof of tenancy at a stated address; and,
- proof of enrollment in an educational institute; and/or,
- proof of employment.

Q What if my son missed the deadline when he was supposed to register or if he simply refused to register?

A In either case, the consequences could be quite serious. However, there are some differences. If your son missed the deadline by which he was supposed to register, he might still be allowed to do a late registration without any consequences. It is also possible, however, that he could be placed into removal proceedings. Often, it depends upon how late he is in registering and what his reason is for missing the deadline. The immigration officer will be looking to see if he had a good reason for missing the deadline or whether he did so willfully.

Whereas, if your son simply refuses to register, he will be considered to be out of status and may be subject to arrest, detention, fines and/or removal from the United States.

Q Do I need to notify anyone if I have moved since I registered?

A Absolutely. Even though the deadlines have already passed for those individuals required to register, there is still an on-going obligation for registrants to provides updates on their address, employment and/or school information. Further, there is also a continuing obligation to follow the rules and regulations regarding special registrants who leave the United States.

Q I have been in the United States for eight months now and have complied with all the requirements for *Special Registration*. My business in the United States is finished and I am ready to return to my home country. Is there anything special I need to do?

A Yes. The first issue to consider is that you may only leave the United States from a *designated port of departure*. You can get a list of designated points of departure by calling the National Customer Service Center or by going online to the Special Registration section of the BCIS website at:
www.immigration.gov/graphics/shared/lawenfor
/specialreg/List_interview.pdf

Furthermore, you must appear in person at the port of departure to be inspected by an immigration officer before you leave the country. (If you do not follow the proper procedures when departing from the United States, you may be found inadmissible should you try to come back at a later date. This requirement applies even if you are just traveling to Mexico, Canada, or adjacent islands.)

Q My husband was called in for *Special Registration* and questioned about what he is doing in the United States, particularly with some of the Muslim organizations he is part of. We are not sure what will happen, but I wonder what my status is as his spouse. Will my visa be affected?

A Yes, it might. The *U.S.A. Patriot Act* has made a number of significant changes to the immigration laws. One of the biggest changes is that the Patriot Act makes the spouse and children of anyone inadmissible on terrorist-related grounds also inadmissible. So, under a worst case scenario, if the questioning by the BCIS leads to a deportation proceeding on a terrorist-related ground and your husband is found inadmissible, you could be deported as well.

8.

Benefits Available to Immigrants and Nonimmigrants

Whether you are in the United States legally or illegally, seeking asylum or refugee status, as a visitor, temporary worker, or a permanent resident, you have rights and benefits you may not know about. These rights may include the right to have a hearing before any decision is made about your immigration status; the right to have your lawyer present at immigration proceedings; the right to appeal certain immigration decisions; and, the possibility of applying for temporary protected status. Benefits available to you may include public aid and food stamps. This chapter answers questions about these rights and benefits.

As in most areas of immigration law, the past few years have brought many changes to the rights and benefits available. The "U.S.A. Patriot Act" has reduced the possibility for applicants to review and appeal some immigration decisions. The "Domestic Security Enhancement Act of 2003" (also called "Patriot II" which has not yet been passed), will likely reduce the due process available to lawful permanent residences and other non-U.S. citizens even more.

The Q&As that follow will give you some real-life examples of how these changes are affecting immigrants in the United States.

U.S. Immigration and Citizenship Q&A

RIGHTS AND BENEFITS OF VISITING FOREIGNERS

Q My cousin is from Germany. He says he has a legal right to enter the United States because of the Visa Waiver Program. Is this correct?

A No. If he came here on the Visa Waiver Program (without the need to apply for a visa), he might easily *assume* that he had a legal right to enter the United States. But, he is mistaken. An alien outside of the United States has no constitutional right to enter the United States. However, because he is a national of Germany, and Germany participates in the Visa Waiver Program, he has the *privilege* of entering the United States without obtaining a visa prior to entry.

Q If my German cousin gets turned down at the border, does he have the right to a lawyer?

A Usually not. He has two significant barriers. If he is refused entry into the United States under the Visa Waiver Program, he has no legal right of appeal. Second, even if he were traveling under a regular tourist visa where he would have a chance of appeal, United States law puts the burden of proof on him in these matters. As the person who wants to come into the United States, he has to prove that he is *not inadmissible*. There is no *right* to have a lawyer represent him when he tries to come into the United States. However, if something goes horribly wrong with his trip to the United States and he is charged with a crime, then he has the right to a lawyer.

Q **My uncle has seen every NYPD Blue episode. When he crossed the border recently, the immigration officer asked him how long he was going to stay in the United States. He said on the show the police always read people their rights before they asked them questions and that the border inspection officer should have read him his rights, too. Was he correct?**

A No, you are asking about his *Miranda rights*. Miranda was the case in which the right to have constitutional guarantees read to *arrestees* was established. Immigration authorities at the border are not making an arrest. Aliens seeking to come into the United States do not have to have their rights read to them

Q **My uncle says if we drive our car in from Mexico that the United States inspection officers need a search warrant to search our car. Is that true?**

A Once you are on United States soil, you *do* have far more rights protecting you from unreasonable searches than you did on the Mexican side of the border. However, and this applies to United States citizens as well, when you are crossing a border you have a very *low expectation of privacy*. Governments maintain borders, so they have a right to search people and their cars *without warrants*. The BCIS does not need a warrant to search your car as part of its mission of keeping the United States border safe.

Q I am coming to the United States from my home country. I am 19. In my country I drink beer all the time. Do I have to follow United States liquor laws while I am visiting?

A Yes. You must follow **all** the laws of the United States while you are visiting. You may ignore laws that only apply to citizens of the United States. An example of laws like these would be voting requirements since only citizens may vote. Liquor laws apply to everyone.

Q My cousin came to see me in the United States. We are both nationals of the United Kingdom. He got arrested in a bar fight. Does he have any rights in the United States?

A Yes he does. As the citizen of a signatory nation to the *Vienna Convention on Consular Relations*, he has the right to see a British consular official. The British consular officer can help him find a United States lawyer.

Benefits Available to Immigrants and Nonimmigrants

Q I am a temporary visitor in the United States, but I have lived in my community long enough to want to take a stand on certain political issues. Can I vote?

A No, you may absolutely not vote. Do not vote. Do not register to vote. If someone tries to get you to register to vote, say no. Only citizens of the United States citizens may vote. Improperly voting in a United States election is a major problem if you want to become a lawful permanent resident alien or if you want to apply for naturalization.

Q While I am in the United States visiting my brother, he has explained his anger to me regarding the U.S. government. I am a citizen of the United Kingdom, but I want to join my brother in a speech denouncing the foreign policy of the United States. May I do that?

A Yes, certain freedoms under the Constitution of the United States are so pervasive that they apply to everyone. As a visitor, you may clearly exercise the *right of free speech* in this country to criticize the government.

Q My grandfather came to the United States to farm after World War II. He died and left me the farm. Now the government wants to take it to build a highway. Do they have to pay me, even though I am an alien?

A Yes. Property in the United States may not be taken from its owner without *just compensation*. Even though you are an alien, you are still entitled to just compensation from the government if it takes your property.

Q I am working in the United States for a pharmaceutical company on an H-1B Visa. The company has not been paying me everything that it promised, but when I complain they always say something like, "well you can always go back home if you don't like it here." Is there anything I can do about this without risking my visa?

A Yes. If your employer is not complying with the terms and conditions of the *Labor Condition Application* (LCA), you can file a complaint with the *Wage and Hour Division* of the Department of Labor. You can do this in writing by letter or by calling the Department of Labor. You can even ask that your identity not be revealed so your employer will not know if you made a complaint or if the Department of Labor is just conducting a routine examination. Once they receive your complaint, the Wage and Hour Division will investigate and make a determination. Before you start the process, however, examine the LCA carefully to make certain you have a reasonable basis for your complaint. In other words, make certain that it is clear from the LCA that you are not being paid the wage specified.

RIGHTS AND BENEFITS OF PERMANENT RESIDENTS

Q Do I have any rights as a permanent resident alien?

A Yes, as a permanent resident alien, you have many rights. In fact, you have nearly the same rights as a citizen. However, your rights may play out somewhat differently than a U.S. citizen.

Q My wife and I disagree about this. We are permanent resident aliens and she thinks we have the same rights as U.S. citizens regarding having our home searched. Is she correct?

A Yes she is. As lawful permanent residents you have the same legal protections regarding searches of your home that U.S. citizens have—but your house can still be searched. The U.S. Constitution protects people against *unreasonable* searches and seizures. However, *reasonable* searches and seizures are permitted.

Q As a lawful permanent resident can I come into the United States with the same rights as a U.S. citizen?

A No, absolutely not. You are still not a citizen of the U.S. Only a citizen has a clear and nearly absolute right to enter the U.S. As a lawful permanent resident, you may travel outside of the U.S. and generally you may reenter the U.S. with no requirements for a visa. As a lawful permanent resident you have procedural safeguards that help to make sure you can return to the United States, but you can still be removed from the United States or denied entry.

Q Do I have the right to work in the U.S. if I have a Green Card?

A Yes. As a lawful permanent resident you may legally work at any occupation in the United States. You may not work in positions which require U.S. citizenship. And, like U.S. citizens as well, you are subject to any licensing or qualification requirements of your occupation.

Q My family are lawful permanent residents. We want to move out of the city and buy a house in the suburbs, but nobody will sell to us. Do we have any rights in the United States in a situation like this?

A Yes. As a permanent resident alien living in the U.S., you enjoy protection under federal civil rights statutes that extend to housing. If you believe you are being discriminated against in housing, you may use these laws to make sure you are treated fairly.

Q: I worked here legally and I am entitled to Social Security benefits. If I become disabled, can I claim those benefits without it harming my immigration status?

A: Some cash benefits are acceptable. Social Security is one of them. Whether or not the benefit is earned is the crucial question.

Q: I have a friend from another country who is worried because she heard a rumor that she could be deported if she accepted government benefits. Is this true?

A: Technically is it true. Immigrants who accept certain benefits can be deported. However, in practice, is it very rare. And, if the immigrant can show that they only became public charges because *something happened after* they entered the United States, then they may be able to stay.

RIGHTS AND BENEFITS OF ASYLEES AND REFUGEES

Q What is a refugee?

A You may qualify for *refugee status* if you are a person who meets the following requirements:
- the President of the United States has designated you as a refugee;
- you are outside of your country; or,
- you have no country and you are outside of the country you used to live in; and,
    - you are unable or unwilling to stay in the country you are in because you are afraid you will be persecuted or
    - you have a well-founded fear of persecution that is based on account of your race, religion, nationality, membership in a particular social group, or because of your political opinions.

Q Who qualifies to enter the United States as a refugee?

A To come to the United States as a refugee, you must have a pressing need for protection. The preference of the United States would be to see you safely resettled in your own country. However, if that is not an option, then perhaps resettlement in the United States is an option. For you to be considered

Benefits Available to Immigrants and Nonimmigrants

a refugee, you have to be *away* from your home country. You also have to have a well-founded fear that you will be prosecuted in your home country because of your race, religion, nationality, gender membership in a particular social group, or political opinion.

Q: My brother and I have been arguing. He says that a refugee and an asylees are basically two ways to describe the same thing. I say that although you often hear the two spoken of at the same time, they are two different things. Who is correct?

A: You are quite correct. A *refugee* is someone who is *outside* the United States and who wants to be allowed to come to the United States because they have been persecuted or have a well-founded fear of persecution. An *asylee* or someone who is seeking asylum is a person who is currently *inside* the United States or at the borders and does not want to be returned to his or her home country because he or she has been persecuted or has a well-founded fear of being persecuted if they go back.

Q: My son is a gay man in Brazil. I am terrified that if the homophobic thugs do not kill him, the police will. Can he come to the United States?

A: You should definitely explore the possibility that he might qualify for refugee status in the United States. To do that, your son must contact the United Nations High Commission on Refugees or another international non-profit voluntary agency. If he cannot reach an international not-for-profit or the UN, he should attempt to contact the American embassy or consulate directly.

The UN or someone from the American embassy will talk to him and gather information about his situation. If they think he might be able to apply for *resettlement* as a refugee, then he will complete the paperwork and have an interview with BCIS. If the BCIS concludes he is eligible for resettlement in the United States, they and the State Department will work to resettle him in the United States.

Q: I am originally from Sudan, but because of the constant warfare in my country, I left and made my way to the United States. I have been in the United States for two months now and want to apply for asylum. Since I've already been here for a while, do I have a pretty good chance of being granted asylum?

A: It depends. The United States would much rather try to help return you to your country, if possible. The United States will also look at possible resettlement countries of asylum *within the region* of your home country.

Q: I just received word today that my application for asylum has been approved. Is there any way that I can petition for my family to join me here in the United States?

A. Yes. You may file an application for your wife and children to be granted *derivative asylum status*. This means that your wife and children may be granted asylum status based on your asylum status. You may apply for derivative status for your family within two years of your being granted asylum status. If your spouse or children are already in the United States, they may be eligible for derivative asylum benefits regardless of whether they are in the country legally or illegally. The relationship between you and your spouse and children must have existed when you were granted asylum and must continue to exist when you file Form I-730 *Refugee/Asylee Relative Petition* and when your spouse and children are admitted to the United States as derivative asylees.

If your children are outside the United States and have been approved for derivative asylum benefits, your children will be able to come to the United States as asylees at any time as long as they are under 21, unmarried, and maintain their relationship with you. If your spouse is outside the United States and has been approved for derivative asylum benefits, your spouse will be able to come to the United States as an asylee, at any time, as long as your spouse remains married to you.

Q. After being stopped at the border by United States immigration officials, I was informed that I probably could not qualify for refugee status or asylum, but that since I am from El Salvador, I might qualify for Temporary Protected Status (TPS). What is the difference between TPS and refugee/asylee?

A *Temporary Protected Status* is a temporary immigration designation that does not lead to permanent residency. This status is granted to individuals who are in the United States and are temporarily unable to return to their homeland because of warfare, a natural disaster, or some other temporary condition. In contrast, if an individual is granted refugee/asylees status, he or she most likely cannot return to his or her own country

Q Who is eligible for Temporary Protected Status (TPS)?

A The Secretary of the Department of Homeland Security may provide TPS to those countries he or she may designate as having temporary and extraordinary conditions. At the time of publication, the nationals of the following countries may apply for TPS: Burundi, El Salvador, Honduras, Liberia, Montserrat, Nicaragua, Sirre Leon, Somalia, and Sudan.

Q My family and I have been granted refugee status to the United States. We have had a difficult time adjusting to life in the United States and are experiencing some financial problems. Is there anything we can do?

A Yes. The first thing you should know is that pursuant to your refugee status, you and/or your spouse are authorized to work. You can obtain an *Employment Authorization Document* by filing Form I-765 with the BCIS.

Benefits Available to Immigrants and Nonimmigrants

Q I have been in the United States as a refugee for two years now. I know there is a five-year wait before I can apply for any public benefits, but what should I do in the meantime?

A Although most aliens, including lawful permanent residents, have to wait at least five years from the time they entered the United States before applying for public benefits, *this five-year ban* does not apply to refugees or asylees. Refugees and asylees are eligible for federally funded food stamps during the first seven years after their entry as a refugee/asylees.

Q If my family comes from Ethiopia as refugees, are they eligible for benefits in the United States? If so, what benefits could we receive?

A There are several government programs available to assist you and your family members. Under the *State Children's Health Insurance Program* (SCHIP), funds are allocated to states to provide health insurance coverage for uninsured, low-income children. Further, under the *Temporary Assistance for Needy Families* (TANF) program, cash payments, vouchers, social services and other assistance is available to low-income families with children.

Immigrants who entered the United States on or after August 22, 1996, are ineligible for non emergency Medicaid, SCHIP or TANF assistance until five years after the date they became a qualified immigrant. However, this five-year bar does not apply to refugees, asylees, those granted withholding of deportation,

Amerasians, Cuban/Haitian entrants, and those who qualify for a veteran's exemption.

Q What if I live in a state that limits or denies benefits to immigrants?

A The *Personal Responsibility and Work Opportunity Reconciliation Act of 1996 (Welfare Act)* gives the states the option to deny TANF and Medicaid to immigrants, but a state may not deny such benefits to refugees, asylees, veterans, or those aliens who have worked for forty qualifying quarters.

Q I am a single mother of two children and I just got a job. However, I need childcare in order to be able to go to work. Is there any program that would assist me, even though I am just a refugee?

A Title XX of the *Social Security Act* provides for childcare, in-home care for disabled persons, programs to combat domestic violence and programs for abused and neglected children. While states have the right to restrict the eligibility of immigrants for Title XX programs in the same way as Medicaid and TANF, states may not restrict such rights to refugees.

Benefits Available to Immigrants and Nonimmigrants

Q When I first came to the United States from China as a refugee, several families in my community were very kind and provided me with food and shelter. However, it is now time for me to stand on my own two feet. The only problem is that I don't think I will be able to afford an apartment on my own. Is there any organization that can give me some assistance with this?

A Yes. Refugees and asylees are eligible to participate in certain rental housing programs financed by the Department of Housing and Urban Development.

Q It's tax time again and I have heard about something called an *earned income credit* that I think I might be eligible for. However, my neighbor assures me that I am not eligible for this credit because I am an asylees. Is she right?

A Maybe not. Refugees and asylees do qualify to apply for the *earned income tax credit* if they have BCIS-issued employment authorization and if they have a social security number that allows them to post earnings and qualifying hours to their social security account.

9.

Consular Processing

Do I need a visa? This is the first question that crosses most people's minds when they think about traveling to a foreign country.

Consular processing is all about getting visas to come to the United States. For the vast majority of visitors and immigrants to the United States, the first step in the journey to the United States is a visit in person or by mail to a U.S. consulate abroad.

With few exceptions, getting into the United States is a two-step process. Get a visa at the consulate and then get inspected at the border. The first step in this process—issuing visas—is the job of the U.S. Department of State, its Bureau of Consular Affairs and its Visa Office. The second step is controlled by the Department of Homeland Security, its BCIS, Bureau of Customs and Border Protection and its Bureau of Immigration and Customs Enforcement. Many visas require cooperation and communication between the consulate and BCIS before they can be issued.

In this chapter, we take you through all aspects of consular processing. If you have not already done so, you may wish to review Appendix A, which describes the various family-based immigration visas, employment-based immigration visas, as well as the temporary, nonimmigrant visas that can be issued. We then discuss: how visa processing really works; who makes decisions about your visa; how much authority a consular officer has; where consular officers get *information about you; how you can do consular processing from inside the United States; and, much more.*

Finally, we help you deal with the U.S. consulate including offering guidance on what to do and say at interviews.

VISA PROCESSING

Q What visas can I apply for at a U.S. consulate overseas and what forms do I need?

A You can apply for any and all visas at U.S. consulates abroad. In fact, only the U.S. Department of State through its Consular Services can issue visas. Most of the time, when you apply for a *visa* in the United States, you are actually *adjusting your immigration status* with the BCIS, not really applying for a visa.

Whether or not you start or complete your processing at a U.S. consulate abroad, will depend on where you are when you start the process, what kind of immigration status you already have, and the type of visa or immigration status you apply for.

Q What is consular processing?

Consular Processing

A *Consular processing* simply refers to the steps taken by a U.S. consulate abroad to accept visa applications, review the applications, make decisions about the applications, interview applicants, and issue visas. People living outside the United States normally go to the U.S. consulate to apply for a visa and have it processed. People in the United States can often apply for adjustment of status, which is a procedure administered and processed by the BCIS. Many types of visas require both the U.S. consulate and the BCIS to take action before they can be issued.

Q What actually happens to my visa application at the consulate?

A When you turn in your completed visa application to the consulate, either by mail or in person, it is first routed within the consulate to the appropriate section. Usually, there are two sections: one handling nonimmigrant visas and one handling immigrant visas. Large posts may have more subsections and small posts may not have any sections. Your application is usually first reviewed by a *Foreign Service National* (FSN), a local of the country working in the consular section, to make sure it is complete, the proper supporting documents are included, it is signed, and the fee is enclosed. Your application then goes to a *consular officer* who makes a preliminary decision on whether to issue or deny the visa. This officer is usually referred to as the *adjudicating officer*. If a decision is made to issue the visa, your application goes to an *issuing officer* who authorizes the printing of the visa into your passport.

Q: Who can be an issuing officer?

A: Only consular officers, consular associates, and professional associates who have been specifically designated by the office of consular affairs as *consular officers for visa purposes* are allowed to authorize the printing of a visa. These persons must be U.S. citizens and must have completed the consular course. The issuing officer may or may not be the same as the adjudicating officer, but, in any case, he or she is responsible for compliance with the *Visa Lookout Accountability* (VLA) requirement.

Q: What is the *Visa Lookout Accountability* requirement? What does it mean to me, the applicant?

A: A *Visa Lookout Accountability* (VLA) requirement requires the consular officer to take certain action on each application. These are steps in the process you do not see from the outside. The primary requirement, in all cases, is to check the *Consular Lookout and Support System* (CLASS) and any other appropriate post records to see if your name appears. Depending upon the results of this search, the consular officer may be required to take other action such as completing *clearance procedures* with other posts. A clearance procedure is nothing more than the process of obtaining information about your potential visa eligibility from other posts or from the Department of State or other government agencies. Such information might include, for example, a previous visa application filed at a different U.S. consulate. Again, depending on the results of the CLASS search and other information, the consular officer may have to request additional name checks, request security advisory opinions from the U.S. State Department, or even forward the original visa application to the FBI or other law enforcement agency.

Moreover, if there are any other issues about the application that are not in the discretion of the consular officer to decide, he or she will request guidance and/or waivers from the Department of State before approving the visa. These measures are normally called *necessary administrative processing*. The consular officer will also decide if a personal interview is required and/or if further information and documents need to be submitted.

Once all these steps are successfully completed to the satisfaction of the consular officer responsible for your application, your visa can be issued. Obviously, the need to perform these measures means that the visa processing time for your visa can be longer or shorter depending on your individual circumstances.

Q How long does consular processing take?

A This will depend upon the consulate, your nationality, and the type of visa. For example, you can get a tourist visa at most U.S. consulates in western Europe on the same day you apply. On the other hand, an immigration visa typically takes five to seven months to process.

U.S. Immigration and Citizenship Q&A

Q Can I have the U.S. consulate in my home country process my visa, even if I live in the United States?

A Yes. As long as you are legally living in the United States you can choose either *consular processing* or *adjustment of status*.

Q My wife and I want to adjust our status. We are already in the United States. Is there any reason we should use consular processing rather than adjustment of status with the BCIS?

A Yes. There may be considerable time savings. Adjustment of status applications have been taking us to two years whereas consular processing can take only five to seven months.

Q We have been sponsored for a family immigration visa. Our Form I-130 *Petition for Alien Relative* has been filed. We have already received Form I-797 *Notice of Approval* from the BCIS. We already live in the United States and thought we were going to adjust our status, but now we would like the U.S. consulate to process the visas. Is there any way we can change to consular processing?

A Yes. You should file Form I-824 *Application for Action on Approved Application or Petition* with the BCIS Service Center requesting them to switch your case to consular processing.

You should be aware that because you started the process as an adjustment of status, the switch after approval will delay consular processing somewhat, in some cases by as much as six months.

Q What are some of the problems with consular processing?

A From the applicant's point the view, the biggest problem or disadvantage is that consular decisions are not reviewable. If you are denied your visa, you have very few choices. On the other hand, there is an appeals process for decisions made by the BCIS on your adjustment of status application. Consular processing can also be less convenient and more expensive because you have to travel to your home country to finish the procedure. U.S. consulates require an interview with you and with all your family members as well.

An adjustment of status application can simply be mailed to the BCIS office, and BCIS often waives the interview requirement. If you are working in the United States, the adjustment of status application lets you and your spouse get *Employment Authorization Documents* to work while your application is being processed as soon as you file. Consular processing does not.

Also, under the *American Competitiveness in the 21st Century Act*, adjustment of status applicants can take advantage of new *portability provisions*. The new law allows the adjustment of status applicant to change jobs if the adjustment of status application has been pending for 180 days or more. Adjustment of status applicants can also apply for permission to travel outside of the United States and return in the same immigration status they currently enjoy (*advance parole*).

Adjustment of status applicants who hold H or L Visas can even travel temporarily outside the United States without obtaining *advanced permission*. This is not available to applicants using consular processing. If you travel out of the United States, you may not be able to get back in on your current visa until your immigration visa has been processed and approved.

Q **Where does the consulate get information about me in order check if I am telling the truth on my application?**

A These sources of information start with the *Consular Lookout and Support System* (CLASS) and any records the consulate itself may have. They extend to the records of other U.S. consulates and embassies and to the institutional knowledge of the diplomats and consular officers who work in those posts.

The U.S. consulate can also access the full investigative resources of the U.S. Department of State including doing name checks in the databases of U.S. government agencies and requesting security advisory opinions. Most U.S. consulates maintain contact with local police and security authorities and can obtain information from them. Department of State regulations also allow consular officers to use any other resources that may be available as sources of information.

Thus, the consular officer can check the World Wide Web and other publicly available materials to find information that may be relevant to your petition. The consulate can indeed pull together information from all over the world to verify that you are telling the truth on your application.

Q Where does the information in the CLASS system come from?

A Sources for information in the Consular Lookout and Support System (CLASS) include: the State Department's database of visa refusals, the State Department's interagency watch list for terrorists, known as TIPOFF, and several other law enforcement and intelligence sources. CLASS also uses Arabic and Russian/Slavic language algorithms to help increase the likelihood that the name check will find a person's name if it is in the database. The CLASS name check system includes information from the TIPOFF terrorist watch list that is managed by the State's Bureau of Intelligence and Research. This list contains declassified biographical information, such as name, birth date, or passport number on thousands of suspected terrorists. This information is drawn from sensitive all-source intelligence and law enforcement data provided by the FBI, the CIA, and other intelligence community agencies.

Q I am applying for a nonimmigrant visa at the U.S. consulate in Delhi. I have been looking at the application Form DS-156 and I notice questions like "Do you seek to enter the United States to engage in terrorist activity?" Does the U.S. government really believe a terrorist will answer yes to a question like this? I don't think anyone planning to do something illegal would ever answer the questions truthfully. Why do they ask these questions?

A The questions about terrorism and criminal activity are asked for two reasons. The first reason is that lying on a visa petition is, in and of itself, a crime and can lead to denial of entry into the United States or deportation from the United States after entry. This gives the U.S. government an independent reason to exclude or deport the person. They do not have to wait until the person commits a criminal act in the United States.

The second reason these questions are asked is to give visa applicants a chance to explain a situation that otherwise might lead to a visa denial. For example, one question is "have you ever been arrested or convicted of a crime...?" If this question were not asked, an applicant might not think this information is important to his or her application and might leave out information about a past conviction. The U.S. consulate would do a background check, find out about the conviction, and deny the visa. But, with the question included on the visa application form, the applicant knows that the past conviction is a matter that must be addressed and he or she has the chance to explain the circumstances of the past criminal matter. There are many exceptions to the exclusion for past crimes, so the applicant still has the possibility of getting the visa.

Q My husband and I are from Pakistan. We would like to apply for a visa to go to the United States, but we have heard that the U.S. consulate will now make it harder for us because we come from Pakistan. What makes it so hard?

A The Department of Homeland Security, including the BCIS and the Department of State, have strengthened the screening of visa applicants from certain countries, including your country, Pakistan.

One visible form of this screening is the *Visas Condor Program,* which is a name check procedure that is initiated when an applicant fulfills certain classified criteria. To help the consular officer determine whether Visas Condor criteria have been met, the State Department, in January, 2002, began to require all 16 to 45-year-old males from certain national groups, including Pakistan, to fill out a supplemental visa application form. This new Form (DS-157) provides additional information such as an applicant's travel and educational history, employment information, and military service. Under the Visas Condor process, the post sends an applicant's information to the FBI National Name Check Program where it is run against FBI databases. Some of the information in these databases comes from the FBI's Foreign Terrorist Tracking Task Force. In the event of a possible match, the information is sent back to the State Department. The consular officer cannot issue a visa to an applicant meeting Visas Condor criteria without an affirmative response from the Department of State. Obviously this process can take some time, so in that sense it may seem harder to get a visa.

Q My family applied for an immigration visa through the U.S. consulate in Bombay, India. Our son is 20 years old. We have heard from our relatives in the United States that there is a way to keep him on our application even if he turns 21 before we get the visa. Does this work through the U.S. consulate or do we have to apply through the BCIS?

A The law that you refer to is the *Child Status Protection Act* (CSPA). It could help in your situation by locking your child's age at 20 even if processing the visa takes place after he turns 21. The Department of State recognizes that Section 3 of the CSPA applies to derivative applicants in family-based and employment-based preference cases, as well as those in DV (visa lottery) cases. This applies to your situation, because your son is a *derivative* applicant on your family-based immigration petition. In other words, he gets his immigrant status based on your status. Thus, you can take advantage of this new law when applying at either the U.S. consulate or at the BCIS.

Q My wife and I are U.S. citizens. We are in the process of adopting a baby in the Czech Republic. We already have approval from the BCIS, but now the consular officer does not want to approve the application. Can she stop the application once it has been approved by the BCIS?

A Yes. The U.S. consular officer has the duty and authority to make decisions about the approved petition (Form I-600). The consular officer is particularly concerned with making sure the child is who he or she is supposed to be and making certain that the child is an orphan as defined and required by U.S. immigration law. These kinds of decisions are best made by the consular officer because he or she has local knowledge. In your case, there may be some questions about whether the child's natural parent fully released the child to the orphanage under Czech law.

Usually, the consular officer will give you a chance to submit additional information to resolve this open question. If the additional information does not satisfy him or her, he or she will have to refer the petition back to the BCIS for a decision. At that point, the BCIS will either reaffirm its approval of the petition, ask the U.S. consulate to conduct a field investigation, or deny the petition. If the BCIS denies the petition, you, as the adoptive parent, can file an appeal with the Administrative Appeals Office.

Q I am married to my first cousin. I am a Green Card holder. We are applying for an immigration visa to the United States. What is the procedure at the U.S. consulate?

A Because you wish to process the application at the U.S. consulate, you will file an immigrant visa petition on behalf of your spouse and provide the consulate the documents necessary to prove that your marriage is valid. Because you are married to your first cousin, the consular officer will not be able to automatically and independently determine that your marriage is valid for immigration purposes. He or she will have to ask the BCIS for approval. Once the BCIS approves the marriage, the application should go smoothly.

Q I am a U.K. citizen working in Los Angeles. The company I work for in Los Angeles applied for an extension of my work visa. I got the approval, but was told I had to get the visa at the U.S. consulate in London, so I took a trip home to pick up the visa. This has always been easy before,

but when I went to the consulate there was a sign saying that no visa applicants would be seen without an appointment. Why the changes?

A The U.S. consulate in London now requires in-person, pre-scheduled interviews for first-time visa applicants even for business visa applicants like you. You are considered a first-time applicant because your *extension* of your visa was actually a change in the type of work visa you had. There are exceptions to this requirement.

Many U.S. consulates, including London, have also adopted new processing procedures for security reasons. They are trying to reduce the number of people coming to the consulate, and have control over when and where applicants can come. State Department security officers do not like having long lines of people waiting in line outside the consulate. You probably remember in London that these lines could sometimes be quite long. All applicants doing consular processing should plan ahead, make sure all your documents are in order, get to the consulate early, and be prepared for unexpected delays.

Q I live in a country that has a ban on travel to the United States. My family in America has petitioned for me to get an immigrant visa to the United States and it has been approved. Can I get my visa at the consulate?

A First check your *passport*. If your passport is stamped or endorsed with a statement that it is not valid for travel to the United States or if it contains a statement that you need a special stamp to travel to the United States and you do not have the stamp, the U.S. consulate will not place the immigration visa in your passport. If, however, you travel outside of your country, you may be able to get the visa stamped in your passport at a U.S. consulate in a third country.

Q: Is it possible to get two visas?

A: Yes. If you need to go to the United States for different reasons at different times, you can get two U.S. visas stamped in your passport. But, you may not use the visas to change your principal activity after admission to the United States. You would have to leave the United States and then reenter. For example, a student who wants to study in the United States would get an F Visa. He or she may also want to visit the United States during breaks from school when he or she is otherwise living in his or her home country. For this, the consulate would issue a B-2 Visa. The student would have both visas in his or her passport. But he or she could not enter the United States as a tourist and then switch to being a student without leaving the country.

Q: I have both Indian and U.K. citizenship and passports. Can I get my U.S. visa stamped in both passports?

A: No, not if you mean the same visa. You can have visas of different classifications stamped in each passport. For example, if you are doing a lot of business between the U.K. and the United States and you otherwise qualify for it, you could have a treaty trader E-1 Visa stamped in your U.K. passport and at the same time a visitor visa B-1/B-2 stamped in your Indian passport.

Q What is third country consular processing?

A *Third country consular processing* is applying for a visa or other immigration benefit at a U.S. consulate that is *not* in your *home country*. For example, many visa holders who are in the United States try to avoid a long, overseas trip by going to Mexico or Canada to get a visa or extension if they cannot do it from within the United States.

Q I am in the U.S. and need to renew my visa. I was told I have to do it at a U.S. consulate. I do not want to go all the way home. Can I do it in Canada?

A Yes, but, since 9/11, there are new procedures. First, you will have to schedule an appointment. Walk-ins are no longer accepted. You can get an appointment over the Internet at **www.nvars.com**. It costs $10.00 Canadian. Second, you cannot be a national of one of the countries designated as state sponsors of terrorism. Third, you cannot be *out of status* or in an *overstay* situation. Finally, you cannot be applying for an E *treaty trader* or *treaty investor visa*.

Q I am from Turkey. When I was in Germany on vacation, I wanted to get a visa to come to the United States, but the U.S. consulate said I had to get it in Ankara, Turkey. Why?

A U.S. consulates are not required to issue visas or take visa applications from third country nationals. The U.S. consulates in Germany will always accept applications from German nationals, but you are Turkish and not German. The reason the U.S. consulate refused to process your application could either be because of their standard policy (no third country consular processing) or because of the type of visa you want. The State Department recognizes that, for many visas, the U.S. consulate in the country of which you are a national is in the best position to make an informed decision on your visa application. Local knowledge and local input are key factors in evaluating visa applications.

DEALING WITH THE U.S. CONSULATE

Q My family is applying for an immigration visa. The U.S. consulate asked us to come for an interview. What should we expect?

A You can expect the consular officer to conduct the interview fairly and sympathetically. You will not be grilled or cross examined. The consular officer may ask a lot of questions, especially if yours is a complicated case. He or she will most likely take careful notes during the interview session.

Q I am applying for a tourist visa. What will the consular officer look for?

A The U.S. consular officer is primarily looking for evidence that:
- you have a residence outside of the United States;
- you do not intend to abandon this residence;
- you intend to depart the United States after your visit; and,
- you have enough money to support yourself during your trip and to get back to your country.

Q How should I prepare for my interview at the U.S. consulate?

A During the interview, the U.S. consular officer is concerned with two main things. The first is to confirm the factual information in your petition to make certain that you are qualified for the visa. The second is to make certain that there is no reason you should be excluded from admission to the United States. So, the first thing you should do to prepare for your interview, is to make certain that you have all the necessary forms, photographs, passports, supporting documentation, and fees. You should also understand all the questions and answers on your petition. It does not happen often, but it does happen that an applicant will answer a question differently at the interview than what is on his or her petition. This will lead to more questioning, maybe a request for more information or documentation, or even to a denial of the visa.

Q What should I say during the interview?

A During the interview, you should answer all questions truthfully and completely, but there is no need to volunteer extraneous information or tell your life story. Keeping focused on the actual visa questions can be particularly important in applying for nonimmigrant visas because of the presumption made under U.S. law. The presumption is that all visa applications are considered to be prospective immigrants unless they can prove they meet one of the nonimmigrant visa categories. (Visa applicants who do not understand this may volunteer remarks that could give the consular officer the impression that the applicant intends to stay in the United States.)

Q How should I act during the U.S. consulate interview? Can I influence the consular officer's decision?

A You should act natural. Just be yourself. Answer the questions in straightforward and open manner. Be helpful in providing supporting documentation, further background information, etc. It does not hurt to be friendly, but this is not a popularity contest. The consular will make his or her decision based on the facts of your case, not on how nice you are. It is important, however, to be cooperative and credible. Your behavior by itself will not get you a visa if the facts are against you, but it may influence the consular officer to use his or her discretion in your favor on close questions. To put yourself in the right frame of mind, it might help to remember that no one has the *right* to immigrate or get a visa to the United States. These are *privileges* granted under U.S. law to certain individuals that meet certain requirements. This may not be fair, but it is the reality.

Q The consular officer has denied my visa. What can I do?

A This is a very difficult situation. Decisions by consular officers are generally **not** reviewable. There is also no appeals process. There are, however, a few things you can try. First of all, you can ask the most senior consular officer at post to review the decision citing the reasons you believe the decision was made in error. If the decision was made by the most senior consular official at post, this will not work. Second, if the denial was based on a mistake in the application of the law, you can ask the Department of State to review the decision. This is difficult and rarely results in a change of the decision. Finally, you can reapply for the visa citing changed circumstances or other evidence that overcomes the reason for the denial.

Q Can we get a refund of our visa application fee if our visa is denied?

A No. The fee is a processing fee and is not refunded if the visa is denied.

Q My family is applying for an immigration visa. Will we all have to go to the interview at the U.S. consulate?

A Maybe not. Regulations permit the U.S. consular officer to waive the personal appearance of children under the age of 14. However, in cases where the *principal beneficiary* of the immigrant petition is a child under 14, he or she would have to go to the interview.

Q My wife and I are scheduled for an interview at the U.S. consulate in our country for an immigrant visa. We have had a few problems in the past. Can we take our lawyer with us to the interview?

A Each U.S. consulate and sometimes even each U.S. consular officer has its own policy regarding if and when a visa applicant may bring his or her lawyer to the consulate. Sometimes, decisions are made on a case-by-case basis, and there is a blanket policy either allowing or not allowing in-person representation. Some consulates do not even permit a lawyer to enter the consulate with an applicant, let alone attend an interview. The consulate is not required to let you have a lawyer with you. Your lawyer probably knows whether the consulate is currently allowing lawyers to attend interviews. If not, you should check with the consulate before going to the interview.

Q How long does it take the U.S. consulate to process my visa? We have been waiting a long time.

A The processing time is usually dependent on two things: the U.S. consulate where you are applying and the type of visa you are applying for. Most consular posts are more than willing to let you know the approximate time it will take to process your visa application; so just ask.

Q I think I am about to be refused an immigrant visa at the U.S. consulate in my home country due to some health problems. I have been told that for a nonimmigrant visa I would not have to talk about my health problem and might be able to get a visa. Should I try to go to another consulate and apply?

A No. Your idea is sometimes referred to as *visa shopping* and it is full of problems. The first problem is that many consulates will not issue visas to *third country nationals*, that is someone who is not a national of the country where the consulate is located, except under special or emergency situations. So, your first problem in visa shopping is to explain why you are not applying at the consulate in your country. The next problem you have is that you have applied for an immigrant visa at the U.S. consulate in your home country, but now are considering applying for

Consular Processing

a nonimmigrant visa at another consulate. If you look at the nonimmigrant visa application Form (DS-156) you will see there is a question "Have you ever been refused a U.S. visa." You may have difficulty with this question. But, even if you somehow overcome these first two problems, you have a third one—CLASS, the Department of State's computerized database lookup system. It stands for *Consular Lookout and Support System*. Even before the consulate refuses your visa, it will most likely enter your name into CLASS with a P1A1 code which signifies a quasi refusal of the visa you applied for. This information will be available to other consulates.

Q Can a consular officer overrule a BCIS decision not to grant me a visa?

A No. At least not if the BCIS has made a definitive finding that you are ineligible for a visa. BCIS would ordinarily enter the definitive finding into the Treasury Enforcement Communication System and the entry would pass into the Department of State's CLASS lookout system. When the consular officer sees the entry, he or she is not suppose to reconsider the matter or look behind the BCIS reasoning for the refusal.

There are some exceptions. If the reason for ineligibility is *nonpermanent* and could be overcome through *changed circumstances*, the consular office can consider whether new circumstances might make you eligible for a visa. For example, if the entry was made because you were sick or because you were thought to have a particular disease and now you do not have it anymore, the consular officer can consider this in making a decision about your visa. Also, if the BCIS entry was not a definitive refusal, but a *quasi refusal*, the consular officer can make a decision about your visa that is different from the BCIS.

Q My wife is a registered nurse and recently got a temporary visa to work in the United States in a special program for nurses. The visa was approved and everything went smoothly, but now, just before we are ready to leave for the United States, we received a notice from the U.S. consulate that we have to come in for another interview. Is this normal or do we have a problem?

A It is not normal, but it is also most likely no problem for you. Following the terrorist attacks on September 11th, the State Department strengthened its oversight over visa operations by instituting new inspection measures. One of the new procedures is that an embassy's *nonimmigrant visa chief*, the *visa chief*, or the *consular section chief*, is now required to periodically conduct spot checks of approved visa applications. The extra interview the consulate has requested may be part of these new inspection measures.

Q How can I replace a damaged visa?

A If you are outside of the United States, go to the nearest U.S. consulate. If you are in the United States and you have an E, I, H, L, or O Visa, you can do it by mail with the Visa Office in St. Louis. You will need to submit all documentation and fees as for a new visa and have a police report if the visa was lost.

Appendix A

Visas

This appendix provides an overview of all the visas that a consulate can issue; who qualifies for each visa; and, what forms you need to complete. This summary will also be a useful overview of the sometimes confusing abbreviations used to identify the visas.

The appendix is divided into three sections: family-based immigration visas, employment-based immigration visas, and, temporary nonimmigrant visas.

The forms starting with DS are Department of State forms; the forms starting with I are BCIS forms; and, the forms starting with G are Department of Justice forms.

NOTE: All the forms mentioned are available free of charge either over the Internet, at U.S. consulates, or directly from the government. Never pay for a form.

CONSULAR PROCESSING OF IMMIGRANT VISAS

These are visas issued to aliens who want to live and/or work permanently in the United States. You can qualify for these visas either by having the proper family relationship or through your employment.

FAMILY-BASED IMMIGRATION VISAS

IR-1, IR-2, and IR-5 VISAS

Who qualifies?
Immediate Relatives:
- spouses of U.S. citizens (IR-1);
- unmarried children under 21 years of age of U.S. citizens (IR-2); and,
- parents of U.S. citizens (IR-5). (A U.S. citizen must be over the age of 21 to petition for his or her parent.)

How to apply?
Your U.S. citizen husband, wife, or child over the age of 21, files Form I-130 *Petition for Alien Relative* with Form G-325 *Biographic Information* and Form I-864 *Affidavit of Support* with the BCIS. When approved, the BCIS issues Form I-797 *Notice of Approval*. You, the applicant, fill out Form DS-230 *Application for Immigrant Visa and Alien Registration* and file the form with the U.S. consulate. The consular officers review the form, all supporting documentation, and conduct a personal interview. This visa requires a medical examination. If all requirements are met, the U.S. consulate issues the visa and stamps it in your passport. (There are no numerical limits on the number of these visas that be can be issued.)

IR-3 and IR-4 VISAS

Who qualifies?
Immediate Relatives:
- unmarried children under 16 of a U.S. citizen adopted abroad (IR-3); or,
- to be adopted in the United States (IR-4).

How to apply?
The U.S. citizen parent or parents (who must be at least 25 years old) files Form I-600 *Petition to Classify Orphan as an Immediate Relative* with the BCIS. If the child has not been identified yet, for example when the parents travel to an orphanage abroad to select a child for adoption, they file Form I-600A *Application for Advance Processing of Orphan Petition* with the BCIS. When approved, the BCIS issues Form I-797 *Notice of Approval*. The parent fills out Form DS-230 *Application for Immigrant Visa and Alien Registration* and files the form with the U.S. consulate. The consular officer reviews the application, all supporting documents, and conducts a personal interview with the child present. If all requirements are met, the U.S. consulate issues a

Visas

visa and stamps it in the child's passport. This can be a complicated process because the parent must be sure that he or she has complied with all foreign adoption or guardianship laws. (There are no numerical limits on this visa.)

F1-1 VISA

Who qualifies?
First Preference—Unmarried sons or daughters over 21 years of age of a U.S. citizen.

How to apply?
Your mother or father files Form I-130 *Petition for Alien Relative* and Form I-864 *Affidavit of Support* with the BCIS. When approved, the BCIS issues Form I-797 *Notice of Approval*. You, the applicant, fill out Form DS-230 *Application for Immigrant Visa and Alien Registration* and file the form with the U.S. consulate. The consular officer reviews the form, all supporting documentation, and conducts a personal interview. This visa requires a medical examination. If all requirements are met, the U.S. consulate issues the visa and stamps it in your passport. (The number of these visas is limited and as of June, 2003, there was a waiting list of about four years—longer if you are from Mexico or the Philippines.)

F2-1 and F2-2 VISAS

Who qualifies?
Second Preference (2A)—Spouses (F2-1) and children (F2-2) of Legal Permanent Resident Green Card holders.

How to apply?
Your husband, wife, mother or father who has a Green Card files Form I-130 *Petition for Alien Relative* and Form I-864 *Affidavit of Support* with the BCIS. When approved, the BCIS issues Form I-797 *Notice of Approval*. You, the applicant, fill out Form DS-230 *Application for Immigrant Visa and Alien Registration* and file this form with the U.S. consulate. The consular officer reviews the form, all supporting documentation, and conducts a personal interview. This visa requires a medical examination. If all requirements are met, the U.S. consulate issues the visa and stamps it in your passport. (The number of these visas is limited and as of June, 2003, there was a waiting list of about five years for these visas—longer if you are from Mexico.)

U.S. Immigration and Citizenship Q&A

F2-4 VISA

Who qualifies?

Second Preference(2B)—Unmarried sons or daughters over 21 years of age of Legal Permanent Resident Green Card holders.

How to apply?

Your father or mother who has a Green Card, files Form I-130 *Petition for Alien Relative* and Form I-864 *Affidavit of Support* with the BCIS. When approved, the BCIS issues Form I-797 *Notice of Approval*. You, the applicant, fill out Form DS-230 *Application for Immigrant Visa and Alien Registration* and file this form with the U.S. consulate. The consular officer reviews the form, all supporting documentation, and conducts a personal interview. This visa requires a medical examination. If all requirements are met, the U.S. consulate issues the visa and stamps it in your passport. (The number of these visas is limited and as of June, 2003, there was a waiting time of nine years for this visa—longer if you are from Mexico.)

F3-1 VISA

Who qualifies?

Third Preference—Married children of U.S. citizens.

How to apply?

Your father or mother who is a U.S. citizen files Form I-130 *Petition for Alien Relative* and Form I-864 *Affidavit of Support* with the BCIS. When approved, the BCIS issues Form I-797 *Notice of Approval*. You, the applicant, fill out Form DS-230 *Application for Immigrant Visa and Alien Registration* and file the form with the U.S. consulate. The consular officer reviews the form, all supporting documentation, and conducts a personal interview. This visa requires a medical examination. If all requirements are met, the U.S. consulate issues the visa and stamps it in your passport. (The number of these visas is limited and as of June 2003 there was a waiting time of six years for this visa—longer if you are from Mexico or the Philippines.)

F4-1 VISA

Who qualifies?

Fourth Preference—Siblings (brothers and sisters) of adult U.S. citizens.

How to apply?

Your U.S. citizen brother or sister files Form I-130 *Petition for Alien Relative* and Form I-864 *Affidavit of Support* with the BCIS. When approved, the BCIS issues Form I-797 *Notice of Approval*. You, the applicant, fill out Form DS-230 *Application for Immigrant Visa and Alien Registration* and file this form with the U.S. consulate. The consular officer reviews the form, all supporting documentation, and conducts a personal interview. This visa requires a medical examination. If all requirements are met, the U.S. consulate issues the visa and stamps it in your passport. (The number of these visas is limited and as of June, 2003, there was a waiting time of twelve years for this visa—longer if you are from the Philippines.)

U.S. Immigration and Citizenship Q&A

EMPLOYMENT-BASED IMMIGRATION VISAS

EB-1 VISA

Who qualifies?

First Preference—Priority workers with extraordinary ability, outstanding researchers and professors, and certain multinational executives and managers.

How to apply?

Your employer in the United States files Form I-140 *Immigrant Petition for an Alien Worker* with the BCIS. If you are a person with extraordinary ability or an outstanding professor or researcher, you may file the form on your own behalf. You do not need a sponsor. When approved, the BCIS issues Form I-797 *Notice of Approval*. You, the applicant, fill out Form DS-230 *Application for Immigrant Visa and Alien Registration* and file this form with the U.S. consulate. The consular officer reviews the form, all supporting documentation, and conducts a personal interview. This visa requires a medical examination. If all requirements are met, the U.S. consulate issues the visa and stamps it in your passport. (The number of these visas is limited, but there is currently no waiting time.)

EB-2 VISA

Who qualifies?

Second Preference—Professionals with advanced degrees and persons with exceptional ability.

How to apply?

Your employer in the United States files U.S. Department of Labor Form ETA 750 *Application for Alien Employment Certification* with the State Workforce Agency serving the area where you will work. When approved, your employer files Form I-140 *Immigrant Petition for an Alien Worker* with the BCIS. When approved, the BCIS issues Form I-797 *Notice of Approval*. You, the applicant, fill out Form DS-230 *Application for Immigrant Visa and Alien Registration* and file this form with the U.S. consulate. The consular officer reviews the form, all supporting documentation, and conducts a personal interview. This visa requires a medical examination. If all requirements are met, the U.S. consulate issues the visa and stamps it in your passport. (The number of these visas is limited, but there is currently no waiting time.)

Visas

EB-3 VISA

Who qualifies?

Third Preference—Skilled workers with at least two years training or experience, professionals with Bachelor degrees, and other workers.

How to apply?

The procedure is the same as for the EB-2 VISA. Your employer in the United States files U.S. Department of Labor Form ETA 750 *Application for Alien Employment Certification* with the State Workforce Agency serving the area where you will work. When approved, your employer files Form I-140 *Immigrant Petition for an Alien Worker* with the BCIS. When approved, the BCIS issues Form I-797 *Notice of Approval*. You, the applicant, fill out Form DS-230 *Application for Immigrant Visa and Alien Registration* and file this form with the U.S. consulate. The consular officer reviews the form, all supporting documentation, and conducts a personal interview. This visa requires a medical examination. If all requirements are met, the U.S. consulate issues the visa and stamps it in your passport. (The number of these visas is limited, but there is currently no waiting time.)

EB-4 VISA

Who qualifies?

Fourth Preference—Certain *special immigrants*, including Amerasians fathered by a U.S. citizen, widows and widowers of U.S. citizens, battered or abused spouse or child of a U.S. citizen or Green Card holder, religious workers, certain employees of the U.S. government, certain long-term employees of international organizations, and certain aliens who served in the U.S. Armed Forces.

How to apply?

You file Form I-360 *Petition for Amerasian, Widow(er), or Special Immigrant* with the BCIS Service Center responsible for the area where you will live in the United States. If you are an Amerasian, widow/widower, or Armed Forces member living outside the United States, you can also file Form I-360 at the U.S. consulate. When approved, the BCIS issues Form I-797 *Notice of Approval*. You, the applicant, fill out Form DS-230 *Application for Immigrant Visa and Alien Registration* and file this form with the U.S. consulate. The consular officer reviews the form, all supporting documentation, and conducts a personal interview. This visa requires a medical examination. If all requirements are met, the U.S. consulate issues the visa and stamps it in your passport. (The number of these visas is limited, but there is currently no waiting time.)

EB-5 VISA

Who qualifies?

Fifth Preference—Employment creation investors who invest at least $1 million dollars in a new business that employs at least ten employees.

How to apply?

You file Form I-526 *Immigrant Petition by Alien Entrepreneur* with the BCIS service center responsible for the area where your business will be located. When approved, the BCIS issues Form I-797 *Notice of Approval*. You, the applicant, fill out Form DS-230 *Application for Immigrant Visa and Alien Registration* and file this form with the U.S. consulate. The consular officer reviews the form, all supporting documentation, and conducts a personal interview. This visa requires a medical examination. If all requirements are met, the U.S. consulate issues the visa and stamps it in your passport. (The number of these visas is limited, but there is currently no waiting time.)

CONSULAR PROCESSING OF NONIMMIGRANT VISAS

Nonimmigrant visas are temporary visas issued for a wide range of activities. They can be used to visit the U.S. as a tourist, work in the United States as a nurse, act in a movie made in the United States, study at a U.S. university, and even manage your own business in the United States. In all cases, the spouse and children of the principal visa applicant may accompany or follow the principal visa holder to the United States, although not all of these have been listed as separate visas.

A-1 VISA

Who qualifies?

The A series of nonimmigrant visas is for foreign government officials seeking to enter the United States on official business. It includes ambassadors, public minister, career, diplomatic or consular officer, and members of immediate family (A-1), other foreign government officials and members of their immediate families (A-2), and servants or personal employees of diplomats or officials (A-3).

How do I apply?

Your government, through the foreign ministry or other official office, sends a note to the U.S. consulate requesting issuance of a visa. You file Form DS-1648 *Application for A, G or NATO Visa* with the U.S. consulate. The consular officer reviews the application and supporting documents looking particularly at what your official duties will be in the United States in order to determine the proper A visa. If all requirements are met, the consular officer issues the visa and stamps it in your passport.

Visa Waiver Program

Who qualifies?

Nationals of certain countries seeking to enter the United States temporarily—up to three months for business or tourism purposes. (The countries are currently Andorra, Australia, Austria, Belgium, Brunei, Denmark, Finland, France, Germany, Iceland, Ireland, Italy, Japan, Liechtenstein, Luxembourg, Monaco, the Netherlands, New Zealand, Norway, Portugal, San Marino, Singapore, Slovenia, Spain, Switzerland, and the United Kingdom. This list can change.)

How do I apply?

You don't. If you qualify, you simply travel to the United States.

U.S. Immigration and Citizenship Q&A

B-1 VISA

Who qualifies?

Visitors who are coming temporarily to the United States on business. Normally this visa would be used by visitors from countries not part of the Visa Waiver Program or visitors from countries part of the Visa Program who need to stay in the United States more than six months.

How do I apply?

You file Form DS-156 *Nonimmigrant Visa Application* with the U.S. consulate. The consular officer reviews the application and any necessary supporting documents. The consular officer especially wants to make sure that you intend to leave the United States at the end of your visa. If all requirements are met, the consular officer issues the visa and stamps it in your passport. The B-1 Visa is usually issued together with the B-2 Visa.

B-2 VISA

Who qualifies?

Visitors who are coming temporarily to the United States as tourists.

How do I apply?

You file Form DS-156 *Nonimmigrant Visa Application* with the U.S. consulate. The consular officer reviews the application and any necessary supporting documents. The consular officer especially wants to make sure that you intend to leave the United States at the end of your visa. If all requirements are met, the consular officer issues the visa and stamps it in your passport. The B-2 Visa is usually issued together with the B-1 Visa.

C-1 VISA

Who qualifies?

Aliens in transit through the United States, including aliens in transit directly through the United States (C-1), aliens in transit who are also crewmen or crewwomen on a boat or airplane (C-1D), aliens who are in transit directly to and only to the United Nations headquarters in New York (C-2), foreign government officials in transit (C-3), and aliens in transit without a visa (C-4).

How I do apply?

You file Form DS-156 *Nonimmigrant Visa Application* with the U.S. consulate. The consular officer reviews the application and any necessary supporting documents. The consular officer especially wants to make sure that you are truly only in transit and will not try to stay in the United States. Your travel cannot include a stay in the United States of more than twenty-nine days. If all requirements are met, the consular officer issues the visa and stamps it in your passport. You apply for transit without a visa at specific ports of entry by presenting a nonrefundable ticket for onward travel out of the United States.

D-1 VISA

Who qualifies?

Crewmen and crewwomen on airplanes and ships that arrive and depart from the United States (D-1) and crewmen and crewwomen who are traveling to the United States to join a ship or airplane that is departing from the United States.

How do I apply?

You file Form DS-156 *Nonimmigrant Visa Application* with the U.S. consulate. The consular officer reviews the application and any necessary supporting documents including a letter from your company. The consular officer especially wants to make sure that you intend to leave the United States at the end of your visa. If all requirements are met, the consular officer issues the visa and stamps it in your passport.

E-1 VISA

Who qualifies?

An alien who is coming to the United States to carry on substantial trade (including services) between his or her home country and the United States or works for a company that is engaged in such trade. (The right treaty must exist between the alien's home country and the United States.)

How do I apply?

You file Form DS-156 *Nonimmigrant Visa Application* and Form DS-156e *Nonimmigrant Treaty Trader/Investor Application* with the U.S. consulate. The consular officer reviews the application and any necessary supporting documents. The consular officer especially wants to examine the trade that you and your company are engaged in and the financial situation of your company. If all requirements are met, the consular officer issues the visa and stamps it in your passport. If you want to change your status to this visa while you are in the United States, your company will have to file Form I-129 *Petition for a Nonimmigrant Worker* with the BCIS on your behalf.

E-2 VISA

Who qualifies?

An alien from a treaty country who has invested or is in the process of investing a substantial amount of capital in a business in the United States and is coming to the United States to direct or develop the business or an executive employee of a treaty trader who has the same nationality as the treaty trader.

How do I apply?

You file Form DS-156 *Nonimmigrant Visa Application* and Form DS-156e *Nonimmigrant Treaty Trader/Investor Application* with the U.S. consulate. The consular officer reviews the application and any necessary supporting documents. The consular officer especially wants to make sure that you and/or your company have made or can make the proper investment in a business and that the business is not just established to support yourself. If all requirements are met, the consular officer issues the visa and stamps it in your passport.

F-1 VISA

Who qualifies?

Academic students in colleges, universities, seminaries, conservatories, academic high schools, elementary schools, other academic institutions, and in language training programs.

☞ **NOTE:** As of August 11, 2003, a new **F-3** visa is available to citizens and residents of Mexico and Canada who seek to commute as students to the United States to attend an approved F school.

How do I apply?

You apply to the school you want to attend. If accepted, the school will enter the acceptance into the SEVIS program which automatically generates a SEVIS Form I-20. You take this form along with a Form DS-156 *Nonimmigrant Visa Application* and Form DS-158 *Contact Information and Work History for Nonimmigrant Visa Applicant* to the U.S. consulate and apply for the visa. The consular officer particularly wants to make sure you can finance your education and that you will leave the United States at the end of your studies. If all requirements are met, the consular officer issues the visa and stamps it in your passport.

F-2 VISA

Who qualifies?
Spouses and children of F-1 academic students.

How do I apply?
Your husband, wife, father, or mother will apply for you by giving your names to the school he or she applies to. If accepted, you as the spouse will be issued your own SEVIS Form I-20. You take this form and a completed Form DS-156 *Nonimmigrant Visa Application* to the U.S. consulate and apply for the visa along with the principal family member. If all requirements are met, the consular officer issues the visa and stamps it in your passport.

G-1 VISA

Who qualifies?
Principal resident representatives of foreign governments to international organizations based in the United States, their immediate relatives, and personal employees.

How do I apply?
You file Form DS-1648 *Application for A, G or NATO Visa* at the U.S. consulate. The consular office determines if you are entitled to G status based on your assignment by your government to an international organization. If all requirements are met, the consular officer issues the visa and stamps it in your passport. The Secretary of State must recognize your status after you are admitted to the United States for this visa to be valid.

H-1B VISA

Who qualifies?
Temporary workers in the United States working in specialty occupations with the Department of Defense in a research or development project or as fashion models.

How do I apply?
Your employer must file a Form I-129 *Petition for a Nonimmigrant Worker* with the BCIS and obtain labor certification. When approved, the BCIS issues Form I-797 *Notice of Approval*. You take this form and a completed Form DS-156 *Nonimmigrant Visa Application* to the U.S. consulate and apply for the visa. The consular officer reviews the application and any necessary supporting documents. If all requirements are met, the consular officer issues the visa and stamps it in your passport. (The available number of these visas is limited.)

H-1C VISA

Who qualifies?

Nurses going to work for up to three years in the United States in areas where there is a shortage of health professionals.

How do I apply?

Your employer files Form I-129 *Petition for a Nonimmigrant Worker* at the BCIS Vermont Service Center and obtains labor certification. When approved, the BCIS issues Form I-797 *Notice of Approval*. You take this form and a completed Form DS-156 *Nonimmigrant Visa Application* to the U.S. consulate and apply for the visa. The consular officer reviews the application and any necessary supporting documents. If all requirements are met, the consular officer issues the visa and stamps it in your passport. The consular officer reviews the application and any necessary supporting documents. (The number of these visas available is very limited.)

H-2A VISA

Who qualifies?

Temporary agriculture workers or seasonal workers.

How do I apply?

Your employer or sometimes an agent files Form I-129 *Petition for a Nonimmigrant Worker* at the BCIS Service Center covering the region where you will be working and obtains labor certification. When approved, the BCIS issues Form I-797 *Notice of Approval*. Take this form and a completed Form DS-156 *Nonimmigrant Visa Application* to the U.S. consulate and apply for the visa. The consular officer reviews the application and any necessary supporting documents. If all requirements are met, the consular officer issues the visa and stamps it in your passport. The consular officer reviews the application and any necessary supporting documents.

H-2B VISA

Who qualifies?

Temporary skilled and unskilled workers.

How do I apply?

Your employer or sometimes an agent files Form I-129 *Petition for a Nonimmigrant Worker* at the BCIS Service Center covering the region where you will be working and obtains labor certification. When approved, the BCIS issues Form I-797 *Notice of Approval*. Take this form and a completed Form DS-156 *Nonimmigrant Visa Application* to the U.S. consulate and apply for the visa. The consular officer reviews the application and any necessary supporting documents. If all requirements are met, the consular officer issues the visa and stamps it in your passport. The consular officer reviews the application and any necessary supporting documents. (The number of these visas is limited.)

H-3 VISA

Who qualifies?
Trainees, except for physicians.

How do I apply?
The organization or company that will provide the training files Form I-129 *Petition for a Nonimmigrant Worker* at the BCIS Service Center covering the region where you will be working and obtains labor certification. When approved, the BCIS issues Form I-797 *Notice of Approval*. Take this form and a completed Form DS-156 *Nonimmigrant Visa Application* to the U.S. consulate and apply for the visa. The consular officer reviews the application and any necessary supporting documents. If all requirements are met, the consular officer issues the visa and stamps it in your passport. The consular officer reviews the application and any necessary supporting documents. (The number of these visas available is very limited.)

I VISA

Who qualifies?
Representatives of foreign media television, newspaper journalists, etc. from a country that recognizes a similar visa for representatives of U.S. media.

How do I apply?
You file Form DS-156 *Nonimmigrant Visa Application* with the U.S. consulate. The consular officer reviews the application and any necessary supporting documents including a letter from your company. The consular officer especially wants to make sure that you have the proper connection to a foreign media and are entering the United States to work solely for that media. If all requirements are met, the consular officer issues the visa and stamps it in your passport.

J-1 VISA

Who qualifies?
Persons coming to the United States in an approved exchange program including students, short-term scholars, business trainees, teach-

U.S. Immigration and Citizenship Q&A

ers, professors, research scholars, specialists, international visitors, government visitors, physicians, camp counselors, and au pairs.

How do I apply?

The J-1 Visa application process is similar to the F-1 student visa process. You apply to the program you want to attend and/or are invited by a program to participate. The program must be one approved by the Department of State Bureau of Educational and Cultural Affairs. If accepted, the program will enter the acceptance into the SEVIS program which automatically generates a SEVIS Form I-2019. Take this form along with a Form DS-156 *Nonimmigrant Visa Application* and Form DS-158 *Contact Information and Work History for Nonimmigrant Visa Applicant* to the U.S. consulate and apply for the visa. If all requirements are met, the consular officer issues the visa and stamps it in your passport.

K-1 VISA

Who qualifies?

Fiancé or fiancée of a U.S. citizen who is traveling to the United States to be married to the U.S. citizen within ninety days after entry and the minor children of the fiancé or fiancée (K-2).

How do I apply?

Your U.S. citizen fiancé or fiancée petitions for you to come to the United States using Form I-129F *Petition for an Alien Fiancé(e)* and filing it with the BCIS Service Center covering the region where he or she resides. When approved, the BCIS issues Form I-797 *Notice of Approval*. You take this form along with completed Form 156 *Nonimmigrant Visa Application* and Form 156k *Nonimmigrant Fiancé(e) Visa Application* to the U.S. consulate to apply for the visa. If all requirements are met, the consular officer issues the visa and stamps it in your passport.

K-3 VISA

Who qualifies?

A spouse of a U.S. citizen entering the United States as a nonimmigrant and the child or children of such spouse (K-4).

How do I apply?

Your U.S. citizen spouse must already have a Form I-130 *Petition for Alien Relative* with the BCIS. He or she then files Form I-129F *Petition for an Alien Fiancé(e)* and filing it with the BCIS Service Center in Chicago. When approved, the BCIS issues Form I-797 *Notice of*

Approval. You take this form along with completed Form 156 *Nonimmigrant Visa Application* and Form 156K *Nonimmigrant Fiancé(e) Visa Application* to the U.S. consulate to apply for the visa. If all requirements are met, the consular officer issues the visa and stamps it in your passport.

L-1 VISA

Who qualifies?

Executives, managers (L-1A) and specialized knowledge employees (L-1B) of companies that have a subsidiary, parent company, branch, joint venture, affiliate or start up business in the United States who are being transferred temporarily to the United States.

How do I apply?

Your company files Form I-129 *Petition for a Nonimmigrant Worker* (with L Classification Supplement) and Form I-129S *Nonimmigrant Petition based on Blanket Petition* (if appropriate) with the BCIS Service Center where the work is to be performed. When approved, the BCIS issues Form I-797 *Notice of Approval.* You take this form along with completed Form 156 *Nonimmigrant Visa Application* to the U.S. consulate to apply for the visa. If all requirements are met, the consular officer issues the visa and stamps it in your passport.

L-2 VISA

Who qualifies?
The spouse and children of an L-1 principal visa holder.

How do I apply?

You apply along with your husband or wife (or parent) by filing out Form DS-156 *Nonimmigrant Visa Application* and filing it at the U.S. consulate to apply for the visa. If all requirements are met, the consular officer issues the visa and stamps it in your passport. The L-2 Visa is interesting because it allows you to work in the United States.

M-1 VISA

Who qualifies?
Vocational and other nonacademic students enrolled in a full course of study at a recognized nonacademic institution.

☞**NOTE:** As of August 11, 2003, a new **M-3** visa is available to citizens and residents of Mexico and Canada who seek to commute as students to the United States to attend an approved M school.

U.S. Immigration and Citizenship Q&A

How do I apply?

You apply to the school or course you want to attend. If accepted, the school will enter the acceptance into the SEVIS program which automatically generates a SEVIS Form I-20. You take this form along with a Form DS-156 *Nonimmigrant Visa Application* and Form DS-158 *Contact Information and Work History for Nonimmigrant Visa Applicant* to the U.S. consulate and apply for the visa. The consular officer particularly wants to make sure you can finance your education and that you will leave the United States at the end of your studies. If all requirements are met, the consular officer issues the visa and stamps it in your passport.

N-8 VISA

Who qualifies?

Mother or father or child (N-9) of certain aliens classified as *special immigrants* like returning permanent residents, former U.S. citizens applying for reacquisition of citizenship, certain religious workers, certain alien U.S. government employees, and certain Panama Canal employees.

How do I apply?

You apply by filing out Form DS-156 *Nonimmigrant Visa Application* and filing it at the U.S. consulate to apply for the visa. For returning Green Card holders who have been out of the United States for more than a year and do not have a reentry permit, you will also complete Form DS-117 *Application for Returning Resident Status*. If all requirements are met, the consular officer issues the visa and stamps it in your passport.

NATO-1 through NATO-7

Who qualifies?

Only certain representatives of the North Atlantic Treaty Organization (NATO), officials of NATO member states, NATO employees, experts, and certain other NATO affiliated civilians and staff.

How do I apply?

Your government, through the defense ministry, military, or other official office, sends a note to the U.S. consulate requesting issuance of a visa. You file Form DS-1648 *Application for A, G or NATO Visa* with the U.S. consulate. The consular officer reviews the application and supporting documents looking particularly at what your official duties will be in the United States in order to determine the proper A visa. If all requirements are met, the consular officer issues the visa and stamps it in your passport.

O-1 VISA

Who qualifies?

Aliens who have extraordinary ability in science, art, education, business or athletics such as outstanding researchers, famous artists, well know university professors, authors and athletes who are coming to the United States temporarily to work or perform in their area of ability.

How do I apply?

Your sponsor in the United States (school, art gallery, sports team, etc.) or your U.S. agent files Form I-129 *Petition for a Nonimmigrant Worker*, along with the O *Supplement* and supporting evidence such as a peer review statement that you are well known in your field, with the BCIS Service Center where you will be working or performing. When approved, the BCIS issues Form I-797 *Notice of Approval*. You take this form along with completed Form 156 *Nonimmigrant Visa Application* to the U.S. consulate to apply for the visa. If all requirements are met, the consular officer issues the visa and stamps it in your passport.

O-2 VISA

Who qualifies?

An alien who is coming temporarily to the United States solely to assist in the artistic or athletic performance by an O-1 Visa holder and is an integral part of the performance.

How do I apply?

Your sponsor in the United States (school, art gallery, sports team, etc.) or your U.S. agent files Form I-129 *Petition for a Nonimmigrant Worker*, along with the O *Supplement* and supporting evidence that your skills are critical to the performance and not of a general nature, with the BCIS Service Center where you will be working or performing. When approved, the BCIS issues Form I-797 *Notice of Approval*. You take this form along with completed Form 156 *Nonimmigrant Visa Application* to the U.S. consulate to apply for the visa. If all requirements are met, the consular officer issues the visa and stamps it in your passport.

U.S. Immigration and Citizenship Q&A

P-1 VISA

Who qualifies?

Internationally recognized individual or team athletes and entertainment groups.

How do I apply?

Your sponsor in the United States (sports team or agent) files Form I-129 *Petition for a Nonimmigrant Worker*, along with the *P Supplement*. with the BCIS Service Center where you will be working or performing. The petition must show that the appropriate labor organization has been consulted about the nature of the work and your qualifications. When approved, the BCIS issues Form I-797 *Notice of Approval*. You take this form along with completed Form 156 *Nonimmigrant Visa Application* to the U.S. consulate to apply for the visa. If all requirements are met, the consular officer issues the visa and stamps it in your passport.

P-2 VISA

Who qualifies?

Artists and entertainers in reciprocal exchange programs.

How do I apply?

Your sponsor in the United States (sports team or agent) files Form I-129 *Petition for a Nonimmigrant Worker*, along with the *P Supplement*. with the BCIS Service Center where you will be working or performing. The petition must show that the appropriate labor organization has been consulted about the nature of the work and your qualifications. You must also show that a reciprocal agreement exists. When approved, the BCIS issues Form I-797 *Notice of Approval*. You take this form along with completed Form 156 *Nonimmigrant Visa Application* to the U.S. consulate to apply for the visa. If all requirements are met, the consular officer issues the visa and stamps it in your passport.

P-3 VISA

Who qualifies?

Artists and entertainers in culturally unique programs.

How do I apply?

Your sponsor in the United States files Form I-129 *Petition for a Nonimmigrant Worker*, along with the *P Supplement* with the BCIS Service Center where you will be working or performing. The petition must show that the appropriate labor organization has been consulted about the nature of the work and your qualifications. When approved, the BCIS issues Form I-797 *Notice of Approval*. You take this form along with completed Form 156 *Nonimmigrant Visa Application* to the U.S. consulate to apply for the visa. If all requirements are met, the consular officer issues the visa and stamps it in your passport.

Q-1 VISA

Who qualifies?
International cultural exchange visitors.

How do I apply?
Your sponsor employer in the United States files Form I-129 *Petition for a Nonimmigrant Worker*, along with the *Q Supplement*. with the BCIS Service Center where you will be working, training or performing services. When approved, the BCIS issues Form I-797 *Notice of Approval*. You take this form along with completed Form 156 *Nonimmigrant Visa Application* to the U.S. consulate to apply for the visa. If all requirements are met, the consular officer issues the visa and stamps it in your passport.

Q-2 VISA

Who qualifies?
Participants in the Irish Peace Process Cultural and Training Program.

How do I apply?
You must get a *Certification Letter* from the Department of State showing that you have been accepted into this program. You take this along with completed Form 156 *Nonimmigrant Visa Application* to the U.S. consulate to apply for the visa. If all requirements are met, the consular officer issues the visa and stamps it in your passport. (The number of these visas is limited.)

R-1 VISA

Who qualifies?
Religious workers who are members of a religious denomination having a bona fide nonprofit religious organization in the United States who are entering the United States temporarily to carry on religious activities.

How do I apply?
You complete Form 156 *Nonimmigrant Visa Application* and take it, along with proof that your U.S. religious organization is nonprofit and proof of your status in the organization, to the U.S. consulate to apply

for the visa. If you are male and between the ages of 16 and 45, you must also complete Form DS-157 *Supplemental Nonimmigrant Visa Application* regardless of your nationality or where you apply for the visa. If all requirements are met, the consular officer issues the visa and stamps it in your passport. If you are in the United States, your church or religious organization files Form I-129 *Petition for an Alien Worker* and the R *Supplement* on your behalf.

T-1 VISA

Who qualifies?

Victims of severe forms of trafficking in persons and their spouse (T-2), children (T-3) and sometimes parents (T-4).

How do I apply?

If you are already in the United States and unfortunate enough to be a victim of trafficking in persons, this visa *may* give you some relief by allowing you to remain temporarily in the United States and receive federal and state benefits. You apply for yourself by filing Form I-914 *Application for T Nonimmigrant Status* with the BCIS Vermont Service Center.

TN VISA

Who qualifies?

Canadian and Mexican citizens who are defined as *professionals* under the North American Free Trade Agreement (NAFTA) and are coming to the United States as nonimmigrants to work for U.S. employers.

How do I apply?

There are different procedures depending on whether you are Canadian or Mexican. If you are Canadian, you apply at the border port of entry by showing a letter from a U.S. employer that proves you have a job offer that is considered a professional position under NAFTA. You will also need copies of your college degree and employment history. If all requirements are met, you do not actually get a visa, but you will be granted TN status by the BCIS at the port of entry. If you are Mexican, your U.S. employer must file a Labor Certification Application with the Department of Labor and file Form I-129 *Petition for a Nonimmigrant Worker* with the BCIS. When approved, the BCIS issues Form I-797 *Notice of Approval*. You take this form and a completed Form DS-156 *Nonimmigrant Visa Application* to the U.S. consulate and apply for the visa. The consular officer reviews the application and any necessary supporting documents. If all requirements are met, the consular officer issues the visa and stamps it in your passport.

V-1 VISA

Who qualifies?

Spouse (V-1) or child (V-2) of a Legal Permanent Resident who is the principal beneficiary of a family-based (second preference) petition (Form I-130 *Petition for Alien Relative*) which was filed prior to December 21, 2000, and has been pending for at least three years. (This is a relatively new visa made possible by the *Legal Immigration Family Equity Act of 2000*.)

How do I apply?

You can apply for this visa at the U.S. consulate with Form DS-156 *Nonimmigrant Visa Application* by showing documents that prove you meet the requirements. The consular officer will review the documents and, if everything is in order, stamp the visa in your passport.

OTHER VISAS

DV-1 Visa

Who qualifies?

Diversity visa applicants who were picked in the Green Card lottery that is open to nationals of certain countries.

How do I apply?

If you win the Green Card lottery you will receive Form DS-122 *Supplemental Registration for the Diversity Immigrant Visa.* You fill out this form and fill out Form DS-230 *Application for Immigrant Visa and Alien Registration* and send them to the Diversity Visa Program office in Kentucky. When approved, they will advise you of the date you have to go to the U.S. consulate to finish your processing. This visa requires a medical examination. If all requirements are met, the U.S. consulate issues the visa and stamps it in your passport.

Specialized Visas

There are other specialized visas not in common use that may be available to you depending on your circumstances. **S-5** and **S-6** Visas are available to informants of criminal organizations or terrorism. **U-1** through **U-4** Visas are available to victims of certain crimes who are cooperating with law enforcement authorities. If you qualify for these visas, law enforcement authorities will usually be able to help you with the processing.

Appendix B

Finding Forms

The Internet and toll-free telephone numbers make it easy to contact the BCIS and other immigration-related agencies to get forms, ask questions, and check on your case. This easy access can make your life easier and save you money. One word of advice, however, it doesn't hurt to be a little cautious these days in contacting the Bureau of Citizenship and Immigration Services.

If you have an immigration question, only give the BCIS information about yourself or contact the BCIS if you know for sure you are in perfect immigration compliance and status.

✏️**NOTE:** The BCIS has two roles: the first is to help people enter the country; the second is to get people out of the United States.

Finding and accessing immigration forms has gotten a lot easier. Forms may be acquired from several different sources. For individual use, they may be downloaded from the Internet or ordered by phone. If you have access to the Internet, you will find the forms easy to access. The forms you may need are located at:

BCIS forms: (These are forms starting with "I" or "AR")
    www.immigration.gov/graphics/index.htm
       or
    www.bcis.gov/graphics/index.htm

Department of State/U.S. consulate forms: (These are forms starting with "DS")
    www.travel.state.gov

U.S. Immigration and Citizenship Q&A

Department of Labor Forms: (These are forms starting with "ETA")
www.dol.gov

Never pay for an immigration form! Every form you will ever need is available *free of charge* from the U.S. government. If you have access to the Internet, you can even download every form free of charge and fill in the forms on your computer.

(It is suggested that you get the forms from the website, but you can order them by phone by calling **800-870-3676** for delivery by mail.)

Not all forms can be filed electronically. Applications that can be filed online are forms I-765 *Application for Employment Authorization* and I-90 *Application for Replacement of Green Card*. These two forms represent approximately 30% of the total number of benefit applications filed with BCIS annually, so the odds are about 1 in 3 that one of these is the form that you need. When filing electronically, get a confirmation number to verify that a form has been sent. Save it, as well as the paper one that the BCIS will mail to you

The BCIS intends to add electronic filing capabilities for additional forms in the Fall of 2003. These forms include: Form I-129 *Petition for Nonimmigrant Worker*; Form I-131 *Application for Travel Document*; Form I-140, *Immigrant Petition for Alien Worker*; Form I-539 *Application to Extend/Change Nonimmigrant Status*; Form I-821 *Application for Temporary Protected Status*; and Form I-907 *Request for Premium Processing*.

The BCIS has also expanded its e-services by introducing *Case Status Online*. Customers who have a receipt number for an e-filed application or an application or petition filed at a Service Center can check the status of their pending case online through the BCIS website **www.bcis.gov** and avoid prolonged waits on the phone or at a local office.

(The BCIS also plans to allow credit card payments, but currently it does not offer this option.)

Appendix C

Official Government Websites

If you have access to the Internet, you can find immigration laws, immigrations forms, immigration lawyers, immigration chat rooms, and articles about immigration. To help you start your journey, we have provided some of the more important websites. There are many more. If you want to explore for yourself, simply use one of the many search engines available. Some that we use, include:

www.metacrawler.com
www.google.com
www.askjeeves.com
www.dogpile.com
www.lycos.com

U.S. immigration law is federal law. So, the most important and absolutely essential websites for you are the U.S. government ones. Everything you need as a starting point for immigration matters is available free-of-charge on U.S. government websites.

✏**NOTE:** You must have Adobe Acrobat in order to successfully print many of the forms or documents you find. You can download a free version of the software at www.adobe.com.

(The agencies listed in this appendix are arranged roughly in their order of direct involvement in immigration matters.)

Department of Homeland Security—www.dhs.gov
    This is now probably the largest government agency in terms of physical resources, but it has the newest, roughest, and least useful site for immigration purposes, but its directorate, the BCIS makes up for this drawback.

U.S. Immigration and Citizenship Q&A

Bureau of Citizenship and Immigration Service—www.bcis.gov

If you only have time for one immigration website, make this the one you spend your time on. It is about the closest to a one stop shopping location for immigration information that you are likely to find on the web.

This site has it all. There are press releases, forms, guides to the forms, and the law. Before this site was created, acquiring immigration forms used to be a time consuming and frustrating experience. One of handiest features on the forms page is the section that states which version of the form is acceptable.

Bureau of Immigration and Customs Enforcemen—www.bice.immigration.gov

This agency brings together most of the federal agencies that focus on border and immigration control and enforcement. The website has very helpful guides on its immigration section, including how to post bond for an alien detainee.

Bureau of Customs and Border Protection—www.cbp.gov

This site does a good job of organizing customs data, but it is not as helpful for acquiring immigration information.

Special Registration—www.immigration.gov/graphics/shared /lawenfor/specialreg/srindividuals.pdf

Special Registration is a complex area and this site helps to explain it. It also includes a list of port of entries for check-out. For a list of offices that process Special Registrants go to:

www.immigration.gov/graphics/shared/lawenfor/specialreg /List_interview.pdf

U.S. Department of State—www.state.gov

Compared to the superb BCIS site, this site is not as strong for comprehensive immigration information. But for the consulate and embassy info alone, it is well worth a look. You will find links to embassies and consulates and their web pages, as well as the visa bulletin and other general information about visas.

Department of Justice—www.usdoj.gov

This site is handy to have because even though the Department of Justice no longer oversees immigration, it does continue to administer the Executive Office of Immigration Review. So, it has a link to that site as well as some of their decisions.

Official Government Websites

**Pro bono attorneys for immigration cases by state—
www.usdoj.gov/eoir/probono/states.htm**

This site is a gold mine of information for people who are looking for no-cost or low-cost legal assistance with immigration problems.

Executive Office of Immigration Review—www.usdoj.gov/eoir

If you are without funds to pay an attorney, you should definitely keep this website in mind. The EOIR will not help you, but their website will. They have an absolutely superb list of pro bono legal providers. A pro bono legal provider will help you for free or for a much lower cost than a private attorney. See www.usdoj.gov/eoir/probono/probono.htm.

Department of Labor—www.dol.gov

The Department of Labor has a good website. However, you'll need the link below to find the information about employment based immigration.

**Labour Condition Processing (LCB)—
www.workforcesecurity.doleta.gov**

If you are interested in immigration through employment, this site is absolutely essential. It has some information on the visas such as the H-1 which are employment based. In addition, it has a lot of information on how labor certification works. But please note that you have to click the foreign worker tab in order to access it.

Department of Health and Human Services—www.hhs.gov

This website has some information on what benefits immigrants can receive from the federal government. Aliens are eligible to receive some federal benefits and its helpful to know which ones.

Social Security Administration—www.ssa.gov

One of the most challenging aspects of living in the United States is the need for a social security number. This site can help make it all clear. It has a drop down menu where you can select the immigration box.

Appendix D

Associations and Non-Profit Immigration Organizations

This appendix will provide some of the resources available that can help guide you through the immigration and nationality jungle. It gives you an extensive list of Internet websites on various immigrant associations, information services, and more. It will help you find organizations and groups that can help you with immigration problems and cultural adaptation.

American Immigration Lawyers Association—www.aila.org
AILA is the premier association of United States immigration attorneys. It has helpful links and helpful background material in the media section and a search function to find immigration attorneys in your area.

American Immigration Law Foundation—www.ailf.org
This foundation is designed to help immigrants with their legal questions.

Asylumlaw.org—http://asylumlaw.org
If you're interested in asylum, this is a very good site to go to. It covers the topic from more than just the U.S. perspective as well.

Catholic Charities, U.S.A.—www.catholiccharitiesusa.org
To us, it's not very easy to use, but it is a resource for immigrants to the United States

Hebrew Immigrant Aid Society—www.hias.org
They've been around since the 1880s; it's well worth taking a look at them if you're interested in resettlement issues.

U.S. Immigration and Citizenship Q&A

Lutheran Immigration and Refugee Service—www.lirs.org
An old refugee service and very much worth the look if you are interested in refugee matters.

National Immigration Law Canter—www.nilc.org
A national support center, whose mission is to protect the rights of low-income immigrants and their families.

**Office of Refugee Resettlement—
www.acf.hhs.gov/programs/orr/geninfo/index.htm**
This site takes a while to load but is definitely worth it.

Refugee Law Center—www.refugeecenter.org
This center serves Africans seeking refuge.

Appendix E

BCIS Offices

Even though it has just been born, the BCIS is a very large agency, and it performs many different functions. This is not a comprehensive list of every facility that the BCIS operates. However, it lists some of the main offices that a person might have contact with and tells how to find the other offices. The addresses are also available on the BCIS website, but the list on the website is not as accessible as other parts of the website, so we have included the addresses here for your easy reference.

Before you go to a BCIS facility you should absolutely confirm the hours and check to see no security concern or other unanticipated event has caused them to close that day. Before you mail anything with a fee, verify on the website or with the customer service number that you are sending the right amount to the right place.

Also, before you actually send your application, fee or other mailing to the BCIS, call or go on their website to verify the information below. **BCIS procedures are constantly changing.** You can reach their website at www.bcis.gov. The customer service number is 800-375-5283.

BCIS SERVICE CENTERS

WESTERN U.S.
U.S. BCIS California Service Center
P.O. Box 30080
Laguna Niguel, CA 92607-0080

Overnight Delivery Address:
U.S. BCIS California Service Center
2400 Avila Road
Laguna Niguel, CA 92677

U.S. Immigration and Citizenship Q&A

(*This address should be used for people from Arizona, California, Hawaii, Nevada, Territory of Guam, or the Commonwealth of the Northern Mariana Islands.*)

MIDWEST
U.S. BCIS Nebraska Service Center
P.O. Box 87400
Lincoln, NE 68501-7400

Overnight Delivery Address:
U.S. BCIS Nebraska Service Center
850 S. Street
Lincoln, NE 68508

(*People from the following states will use this center: Alaska, Colorado, Idaho, Illinois, Indiana, Iowa, Kansas, Michigan, Minnesota, Missouri, Montana, Nebraska, North Dakota, Ohio, Oregon, South Dakota, Utah, Washington, Wisconsin, or Wyoming.*)

MIDSOUTH
U.S. BCIS Texas Service Center
P.O. Box 851204
Mesquite, TX 75185-1204

Overnight Delivery Address:
U.S. BCIS Texas Service Center
4141 North St. Augustine
Dallas, TX 75227

(*The Texas Service Center handles paperwork for the following states: Alabama, Arkansas, Florida, Georgia, Kentucky, Louisiana, Mississippi, New Mexico, North Carolina, Oklahoma, Tennessee, or Texas.*)

EAST COAST
U.S. BCIS Vermont Service Center
75 Lower Weldon Street
St. Albans, VT 05479-0001

Overnight Delivery Address:
U.S. BCIS Vermont Service Center
75 Lower Weldon Street
St. Albans, VT 05479-0001

(This Service Center handles Connecticut, District of Columbia, Delaware, Maine, Maryland, Massachusetts, New Hampshire, New Jersey, New York, Pennsylvania, Rhode Island, Vermont, Virginia, West Virginia, Commonwealth of Puerto Rico, or the U.S. Virgin Islands.)

BCIS DISTRICT AND SUBDISTRICT OFFICES

The BCIS also has district and subdistrict offices. Before you travel to an office, check the website to be sure the office is open. Verify your appointment. Verify that you can enter the building.

Some suboffices provide a full range of services. Others are much more specialized. If you are going to a suboffice, go to the BCIS website at **www.bcis.gov** to verify that the service you are going for is offered at that location.

Appendix F

Abbreviations

Your guide to some of the abbreviations and acronyms used in the complex world of U.S. immigration law.

AC21	American Competitiveness in the 21st Century Act of 2000
AEWR	Adverse Effect Wage Rate
BACLA	Board of Alien Certification Appeals (Department of Labor)
BCBP	Bureau of Customs and Border Protection (Department of Homeland Security)
BCC	Border Crossing Card
BCIS	Bureau of Citizenship and Immigration Services (Department of Homeland Security)
BICE	Bureau of Immigration and Customs Enforcement (Department of Homeland Security)
CA	Bureau of Consular Affairs (U.S. Department of State)
CIA	Central Intelligence Agency
CLASS	Consular Lookout and Support System
CONGEN	Consulate General
CSPA	Child Status Protection Act
DCM	Deputy Chief of Mission
DHS	Department of Homeland Security
DOS	Department of State
EAD	Employment Authorization Document
EOIR	Executive Office of Immigration Review (U.S. Department of Justice)
FBI	Federal Bureau of Investigation
FPU	Fraud Prevention Unit
FSN	Foreign Service National

HPSA	Health Professional Shortage Area
HR	Bureau of Human Resources (Department of State)
IBIS	Interagency Border Inspection Service
IIRIRA	Illegal Immigration Reform and Immigrant Responsibility Act of 1996
INA	Immigration and Nationality Act
INRA	Immigration Nursing Relief Act of 1989
INTCA	Immigration Technical Corrections Act of 1994
IV	Immigrant visa
LCA	Labor Certification Application
LPR	Lawful Permanent Resident
MRV	Machine readable visa
MUA	Medically Underserved Areas
MUP	Medically Underserved Populations
NIV	Nonimmigrant visa
NRDAA	Nursing Relief for Disadvantaged Areas Act of 1999
NSEERS	National Security Entry/Exit Registration System
OIG	Office of Inspector General
ORR	Office of Refugee Resettlement (Department of Health and Human Service)
SAO	Security Advisory Opinion
SEVIS	Student and Exchange Visitor Information System
TARP	Travel Agents Referral Program
TPF	Temporary Processing Facility
TSA	Transportation Security Administration
USDA	United States Department of Agriculture
VISIT	Visitor and Immigration Status Indication Technology System

Index

180-day rule, 93
2-year return rule, 124, 125, 126, 128, 129
    waiver, 124
9/11. See September 11th, 2001

A

A Visas, 319
ABCIS, 100
academic students, 131
adjudicating officer, 291
adjustment of status, 28, 76, 77, 85, 88, 91, 93, 95, 102, 128, 142, 143, 150, 166, 167, 180, 188, 201, 245, 263, 290, 294, 295
Administrative Appeals Unit, 111, 148
admissible, 57, 58, 76
admission, 29, 31, 50, 245, 252
adoption, 1, 16–19, 21, 22, 209, 315
advance parole, 89, 187, 295
advance permission, 89, 173, 187
advanced degrees, 143, 317
advanced knowledge, 100

adverse effect wage rate, 133
Affidavit of Support, 153, 154, 250, 314, 315, 316
affiliated companies, 97
aging out, 13
agriculture workers, 325
airlines, 33, 48, 50, 51
airport security, 32, 34
Alien Registration Receipt Card, 168
alimony, 8
amateur sports events, 53
Amerasians, 318
American Competitiveness in the 21st Century Act, 142, 295
American Council on International Personnel, 122
American Evaluation and Translation Service, 145
appeals, 272
Application for a Nonimmigrant Visa, 41, 57, 59, 79, 119–120, 133
Application for a Replacement Card, 171
Application for A, G or NATO Visa, 320, 324, 329

Application for Action on Approved Application or Petition, 294
Application for Advance Processing of Orphan Petition, 314
Application for Alien Employment Certification, 317, 318
Application for Employment Authorization, 125, 188
Application for Immigrant Visa and Alien Registration, 314–319, 334
Application for Naturalization, 218–224
Application for Nonimmigrant Visa, 87, 104, 113
Application for Returning Resident Status, 329
Application for T Nonimmigrant Status, 333
Application to Determine Returning Resident Status, 172
Application to Replace Alien Registration Card, 169
arrests, 230, 261
artists, 84, 331
Association for International Practical Training, Inc., 122
asylees. *See asylum*
asylum, 244, 255, 263, 266, 271, 282–287
athletes, 64, 84, 330, 329
Attorney General, 44

B

B-1 Visas, 25, 28, 46, 56–64, 66, 68, 71, 73, 78, 182, 320
documents, 59
requirements, 58
spouse, 62
working, 60
B-2 Visas, 25, 28, 40, 46, 49, 52–55, 70, 71, 74, 78, 182, 205, 321
background checks, 29, 30, 31, 34, 198, 298
bars to admission, 247
BBS, 238, 239, 242
BCBP, 240, 289
BCIS, 2, 5, 12, 13, 18, 29–33, 35–39, 45, 50, 51, 55, 56, 65, 67, 68, 73, 74, 78, 87, 92, 98, 101, 110, 112, 123, 131, 142, 143, 147, 166, 168–170, 183, 187, 189, 204, 209, 214, 215, 217–221, 225, 231, 237–241, 243, 251, 264, 267, 269, 274, 282, 284, 287, 289, 290, 291, 294, 295, 300, 301, 311, 313
branch office, 97
Forms Center, 170
offices, 241
Service Center, 87, 107, 108, 222, 224, 294, 318
beneficiaries, 175
benefits, 272
asylum, 280
five-year ban, 285
foreigners, 272
permanent resident aliens, 277
refugees, 280
BICE, 67, 237, 240, 242, 243, 261, 262

Biographic Data Sheets, 184
Biographic Information, 314
biometrics, 35, 36, 37, 43, 74
birth, 204, 205, 206, 210
birth certificates, 10, 12, 19, 114, 164, 206, 208
birth records, 11
blanket petitions, 97, 104, 107
board meetings, 62
Board of Immigration Appeals, 244, 257
bona fide father-child relationship, 11, 12, 21, 22
bona fide marriage, 4, 189
bond, 256, 257
Border and Transportation Security Directorate, 239
Border Patrol, 242
born out-of-wedlock, 10, 11, 12, 23, 164
boyfriend, 8
brides, 4
brothers, 1, 23, 160, 163–166, 176, 316
  adopted, 24
Bureau of Customs and Border Protection, 26
Bureau of Educational and Cultural Affairs, 326
Bureau of Intelligence and Research, 297
business manager of exceptional ability, 102
business visas, 25, 47, 56, 57, 60. *See also B-1 Visas*
business visitors, 103
buying property, 67, 68

C

C Visas, 321
Certificate of Citizenship, 184
certificate of eligibility, 55, 121
Certificate of Eligibility for Exchange Visitor status, 125
Certificate of Naturalization, 184, 228, 229, 232
change of address, 40
charging document, 257
Child Citizen Act, 209
Child Status Protection Act, 2, 13, 14, 300
children, 1, 2, 8–14, 16, 17, 19, 91, 160, 161, 283, 315, 323, 328, 332, 333
  abused/battered, 318
  adopted, 16, 18, 21, 24, 314
  alien, 209
  asylum, 283
  childcare, 286
  citizenship, 208
  illegitimate, 11, 20
  married, 14, 161, 175, 316
  preferences, 16
  unmarried, 15, 16, 77, 160, 161, 163, 164, 176, 177, 199, 314
citizen, 3, 7, 10, 12, 13, 15, 17, 20–23, 54, 160–163, 166, 174, 176, 177, 183, 205, 258, 266, 271, 275, 300, 316, 327
citizenship, 203, 204, 206, 207, 209, 210
  renouncing, 234
civil rights statutes, 278
CLASS, 30, 34, 292, 293, 296, 297, 311
clearance procedures, 292

cohabitation, 8
common law marriage, 8
company support letter, 112
concurrent filing, 141
conditional immigrant status, 157
conditional permanent resident, 152, 188, 189, 200, 212
  status, 150, 151
conferences, 25, 53, 59
consular officer, 4, 19, 31, 36, 55, 56, 58–60, 87, 121, 208, 234, 246, 289, 292, 293, 296, 299, 300, 305, 306, 308, 309, 311, 312
consular processing, 105, 290, 291, 293, 294, 295, 310, 313
  interview, 307, 309, 310, 312
  problems, 295
consular section chief, 312
consulate, 3, 4, 12, 18, 19, 25, 30, 31, 36, 42, 51, 52, 54, 55, 57, 60, 74, 105, 110, 129, 134, 150, 166, 282, 290–296, 298, 299–306, 309, 310
  locating, 57
consummate, 5
Contact Information and Work History for Nonimmigrant Visa Applicant, 323, 326, 328
continuous residence, 203, 210, 211, 217
conventions, 53, 61
convocations, 53
corporations, 71
cousins, 6, 162, 179, 301
criminal convictions, 46, 58, 77, 203, 217, 230, 246, 249, 259, 261, 298

D

D-1 Visas, 321
damaged visa, 312
daughters, 9, 14, 16, 160, 161, 163, 176, 177, 315
deeds, 4
deferred inspection, 251, 252
delays, 30
Department of Agriculture, 133, 242
Department of Health and Human Services, 126, 241
Department of Homeland Security, 38, 41, 73, 238, 239, 241–242, 244, 289
  address, 244
Department of Housing and Urban Development, 287
Department of Justice, 313
Department of Labor, 86, 87, 132, 134, 146, 193, 276, 317, 318, 333
dependent visas, 83, 90
deportable, 258
deportation proceedings, 258
derivative asylum status, 283
derivative status, 9
detention centers, 243, 256
Dictionary of Occupational Titles, 192
disabilities, 219
discrimination, 278
diseases, 246
Diversity Immigrant Visa, 334
diversity lottery, 190, 191, 193, 194, 196–200. *See also* Green Card Lottery
divorce, 7, 8, 10, 14, 189, 212
documentation, 4

domestic employees, 63
Domestic Security Enhancement Act, 271
downsizing, 92
driving, 68, 69
dual citizenship, 205, 266
DUI, 69
DV-1 Visas, 190, 334
DWI, 69

E

E Visas, 81
E-1 Visas, 108, 116–119, 322
  requirements, 116
  spouse, 119
E-2 Visas, 108, 322
earned income credit, 287
EB Visas, 145
EB-1 Visas, 148, 317
EB-1B Visas, 147, 148
EB-2 Visas, 317
EB-3 Visas, 318
EB-4 Visas, 318
EB-5 Visas, 152, 319
Electronic Diversity Visa Entry Form, 194, 195
eligibility, 1
embassy, 36, 42, 44, 51, 52, 55, 282, 296
Emergency and Preparedness and Response Directorate, 239
employee of extraordinary ability, 138
Employment Authorization Document, 88, 89, 108, 109, 115, 167, 284, 295
employment creation immigration visa, 152

employment-based immigration visas, 313, 317
  petition, 143
engagements, 181, 182, 185
English test, 215, 216
Enhanced Border Security Act, 239
Enhanced Border Security and Visa Entry Reform Act, 34
entering, 25–29, 32, 244, 245, 246, 250, 272
  permission, 29
  physically, 252
entertainers, 84, 331
EOIR, 243
exceptional ability, 138, 139, 317
exchange programs, 326
Exchange Visitor Program, 121, 122, 126, 131
exchange visitor visa, 120, 121, 123, 124
exclusion proceedings, 258
executive, 96, 99, 100, 105, 106, 109, 111, 116, 138, 140, 317, 327
expectation of privacy, 273
expedited removal, 253, 254, 255
  appeals, 255
  exemptions, 255
extension of stay, 101, 103
extraordinary ability, 140, 317, 329

F

F Visas, 82, 120, 131
F-1 Visas, 128, 323
F-2 Visas, 323
F-3 visas, 323
F1-1 Visas, 315

F2-1 Visas, 315
F2-2 Visas, 315
F2-4 Visas, 316
F3-1 Visas, 316
F4-1 Visas, 316
family, 1, 2, 20
family businesses, 111
family relationship, 159
family-based immigration visas, 313
  petitions, 161
  preferences, 162
fashion models, 84, 324
fiancé/ée, 2, 3, 5, 53, 182–188, 327
fingerprinted, 39, 43, 224, 267
firearms, 75
following to join, 178, 199
foreign degree equivalency, 144
foreign government officials, 319
Foreign Service National, 291
Foreign Terrorist Tracking Task Force, 299
Form 156, 327, 328, 330, 331, 332
Form 156k, 327
Form AR-11, 40
Form DS-117, 172, 329
Form DS-122, 334
Form DS-156, 41, 57, 59, 79, 87, 104, 113, 119, 121, 133, 297, 311, 320–326, 328, 329, 333, 334
Form DS-156e, 322
Form DS-157, 40, 60, 299, 332
Form DS-158, 323, 326, 328
Form DS-1648, 320, 324, 329
Form DS-230, 314–319, 334
Form ETA 750, 132, 317, 318
Form ETA-9035, 86

Form G-325, 314
Form G-325A, 165, 184
Form I-129, 86, 101, 103, 104, 110, 112, 115, 322, 324, 325, 327, 330, 331, 332, 333
Form I-129F, 183, 184, 187, 327
Form I-129S, 327
Form I-130, 12, 13, 14, 165, 166, 185, 294, 314, 315, 316, 327, 333
Form I-140, 138, 141, 142, 143, 144, 146, 147, 317, 318
Form I-20, 55, 323, 328
Form I-2019, 326
Form I-290, 148
Form I-290B, 111
Form I-360, 318
Form I-485, 93, 138, 141, 142, 143, 147, 150, 166
Form I-526, 150, 319
Form I-600, 18, 300, 314
Form I-600A, 314
Form I-730, 283
Form I-751, 188, 189, 212
Form I-765, 108, 115, 125, 167, 188, 284
Form I-797, 88, 104, 110, 113, 294, 314, 315, 316, 317, 318, 319, 324, 325, 327, 328, 330, 331, 333
Form I-824, 107, 294
Form I-829, 151
Form I-864, 153, 154, 314, 315, 316
Form I-90, 169, 171
Form I-907, 106
Form I-914, 333
Form I-94W, 47, 48, 50, 51, 52
Form N-336, 229

Index

Form N-400, 204, 212, 218–223, 230, 232
Form N-565, 229
fraud, 260
free speech, 275
friends, 162, 164, 179

G

G-1 Visas, 323
gambling, 70
girlfriends, 12
godchildren, 179
good moral character, 217, 231
government programs, 123, 125, 126, 128
grandchildren, 178
Green Card, 6, 8, 13–16, 27, 55, 56, 73, 88, 89, 102, 138–141, 141, 145, 146, 150–153, 157, 164–170, 172, 174, 178, 188, 189, 190, 198, 199, 220, 228, 245, 251, 278, 301, 315, 316, 329
  renewal, 169, 170
Green Card lottery, 149, 190, 191, 192, 201, 334. *See also diversity lottery*
  requirements, 192
guns, 75

H

H Visas, 81, 82
  extending, 85, 95
  premium processing, 87
  processing, 86
H-1B Visas, 83, 84, 85, 87, 90, 91, 92, 94, 95, 100, 139, 144, 276, 324
  limits, 84
H-1C Visas, 88, 89, 90, 324
H-2A Visas, 133, 134, 135, 325
H-2B Visas, 325
H-3 Visas, 325
H-4 Visas, 83, 90
half siblings, 23
health. *See medical treatment*
health professional shortage areas, 126
highly skilled employee, 116
hobbies, 55
Homeland Security Act, 237, 238, 239
homosexuality, 281
housing, 278
hunting, 75
husband, 1, 2, 3, 4, 5, 6, 7

I

I Visas, 326
I-9, 66
I-94, 36, 45, 49, 52, 114
IBIS, 30, 38
illegal alien, 170
Illegal Immigration Reform and Immigrant Responsibility Act, 154
immediate relatives, 3, 13, 14, 77, 161, 174–177, 179, 314
  petition, 174
immigrant intent, 25, 27, 28, 49, 68, 73, 74
Immigrant Petition by Alien Entrepreneur, 319
Immigrant Petition for Alien Worker, 138, 141, 144, 146, 317, 318
immigrant visas, 76

immigrating, 159
Immigration and Nationality Act, 137, 162, 175, 199, 258
Immigration Reform and Control Act, 85, 253, 258
impairments, 219
inadmissible, 247–250, 256, 258, 268, 269, 272
  grounds, 250
independent waiver petition, 128
Information Analysis and Infrastructure Protection Directorate, 239
inheritence, 8
INS, 38, 75, 238, 239, 240, 264, 265
inspection, 29
Inter-American driving permit, 69
interested government agency, 127
international cultural exchange visitors, 331
international driving permit, 69
Internet brides, 4, 5
internships, 121
intracompany transfers, 96, 97, 106, 112, 114, 115, 118
investments, 150–152
investors, 319
IR-1 Visas, 314
IR-2 Visas, 314
IR-3 Visas, 314
IR-4 Visas, 314
IR-5 Visas, 314
Irish Peace Process Cultural and Training Program, 332
issuing officer, 291, 292

J

J Visas, 81, 120, 131
J-1 Visas, 121, 123, 126, 130, 326
  extension, 126
J-2 Visas, 123
job descriptions, 114
joint venture, 97
journalists, 326
just compensation, 276

K

K Visas, 3, 53
K-1 Visas, 185, 186, 187, 327
K-2 Visas, 187, 327
K-3 Visas, 327
K-4 Visas, 327

L

L Classification Supplement, 327
L Visas, 81, 98
  documentation, 113, 114
L-1 Visas, 84, 96, 102, 109, 111, 115, 119, 327
  children, 108, 115
  processing, 105
L-2 Visas, 108, 110, 113, 115, 328
labor certification, 100, 134, 241, 324, 325
Labor Certification Application, 94, 146, 333
Labor Certification Approval, 139
Labor Condition Application, 86, 87, 276
lawful permanent resident. *See permanent resident alien*

Index

lectures, 61
Legal Immigration Family Equity Act, 158, 180, 181, 333
legitimating, 12, 20, 164
liquor laws, 274
living together, 6

M

M Visas, 81, 120, 131
M-1 Visas, 131, 328
M-3 Visas, 328
machine readable passport, 42, 47, 74
mail-order brides, 5
Management Directorate, 239
managers, 96, 99, 100, 101, 105, 108, 109, 111, 116, 138, 140, 150, 317, 327
marital status, 11
marriage, 2–6, 8, 9, 12, 301
  ceremony, 5
  certificate, 4
  previous, 10
  proxy, 5
marriage certificate, 164, 165
Marriage Fraud Act, 157
meaningfully interruptive, 92
Medicaid, 286
medical training, 125
medical treatment, 25, 53, 78, 248
medically underserved areas or populations, 126
meetings, 25, 61
military, 11, 54, 213, 214
million dollar visa, 149
Miranda rights, 273
money laundering, 70
multiple entry visas, 32

N

N-8 Visas, 329
NACARA, 190, 263
NAFTA, 35, 333
National Customer Service Center, 226
National Name Check Program, 299
NATO Visas, 329
natural father, 11, 21, 22
natural mother, 10, 22
natural parents, 21, 300
naturalization, 13, 15, 163, 173, 203, 204, 206, 208–214, 218, 233
  additional documents, 225
  application, 218–223
  continuous residence, 223
  fingerprint appointment, 224, 225, 226
  history requirement, 216
  interview, 221, 223, 225, 226, 227
  language requirement, 214, 215, 216
  oath ceremony, 226, 227
  physically present, 223
  revoking, 234
nephews, 179
nieces, 179
no-fly list, 33
no-objection letter, 127
non-profit social services organizations, 107
Nonimmigrant Fiancé(e) Visa Application, 327
Nonimmigrant Petition based on Blanket Petition, 327–328

Nonimmigrant Treaty Trader/Investor Application, 322
Nonimmigrant Visa Application, 320–334
nonimmigrant visa chief, 312
Nonimmigrant Visa Waiver Arrival-Departure Record, 51
nonimmigrant visas, 25, 76, 297
nonimmigrant visitor visa, 28
North American Free Trade Agreement. *See NAFTA*
Notice of Approval, 104, 113, 294, 314–319, 324, 325, 327, 328, 330, 331–332, 333
Notice to Appear, 257, 262
NSEERS, 26, 38
numerical limitations, 174
nurse, 84, 88, 90, 123, 174, 319

O

O Supplement, 330
O Visas, 82
O*Net Online, 192
O-1 Visas, 128, 329
O-2 Visas, 330
Oath Ceremony, 227
ombudsman, 33, 243
one-year continuous employment requirement, 98
open market employment, 89
orphans, 17
overstay, 37, 39, 44, 45, 61, 69, 72, 73, 75, 201, 304

P

P Supplement, 330, 331
P Visas, 82
P-1 Visas, 330
P-2 Visas, 331
P-3 Visas, 331
Panama Canal employees, 329
parent-subsidiary relationship, 97
parents, 1, 14, 18, 20, 21, 22, 77, 160, 161, 163, 176, 206, 314, 332
  adoptive, 22
parking tickets, 77
part-time employment, 147
passenger identification verification form, 33
passports, 42, 43, 47, 114, 171, 184, 208, 228, 232, 251, 254, 291, 302, 303, 304
peak load temporary workers, 84
permanent residence, 46, 56
permanent resident alien, 51, 55, 56, 67, 91, 93, 158–166, 169, 171, 173, 177, 182, 189, 204, 206, 210–215, 217, 218, 232, 233, 245, 254, 255, 258, 265, 266, 271, 275, 277, 278, 315, 316, 333
permissible activities. *See prohibited activities*
Personal Responsibility and Work Opportunity Reconciliation Act, 286
Petition by Entrepreneur to Remove Conditions, 151
Petition for a Nonimmigrant Worker, 322, 324, 325, 327, 330, 331, 333

Index

Petition for Alien Relative, 12, 165, 294, 314, 315, 316, 327, 333
Petition for Amerasian, Widow(er), or Special Immigrant, 318
Petition for an Alien Fiancé(e), 183, 184, 327
Petition for an Alien Relative, 12
Petition for an Alien Worker, 332
petition or sponsor, 159
Petition to Classify Orphan as an Immediate Relative, 18, 314
Petition to Remove the Conditions on Residence, 188, 189
Petition to Request Permanent Residence or Adjust Status, 141
petitions, 6, 9
photographs, 4, 165, 195, 221, 222
physically present, 3, 5, 85, 207, 209, 211
port of departure, 268
port-of-entry, 32, 39, 253
portability provisions, 295
portable, 93
Practical Training Program, 123
preferences, 3, 12, 15, 16, 137, 161, 165, 172, 173, 175–179, 183, 333
   family-based, 173, 176
premium processing, 106
primary inspection, 251
principal beneficiary, 309
principal visa holder, 96, 109, 128, 178, 328
priority date, 16, 180
profession, 99

professionals, 138, 317, 318, 333
professors, 317, 326, 329
prohibited activities, 58, 60, 65, 66, 67, 70, 71
property, 67, 68, 71, 276
proxy, 5
proxy adoption abroad, 18
public charge, 154, 250, 260
public office, 233

Q

Q Supplement, 331
Q Visas, 81–82, 132
Q-1 Visas, 331
Q-2 Visas, 332
quasi refusal, 312

R

R Supplement, 332
R-1 Visas, 332
reacquisition of citizenship, 329
reasonable accommodations, 219
recapture, 95
recreational school, 55
Refugee/Asylee Relative Petition, 283
refugees, 255, 266, 271, 280, 281, 283–287
registered nurses. *See nurses*
relevant practical training, 123
religious workers, 318, 329, 332
removal, 242, 253, 258, 259, 261, 263, 267
   expedited, 253, 254
   hearing, 262
   in absentia, 261
   offenses, 259

Replacement Naturalization Citizenship Document, 229
Request for Hearing on a Decision for Naturalization, 229
research, 61, 120, 147, 317, 324, 326
resettlement, 282
residency, 173, 178
  abandoning, 173

S

S Visas, 334
SCHIP, 285
Science and Technology Directorate, 239
search warrants, 273
searches and seizures, 277
seasonal farm workers, 84
secondary inspection, 251
Secretary of State, 44
seminars, 61
separated, 6, 7, 212
September 11, 2001, 26, 29, 34, 38, 41, 49, 72, 75, 112, 187, 239, 252, 304
SEVIS, 130, 131, 323, 326, 328
siblings, 160, 161, 163, 316
single entry visas, 32
sisters, 1, 2, 23, 160, 163, 176, 316
  adopted, 24
skilled workers, 318, 325
Social Security, 279
Social Security Act, 286
sons, 9, 14, 16, 160, 161, 163, 176, 177, 315
special education programs, 84
special immigrants, 329

special permission, 88
Special Registration, 37, 39, 264–269
specialized knowledge, 96, 99, 100, 101, 105, 108, 109, 111, 112
specialized knowledge employees, 327
Specialized Visas, 334
specialty occupation, 83, 84, 90, 91, 324
specialty worker, 99
specific residency requirements, 172
spouse, 1–3, 5–9, 54, 62, 77, 160, 161, 163, 164, 176, 177, 210, 283, 314, 315, 323, 328, 332, 333
  abused/battered, 318
State Department, 29, 30, 34, 36, 57, 60, 119, 122, 123, 126, 166, 180, 192, 196, 197, 198, 241, 289, 290, 292, 293, 296, 297, 299, 302, 308, 313
staying, 76, 77
stepchildren, 1, 9, 10, 20, 164
stipends, 129
student visas, 10, 120, 131
students, 51, 323, 326
studying, 120
substantial trade, 117, 118, 322
Superstar visa, 140
Supplemental Nonimmigrant Visa Application, 40, 332
Supplemental Nonimmigrant Visa Information, 60
Supplemental Registration, 334

Index

T

T-1 Visas, 332
T-2 Visas, 332
T-3 Visas, 332
T-4 Visas, 332
TANF, 285, 286
tax returns, 4
taxes, 231
teaching, 120, 122, 145, 146
temporary cultural exchanges, 131
temporary nonimmigrant visas, 313, 319
Temporary Protected Status, 283, 284
tenure, 147
territories, 203, 206
terrorists, 2, 30, 33, 34, 38, 235, 242, 246, 260, 269, 297, 298
third country consular processing, 304
TIPOFF, 30, 34, 297
TN Visas, 82, 333
tourist visas, 40, 47, 53–55, 62, 73, 76, 272, 306
tourists, 25, 51, 319
trade shows, 61, 64
trafficking in persons, 332
trainees, 325, 326
training, 61
translating, 4, 145
Transportation Security Administration, 33, 240
treason, 204, 235
Treasury Enforcement Communication System, 311
treaty investor visa, 304
treaty investors, 109
treaty trader visa, 304
treaty traders, 109, 116, 117, 118, 322
troubled business, 150

U

U Visas, 334
U.S.A. Patriot Act, 2, 34, 240, 264, 269, 271
unlawfully present, 61
unmarried, 9
unskilled workers, 325

V

V Visas, 158, 181
V-1 Visas, 333
V-2 Visas, 333
Vienna Convention on Consular Relations, 274
Viper, 34
visa application fee, 308
Visa Bulletin, 165, 180
visa chief, 312
Visa Lookout Accountability, 292
visa lottery. *See diversity lottery*
visa processing, 290, 291, 293
visa shopping, 310
Visa Waiver Arrival Departure Record, 47
Visa Waiver Program, 25, 41, 43–52, 78, 79, 272, 320
requirements, 47
visas, 1, 2, 7, 8
multiple entry, 32
visitor visas, 32
Visas Condor Program, 299
VISIT, 26, 36, 37, 39, 73
visitor visas, 30, 32, 40
vocational program, 131

vocational school, 55
vocational student visa, 120
vocational students, 131, 328
voluntary departure, 253, 263
volunteer service program, 62
voting, 71, 171, 233, 275

W

Wage and Hour Division, 276
waiting time, 15, 179
Welfare Act, 286
widowers, 318
widows, 318
wife, 1, 2, 5, 6, 8, 165
work permits, 167, 188
work visas, 2, 9, 83, 128, 301
working, 65, 66, 67, 81, 278
World Trade Center, 34

About the Authors

Kurt A. Wagner, MBA, JD (Magna Cum Laude) is an attorney, author, university lecturer, and founder of the Law Offices of Kurt A. Wagner with offices in Illinois and Austria. He is a member of the Immigration and International Law Section of the Illinois State Bar Association, the Chicago Bar Association, and the Washington, D.C. Bar Association. He formerly served as a U.S. Department of State Consular Officer with experience in visa processing at U.S. embassies abroad. He teaches classes on legal topics at the University of Klagenfurt and the Carinthia Technical Institute in Austria, and served as Editor-in-Chief of the Southern Illinois University Law Journal.

Debbie M. Schell, JD is an attorney and author who practices with the Law Offices of Kurt A. Wagner. She is a member of the American Immigration Lawyers Association (AILA) and the Immigration and Nationality Law Committee of the Chicago Bar Association. Her experience with immigration began early, when her mother immigrated to the United States from Jamaica and her father came from Belize. She has edited legal forms books as well as works on the law of asylum. Her clients include refugees, as well as individuals and companies seeking help with immigration issues. In addition, she has extensive experience with human rights issues related to employment and housing.

Richard E. Schell, JD is an attorney, author, and serves of Counsel to the Law Offices of Kurt A. Wagner. He has extensive legal editing and researching experience with a major legal publisher and in the areas of international law, immigration law, and agricultural law. He studied international law at the University of Notre Dame in London. He is also a frequent writer and speaker on international legal topics and small business development.

Your #1 Source for Real World Legal Information...

Sphinx® Publishing
An Imprint of Sourcebooks, Inc.®

• Written by lawyers • Simple English explanation of the law
• Forms and instructions included

SOCIAL SECURITY Q&A

This book contains actual questions from individual around the country. Information is included on child, spousal, survivor and retirement benefits.

192 pages; $12.95;
ISBN 1-57248-216-8

U.S. IMMIGRATION STEP BY STEP

Current information regarding procedures, documents, and current laws for immigrants. Blank forms are included.

312 pages; $21.95;
ISBN 1-57248-218-4

What our customers say about our books:

"It couldn't be more clear for the layperson." —R.D.

"I want you to know I really appreciate your book. It has saved me a lot of time and money." —L.T.

"Your real estate contracts book has saved me nearly $12,000.00 in closing costs over the past year." —A.B.

"...many of the legal questions that I have had over the years were answered clearly and concisely through your plain English interpretation of the law." —C.E.H.

"If there weren't people out there like you I'd be lost. You have the best books of this type out there." —S.B.

"...your forms and directions are easy to follow." —C.V.M.

Sphinx Publishing's Legal Survival Guides are directly available from Sourcebooks, Inc., or from your local bookstores.

*For credit card orders call 1–800–432-7444,
write P.O. Box 4410, Naperville, IL 60567-4410, or fax 630-961-2168*

Sphinx® Publishing's State Titles
Up-to-Date for Your State

California

CA Power of Attorney Handbook (2E)	$18.95
How to File for Divorce in CA (4E)	$26.95
How to Make a CA Will	$16.95
How to Probate and Settle an Estate in CA	$26.95
How to Start a Business in CA (2E)	$21.95
How to Win in Small Claims Court in CA (2E)	$18.95
The Landlord's Legal Guide in CA	$24.95
Make Your Own CA Will	$18.95
Tenants' Rights in California	$21.95

Florida

Child Custody, Visitation and Support in FL	$26.95
How to File for Divorce in FL (7E)	$26.95
How to Form a Corporation in FL (6E)	$24.95
How to Form a Limited Liability Company in FL (2E)	$24.95
How to Form a Partnership in FL	$22.95
How to Make a FL Will (6E)	$16.95
How to Probate and Settle an Estate in FL (5E)	$26.95
How to Start a Business in FL (7E)	$21.95
How to Win in Small Claims Court in FL (7E)	$18.95
Land Trusts in Florida (6E)	$29.95
Landlords' Rights and Duties in FL (9E)	$22.95

Georgia

How to File for Divorce in GA (5E)	$21.95
How to Make a GA Will (4E)	$21.95
How to Start a Business in GA (3E)	$21.95

Illinois

Child Custody, Visitation, and Support in IL	$24.95
How to File for Divorce in IL (3E)	$24.95
How to Make an IL Will (3E)	$16.95
How to Start a Business in IL (3E)	$21.95
The Landlord's Legal Guide in IL	$24.95

Maryland, Virginia and the District of Columbia

How to File for Divorce in MD, VA and DC	$28.95
How to Start a Business in MD, VA or DC	$21.95

Massachusetts

How to File for Divorce in MA (3E)	$24.95
How to Form a Corporation in MA	$24.95
How to Make a MA Will (2E)	$16.95
How to Start a Business in MA (3E)	$21.95
The Landlord's Legal Guide in MA	$24.95

Michigan

How to File for Divorce in MI (3E)	$24.95
How to Make a MI Will (3E)	$16.95
How to Start a Business in MI (3E)	$18.95

Minnesota

How to File for Divorce in MN	$21.95
How to Form a Corporation in MN	$24.95
How to Make a MN Will (2E)	$16.95

New Jersey

How to File for Divorce in NJ	$24.95

New York

Child Custody, Visitation and Support in NY	$26.95
How to File for Divorce in NY (2E)	$26.95
How to Form a Corporation in NY (2E)	$24.95
How to Make a NY Will (2E)	$16.95
How to Start a Business in NY (2E)	$18.95
How to Win in Small Claims Court in NY (2E)	$18.95
The Landlords' Legal Guide in NY	$24.95
New York Power of Attorney Handbook	$19.95
Tenants' Rights in NY	$21.95

North Carolina

How to File for Divorce in NC (3E)	$22.95
How to Make a NC Will (3E)	$16.95
How to Start a Business in NC (3E)	$18.95
Landlords' Rights & Duties in NC	$21.95

Ohio

How to File for Divorce in OH, 2E	$24.95
How to Form a Corporation in OH	$24.95
How to Make an OH Will	$16.95

Pennsylvania

Child Custody, Visitation and Support in PA	$26.95
How to File for Divorce in PA (3E)	$26.95
How to Make a PA Will (2E)	$16.95
How to Start a Business in PA (2E)	$18.95
The Landlord's Legal Guide in PA	$24.95

Texas

Child Custody, Visitation, and Support in TX	$22.95
How to File for Divorce in TX (3E)	$24.95
How to Form a Corporation in TX (2E)	$24.95
How to Make a TX Will (3E)	$16.95
How to Probate and Settle an Estate in TX (3E)	$26.95
How to Start a Business in TX (3E)	$18.95
How to Win in Small Claims Court in TX (2E)	$16.95
Landlords' Rights and Duties in TX (2E)	$21.95

For credit card orders call 1–800–432-7444,
write P.O. Box 4410, Naperville, IL 60567-4410, or fax 630-961-2168

Sphinx® Publishing's National Titles
Valid in All 50 States

Legal Survival in Business

The Complete Book of Corporate Forms	$24.95
The Complete Patent Book	$26.95
The Entrepreneur's Internet Handbook	$21.95
How to Form a Limited Liability Company (2E)	$24.95
Incorporate in Delaware from Any State	$24.95
Incorporate in Nevada from Any State	$24.95
How to Form a Nonprofit Corporation (2E)	$24.95
How to Form Your Own Corporation (4E)	$26.95
How to Form Your Own Partnership (2E)	$24.95
How to Register Your Own Copyright (4E)	$24.95
How to Register Your Own Trademark (3E)	$21.95
The Small Business Owner's Guide to Bankruptcy	$21.95
Most Valuable Corporate Forms You'll Ever Need (3E)	$21.95

Legal Survival in Court

Crime Victim's Guide to Justice (2E)	$21.95
Grandparents' Rights (3E)	$24.95
Help Your Lawyer Win Your Case (2E)	$14.95
Jurors' Rights (2E)	$12.95
Legal Research Made Easy (3E)	$21.95
Winning Your Personal Injury Claim (2E)	$24.95
Your Rights When You Owe Too Much	$16.95

Legal Survival in Real Estate

Essential Guide to Real Estate Contracts	$18.95
Essential Guide to Real Estate Leases	$18.95
How to Buy a Condominium or Townhome (2E)	$19.95
How to Buy Your First Home	$18.95
Working with Your Homeowners Association	$19.95

Legal Survival in Personal Affairs

The 529 College Savings Plan	$16.95
The Antique and Art Collector's Legal Guide	$24.95
The Complete Legal Guide to Senior Care	$21.95
Family Limited Partnership	$26.95
Gay and Lesbian Rights	$26.95
How to File Your Own Bankruptcy (5E)	$21.95
How to File Your Own Divorce (5E)	$26.95
How to Make Your Own Simple Will (3E)	$18.95
How to Write Your Own Living Will (3E)	$18.95
How to Write Your Own Premarital Agreement (3E)	$24.95
Living Trusts and Other Ways to Avoid Probate (3E)	$24.95
Mastering the MBE	$16.95
Most Valuable Personal Legal Forms You'll Ever Need	$24.95
Neighbor v. Neighbor (2E)	$16.95
The Nanny and Domestic Help Legal Kit	$22.95
The Power of Attorney Handbook (4E)	$19.95
Repair Your Own Credit and Deal with Debt (2E)	$18.95
Sexual Harassment: Your Guide to Legal Action	$18.95
The Social Security Benefits Handbook (3E)	$18.95
Social Security Q&A	$12.95
Teen Rights	$22.95
Unmarried Parents' Rights (2E)	$19.95
U.S. Immigration and Citizenship Q&A	$18.95
U.S. Immigration Step By Step	$21.95
U.S.A. Immigration Guide (4E)	$24.95
The Visitation Handbook	$18.95
Win Your Unemployment Compensation Claim (2E)	$21.95
Your Right to Child Custody, Visitation, and Support (2E)	$24.95

Legal Survival in Spanish

Cómo Hacer su Propio Testamento	$16.95
Cómo Restablecer su propio Crédito y Renegociar sus Deudas	$21.95
Cómo Solicitar su Propio Divorcio	$24.95
Guía de Inmigración a Estados Unidos (3E)	$24.95
Guía de Justicia para Víctimas del Crimen	$21.95
Inmigración a los EE. UU. Paso a Paso	$22.95
Manual de Beneficios para el Seguro Social	$18.95

SPHINX® PUBLISHING ORDER FORM

	SHIP TO:

	Terms	F.O.B.	Chicago, IL	Ship Date

Charge my: ☐ VISA ☐ MasterCard ☐ American Express   ☐ Money Order or Personal Check

Credit Card Number   **Expiration Date**

ISBN	Title	Retail	Qty	ISBN	Title	Retail
	SPHINX PUBLISHING NATIONAL TITLES			1-57248-220-6	Mastering the MBE	$16.95
1-57248-238-9	The 529 College Savings Plan	$16.95		1-57248-167-6	Most Val. Business Legal Forms You'll Ever Need (3E)	$21.95
1-57248-349-0	The Antique and Art Collector's Legal Guide	$24.95				
1-57248-347-4	Attorney Responsibilities & Client Rights	$19.95		1-57248-360-1	Most Val. Personal Legal Forms You'll Ever Need (2E)	$26.95
1-57248-148-X	Cómo Hacer su Propio Testamento	$16.95				
1-57248-226-5	Cómo Restablecer su propio Crédito y Renegociar sus Deudas	$21.95		1-57248-098-X	The Nanny and Domestic Help Legal Kit	$22.95
				1-57248-089-0	Neighbor v. Neighbor (2E)	$16.95
1-57248-147-1	Cómo Solicitar su Propio Divorcio	$24.95		1-57248-169-2	The Power of Attorney Handbook (4E)	$19.95
1-57248-166-8	The Complete Book of Corporate Forms	$24.95		1-57248-332-6	Profit from Intellectual Property	$28.95
1-57248-229-X	The Complete Legal Guide to Senior Care	$21.95		1-57248-329-6	Protect Your Patent	$24.95
1-57248-201-X	The Complete Patent Book	$26.95		1-57248-344-X	Repair Your Own Credit and Deal with Debt (2E)	$18.95
1-57248-369-5	Credit Smart	$18.95		1-57248-350-4	El Seguro Social Preguntas y Respuestas	$14.95
1-57248-163-3	Crime Victim's Guide to Justice (2E)	$21.95		1-57248-217-6	Sexual Harassment: Your Guide to Legal Action	$18.95
1-57248-251-6	The Entrepreneur's Internet Handbook	$21.95		1-57248-219-2	The Small Business Owner's Guide to Bankruptcy	$21.95
1-57248-346-6	Essential Guide to Real Estate Contracts (2E)	$18.95		1-57248-168-4	The Social Security Benefits Handbook (3E)	$18.95
1-57248-160-9	Essential Guide to Real Estate Leases	$18.95		1-57248-216-8	Social Security Q&A	$12.95
1-57248-254-0	Family Limited Partnership	$26.95		1-57248-221-4	Teen Rights	$22.95
1-57248-331-8	Gay & Lesbian Rights	$26.95		1-57248-335-0	Traveler's Rights	$21.95
1-57248-139-0	Grandparents' Rights (3E)	$24.95		1-57248-236-2	Unmarried Parents' Rights (2E)	$19.95
1-57248-188-9	Guía de Inmigración a Estados Unidos (3E)	$24.95		1-57248-362-8	U.S. Immigration and Citizenship Q&A	$18.95
1-57248-187-0	Guía de Justicia para Víctimas del Crimen	$21.95		1-57248-218-4	U.S. Immigration Step by Step	$21.95
1-57248-103-X	Help Your Lawyer Win Your Case (2E)	$14.95		1-57248-161-7	U.S.A. Immigration Guide (4E)	$24.95
1-57248-164-1	How to Buy a Condominium or Townhome (2E)	$19.95		1-57248-192-7	The Visitation Handbook	$18.95
1-57248-328-8	How to Buy Your First Home	$18.95		1-57248-225-7	Win Your Unemployment Compensation Claim (2E)	$21.95
1-57248-191-9	How to File Your Own Bankruptcy (5E)	$21.95				
1-57248-343-1	How to File Your Own Divorce (5E)	$26.95		1-57248-330-X	The Wills, Estate Planning and Trusts Legal Kit	$26.95
1-57248-222-2	How to Form a Limited Liability Company (2E)	$24.95		1-57248-138-2	Winning Your Personal Injury Claim (2E)	$24.95
1-57248-231-1	How to Form a Nonprofit Corporation (2E)	$24.95		1-57248-333-4	Working with Your Homeowners Association	$19.95
1-57248-345-8	How to Form Your Own Corporation (4E)	$26.95		1-57248-162-5	Your Right to Child Custody, Visitation and Support (2E)	$24.95
1-57248-224-9	How to Form Your Own Partnership (2E)	$24.95				
1-57248-232-X	How to Make Your Own Simple Will (3E)	$18.95		1-57248-157-9	Your Rights When You Owe Too Much	$16.95
1-57248-200-1	How to Register Your Own Copyright (4E)	$24.95			**CALIFORNIA TITLES**	
1-57248-104-8	How to Register Your Own Trademark (3E)	$21.95		1-57248-150-1	CA Power of Attorney Handbook (2E)	$18.95
1-57248-233-8	How to Write Your Own Living Will (3E)	$18.95		1-57248-337-7	How to File for Divorce in CA (4E)	$26.95
1-57248-156-0	How to Write Your Own Premarital Agreement (3E)	$24.95		1-57248-145-5	How to Probate and Settle an Estate in CA	$26.95
				1-57248-336-9	How to Start a Business in CA (2E)	$21.95
1-57248-230-3	Incorporate in Delaware from Any State	$24.95		1-57248-196-X	The Landlord's Legal Guide in CA	$24.95
1-57248-158-7	Incorporate in Nevada from Any State	$24.95		1-57248-194-3	How to Win in Small Claims Court in CA (2E)	$18.95
1-57248-250-8	Inmigración a los EE.UU. Paso a Paso	$22.95		1-57248-246-X	Make Your Own CA Will	$18.95
1-57071-333-2	Jurors' Rights (2E)	$12.95		1-57248-241-9	Tenants' Rights in CA	$21.95
1-57248-223-0	Legal Research Made Easy (3E)	$21.95			**FLORIDA TITLES**	
1-57248-165-X	Living Trusts and Other Ways to Avoid Probate (3E)	$24.95		1-57248-205-2	Child Custody, Visitation and Support in FL	$26.95
				1-57248-176-5	How to File for Divorce in FL (7E)	$26.95
1-57248-186-2	Manual de Beneficios para el Seguro Social	$18.95		1-57248-356-3	How to Form a Corporation in FL (6E)	$24.95

Form Continued on Following Page   **SubTotal** _____

Qty	ISBN	Title	Retail
___	1-57248-203-6	How to Form a Limited Liability Co. in FL (2E)	$24.95
___	1-57071-401-0	How to Form a Partnership in FL	$22.95
___	1-57248-113-7	How to Make a FL Will (6E)	$16.95
___	1-57248-088-2	How to Modify Your FL Divorce Judgment (4E)	$24.95
___	1-57248-354-7	How to Probate and Settle an Estate in FL (5E)	$26.95
___	1-57248-339-3	How to Start a Business in FL (7E)	$21.95
___	1-57248-204-4	How to Win in Small Claims Court in FL (7E)	$18.95
___	1-57248-202-8	Land Trusts in Florida (6E)	$29.95
___	1-57248-338-5	Landlords' Rights and Duties in FL (9E)	$22.95
		GEORGIA TITLES	
___	1-57248-340-7	How to File for Divorce in GA (5E)	$21.95
___	1-57248-180-3	How to Make a GA Will (4E)	$21.95
___	1-57248-341-5	How to Start a Business in Georgia (3E)	$21.95
		ILLINOIS TITLES	
___	1-57248-244-3	Child Custody, Visitation, and Support in IL	$24.95
___	1-57248-206-0	How to File for Divorce in IL (3E)	$24.95
___	1-57248-170-6	How to Make an IL Will (3E)	$16.95
___	1-57248-247-8	How to Start a Business in IL (3E)	$21.95
___	1-57248-252-4	The Landlord's Legal Guide in IL	$24.95
		MARYLAND, VIRGINIA AND THE DISTRICT OF COLUMBIA	
___	1-57248-240-0	How to File for Divorce in MD, VA and DC	$28.95
___	1-57248-359-8	How to Start a Business in MD, VA or DC	$21.95
		MASSACHUSETTS TITLES	
___	1-57248-115-3	How to Form a Corporation in MA	$24.95
___	1-57248-108-0	How to Make a MA Will (2E)	$16.95
___	1-57248-248-6	How to Start a Business in MA (3E)	$21.95
___	1-57248-209-5	The Landlord's Legal Guide in MA	$24.95
		MICHIGAN TITLES	
___	1-57248-215-X	How to File for Divorce in MI (3E)	$24.95
___	1-57248-182-X	How to Make a MI Will (3E)	$16.95
___	1-57248-183-8	How to Start a Business in MI (3E)	$18.95
		MINNESOTA TITLES	
___	1-57248-142-0	How to File for Divorce in MN	$21.95
___	1-57248-179-X	How to Form a Corporation in MN	$24.95
___	1-57248-178-1	How to Make a MN Will (2E)	$16.95
		NEW JERSEY TITLES	
___	1-57248-239-7	How to File for Divorce in NJ	$24.95
		NEW YORK TITLES	
___	1-57248-193-5	Child Custody, Visitation and Support in NY	$26.95
___	1-57248-351-2	File for Divorce in NY	$26.95
___	1-57248-249-4	How to Form a Corporation in NY (2E)	$24.95
___	1-57248-095-5	How to Make a NY Will (2E)	$16.95
___	1-57248-199-4	How to Start a Business in NY (2E)	$18.95
___	1-57248-198-6	How to Win in Small Claims Court in NY (2E)	$18.95
___	1-57248-197-8	Landlords' Legal Guide in NY	$24.95
___	1-57071-188-7	New York Power of Attorney Handbook	$19.95
___	1-57248-122-6	Tenants' Rights in NY	$21.95
		NORTH CAROLINA TITLES	
___	1-57248-185-4	How to File for Divorce in NC (3E)	$22.95
___	1-57248-129-3	How to Make a NC Will (3E)	$16.95
___	1-57248-184-6	How to Start a Business in NC (3E)	$18.95

Qty	ISBN	Title	R
___	1-57248-091-2	Landlords' Rights & Duties in NC	$2
		OHIO TITLES	
___	1-57248-190-0	How to File for Divorce in OH (2E)	$2
___	1-57248-174-9	How to Form a Corporation in OH	$2
___	1-57248-173-0	How to Make an OH Will	$1
		PENNSYLVANIA TITLES	
___	1-57248-242-7	Child Custody, Visitation and Support in PA	$2
___	1-57248-211-7	How to File for Divorce in PA (3E)	$2
___	1-57248-358-X	How to Form a Corporation in PA	$2
___	1-57248-094-7	How to Make a PA Will (2E)	$1
___	1-57248-357-1	How to Start a Business in PA (3E)	$2
___	1-57248-245-1	The Landlord's Legal Guide in PA	$2
		TEXAS TITLES	
___	1-57248-171-4	Child Custody, Visitation, and Support in TX	$2
___	1-57248-172-2	How to File for Divorce in TX (3E)	$2
___	1-57248-114-5	How to Form a Corporation in TX (2E)	$2
___	1-57248-255-9	How to Make a TX Will (3E)	$1
___	1-57248-214-1	How to Probate and Settle an Estate in TX (3E)	$2
___	1-57248-228-1	How to Start a Business in TX (3E)	$1
___	1-57248-111-0	How to Win in Small Claims Court in TX (2E)	$1
___	1-57248-355-5	the Landlord's Legal Guide in TX	$2

SubTotal This page ___
SubTotal previous page ___
Shipping — $5.00 for 1st book, $1.00 each additional ___
Illinois residents add 6.75% sales tax ___
Connecticut residents add 6.00% sales tax ___

Total ___